*PATTON HIDDEN IN PLAIN SIGHT* SERIES

**BOOK ONE**

# THE BATTLE BEFORE THE WAR

# DENNY G. HAIR

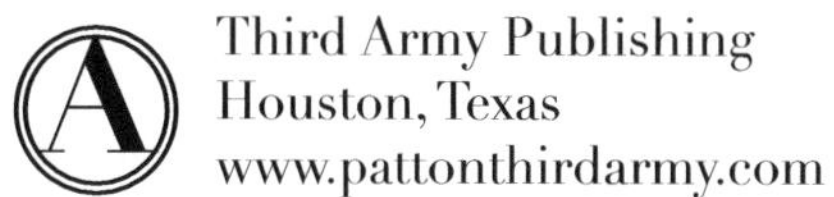

Third Army Publishing
Houston, Texas
www.pattonthirdarmy.com

Third Army Publishing
Houston, Texas

Image Credit: 3rd Army Patch, Author's Personal Collection

Image Credit: Blessing of the Colors, Third Army Headquarters Peover England,
Chaplain James H., O'Neil Blesses Colors with 503 MP Battalion Honor Guard,
June 1944, Library Of Congress, Patton Papers

Cover design by Bri Bruce Productions
(www.bribruceproductions.net)

For more information, visit
www.pattonthirdarmy.com

This book is dedicated to
Carlos and Helen Manning
whose loving support
has made this book possible.

# TABLE OF CONTENTS

# PREFACE



I was urged to write this book by friends who both knew of my love of history and of my high regard for General Patton. From the very beginning of my research, I understood that there were two main reasons General Patton had risen to such prominence; the first was his brilliant war record, in particular, his achievements during World War II as head of the United States Third Army; the second was the 1970 motion picture *Patton*. Regarding the latter, it is not often that a Hollywood movie captures the public's imagination to such a degree that it is the beginning of a man's popularity and place in history instead of the final chapter of his life. Since the release of the movie, its Oscar-winning performances and its now almost cult-like following, General Patton has become an American icon and is increasingly popular. This has lead to a great deal more research into the man's life and generalship; information known about Patton has greatly increased rather than diminished since the movie's release.

Though quite a headliner grabber in WWII, by 1970 the public memory of Patton was fading. Only General Eisenhower had a higher degree of name recognition at the end of the war, which he parlayed into a winning bid for president. By the time Eisenhower had passed in 1969, he had secured his place in America's rich history.  Patton, however, died before he could write the story he wanted to tell.  Patton had been both a friend and a thorn in Eisenhower's side; thus, though Eisenhower had lost a long-time friend and confidant, he'd also lost the need to look over his shoulder, especially when it came to questions regarding his military decisions in WWII.  Had Patton not died in 1945, there are many reasons to believe that Eisenhower would not have been elected President. In fact, there was a movement to draft Patton as the nominee after Truman and even mention of giving him the Congressional Medal of Honor.  Patton never did receive this honor, and it is doubtful that he would have run for president. I mention this to give a historical perspective of the popularity of these two juggernauts during WWII.

In 1945, Patton was a highly visible, controversial and popular general. Yet, except in the minds and hearts of those who served with and under him, his memory had been dimmed by time. Supporters continued to write books and push for another movie about him.  Rather than serving as a capping point on Patton, the 1970 movie seeded additional research and inquiries about the man, his character and his generalship; therefore, had the movie not been made, nor been both a great commercial and critical success, winning multiple academy awards, Patton may have forever been relegated to footnote status in the WWII European Theater. The movie sparked a new interest in this flamboyant figure; a new generation wanted to know more.

Far more important than the movie are the *Patton Papers*, a set of books by renowned author and historian Martin Blumenson.  In these volumes, Blumenson chronicled Patton's life utilizing Patton's diary and personal letters. The Patton Papers caused historians to sit up and take notice of this dynamic figure. By reading the General's own words and analyzing the dynamics of his frustrations on issues he dared not voice while serving in the army, the historical accounts regarding how the war was prosecuted in the European Theater were beginning to be reexamined. If General Patton's accusations and writings were a correct reflection of historical events, history would have to be rewritten. Though many books followed based on Blumenson's work, and interviews with Patton's children and family members soon sparked additional books and periodicals, the *Patton Papers* became the most read set of books about George Patton.

History can only be fully understood when all facts come to light. Historians have found a wealth of information left behind about General Patton—the majority, written by Patton himself. Thus, in Patton's case, dead men do tell tales. Additionally, many books have been written by Patton's good friends and close associates. Most have not been read widely. They speak of a general that the public did not know and one his superiors hoped would never be known. It is as if they understood that someday Patton would be studied; therefore they left an enormous amount of material, written from their own experiences, in both their and his own words. They explain aspects of his life and what he did and why.

I spent over 30 years as a Houston police officer thus can verify that dead men do tell tales; the truth often surfaces after we're gone. The search for the truth, and bringing that truth to light was my primary objective for this book. I navigated its construction as I would a homicide investigation. As such, I developed a chronology and investigated any and all leads. To those ends, a true image emerged primarily from written accounts by those who knew Patton. Hidden under 75 years of dust, each was meticulously read, reread and cross-referenced for accuracy.

It is my sincere hope that this book will change how Patton has been regarded. It will not change but correct our current historical narratives as it revisits and reexamines many incidents of the war from new perspectives. Typically, a witness tells a story based on what he saw and heard. They tell the story from their perspective. If ten people are all standing at an intersection when an accident occurs, they all see the same thing but they witness the events from the location where they were standing. Witnesses across the street or at opposing angles would view the accident differently. The task of the investigator is to identify and align verifiable constants to uncover the factual sequence of events as they occurred. When put in chronological order, compared and synthesized, a much more in-depth and far more accurate story is revealed. Historic events are equivalent in that information is gathered from multiple sources, most specifically from the details and descriptions of those who witnessed the events. Naturally, this information is derived from individuals and/or groups who experienced the same events from differing perspectives. As well, in war, political influences, career aspirations and the narrative of the victor bury secrets and keep some stories from being revealed.

In writing this book, my good friend, Pascale Craan, suggested the current title. She understood the significance of this book as it reveals an important history that had previously been hidden in print, in plain sight. When ordered chronologically, day-by-day as the events occurred, the real significance is revealed. A great deal of this book is comprised of direct quotes from multiple sources, on corresponding days, by those who lived through these events. Most of these individuals have not previously been cited, and none of it in this manner. For the first time, General Patton and his headquarters staff are allowed to tell their incredible story in their own words. What was placed in text and, thereafter, hidden in dusty old files, now bring to life a story never before assembled in this manner.

General Patton himself was a prolific writer. He kept a daily dairy and corresponded regularly with family, friends and colleagues throughout the war. Late in the day, the last thing before bed, Patton would call his personal secretary in and hand him the notes of the day. These were sometimes just scribbles on a piece of paper. Other times, he would write long letters in his own hand. Yet, few of these documents were revealed until after the movie bearing his name was released. All of his letters and correspondences were kept intact and donated to the Library of Congress. Many have seldom been read, much less used to tell a story of his day-to-day activities during his tenure of command as the commanding General of Third Army.

Both before and after the Patton movie, many of the soldiers that served with or under General Patton wrote about him, understanding that a great man had not been given his just due. Many firsthand accounts were written just after or a few years after the war. These books, memoirs, and magazine articles gave great insight into Patton the man, as they knew him. Many of those who authored these works were good friends who both loved and admired him. Many more wrote of Patton's exploits during WWII after the movie, before they passed away. Though it was against Army regulations to keep a war diary, many did. Ultra intercepts were considered the most secret and were not even to be spoken of unless around others with the same clearance, yet secrets were written down in private journals. These are revealed for the first time ever in print and in the context they were meant to be understood. Additionally, there have been those fringe elements who've perpetuated conspiracy theories through conjecture. Hence, Patton remains as controversial and misunderstood a figure as he was when he was alive.

Some may inquire why it took so long to make a movie about Patton as he'd been quite popular long before 1970. The reason was very simple. He knew way too much, and had he lived and said what he thought, he would have continued to change the outcome of events far into the future. He saw the blunders of the Falaise Gap, the politics and debacle of Operation Market Garden, the folly of static defense and the failure of his superiors to prosecute the war quickly to save lives. He had to fight to fight, a situation he found intolerable. He was, as many historians have now come to believe, convinced the war could have been won by late October or early November of 1944. He would have certainly voiced this had he lived. In fact, there is growing support for this belief. Could the War have been won in 1944? Could some 10 million lives have been spared on both sides, including the civilians who died? Frederick Ayer, Patton's nephew, confronted General Bradley with this question in veiled form during an interview in 1963. "I asked General Bradley if he believed Uncle Georgie could that fall (1944) have driven on into Germany. He answered, You know, he might have … you know your uncle was prone to exaggeration but this time, I could not dispute him."[i] Frederick Ayer was a "Special Agent" in WWII and bureau chief of the FBI for counterintelligence in Europe, part of Eisenhower's staff. Did this mean that Ayer was asking a question he already knew the answer to but was duty bound to keep?

Patton is often depicted as an ancient man caught up in a modern world. Some of this came from the movie. Though the movie was a Hollywood blockbuster, like all films "based on real events," Hollywood exercised its artistic license, in this case, quite liberally. Therefore, much of what was depicted in the movie did not match reality. Patton was a forward thinker. Thus, he was on the cutting edge of advancements and developments of his time. He was not only a modern fighter but far ahead of his time prior to and during the war. He used history to understand the future. He reasoned that man had not changed in his reactions to military conflict, only the tools he used to wage war had changed. He utilized his life-long study of history to predict the reactions of his foes. Patton was also far ahead of his superiors. This was perhaps his biggest problem in executing the war. He often disagreed with their strategies and planning. Because of his lack of tact, he was often seen as irritating and viewed with some contempt. General Eisenhower understood Patton as a war genius, but seldom complimented him; compliments were only offered when Eisenhower was in need of Patton's assistance. Patton's bluntness was not appreciated by his peers; however, they, too, used him to "get their chestnuts out of the fire" when they'd blundered, a not uncommon event. Patton was so angry by the end of the war that he'd stated that he was going to retire and reveal all of this information and events. Had he been able to do so, there is no question that many military and political careers would have taken very different paths.

Patton's wife, Beatrice, loved him with all of her being and protected his reputation after his death. She was against books and movies about him and wanted his memory to be left as it was with his passing. In retrospect, this seems strange. Many great men had wives who carried on their memories after they died. One of the most notable was Libby Custer, the wife of General George Armstrong Custer. She protected him and perpetuated his memory for the rest of her life. Why would Beatrice be against a film about her husband? Beatrice felt that the film would fail to do him justice. As Beatrice was the guardian of the family history, she alone had the power to grant or deny permission to the studios. Beatrice would not grant permission for a film. As much as Beatrice loved "Georgie," she also had two daughters and a son to consider. Her two daughters were married to career military men and both her sons-in-law and her son became generals in the U.S. Army. A Patton movie could have negatively affected their military careers, as well as the careers of Patton's peers and friends, had it revealed the way in which Patton had to prosecute the war due to the barriers set forth by misguided superiors, and the way in which Patton spoke of said issues and persons in his diary and in correspondences with friends and family.

Beatrice was firmly in charge of her Georgie's memory and sought to preserve it through the publication of *War as I Knew It*, the "Patton penned" book released posthumously. Beatrice and Col. Paul Harkins heavily edited what Patton had written in his diary notes. At the time, the book was a best seller. Though Patton is credited as the author, in reality, Patton contributed to the book but did not write it. MSgt Joseph D. Rosevich typed for Patton as his personal secretary; Col. Paul Harkins did the editing, and his wife Beatrice, redacted the parts she felt were inappropriate, e.g. those that were too personal or too political. In 1953, Beatrice died as Patton would have wished to die - riding a horse, free of care, doing what he wanted to do.

On the day of her funeral, a production studio pitched the family on a movie about Patton. The Patton family, still in agreement with Beatrice, denied permission, but in 1970 the studio bought the rights to *Patton: Ordeal and Triumph* by Ladislas Farago and *A Soldier's Story*, the autobiography of General Omar Bradley. The latter was ghost-written in 1951 by General Bradley's Aide de Camp,

Chester Hanson, who was not a fan of Patton.  The family was not at all pleased and registered their objections, which fell on deaf ears.  The movie had a tendency to reflect certain biases that negatively reflected on General Patton; one could argue that it did not show a true understanding of the real Patton.  Though highly popular, the movie reflected Bradley's view of Patton and left out large amounts of historical data … not to mention that Eisenhower was not depicted in the movie.  Though it does capture the imagination, and did make Patton a household name well into the 21st century, it is not historically accurate. Thus, it is not a complete rendering of the man, the war, or the times.

Following his retirement from the army and nearing the end of his life, General Bradley penned another autobiography. This book, *A Soldier's Life*, revealed more of the infighting between Eisenhower, Bradley, and Montgomery. Though mostly ignored by historians when exploring the Patton mystique, put in the chronological context of the war, it too assists in telling a story much different from the one depicted in the Patton movie.

In war, romantic affairs were not uncommon among the soldiers but were dangerous security risks when high-ranking, married officers had girlfriends. If they learned secrets, these girlfriends could be both in real danger to themselves and a political danger had they been discovered. General Eisenhower's driver, Kay Summersby, was one such girlfriend. She was known to be Eisenhower's lover by President Franklin Roosevelt almost at the same time it occurred. This was not a secured secret and it was known about down a long chain of command. What was not known, or at least never considered, was that she too knew many of the secrets Eisenhower knew. She kept a private journal that was lost to history until it surfaced in 2002.  Kay Summersby wrote two books, her first thought to be a book with little to offer to historians, but it does reveals an Ultra secret. The secret was highly classified at the time. This was collaborated by the diary that surfaced in 2002. Her second book reveals her love affair with Eisenhower.  President Truman's revelation to a reporter that Eisenhower was thinking of leaving his wife to marry her added the validity to her claim when she wrote her second book. Many at the time, including General Patton, knew full well she knew way too much. Prime Minister Churchill knew of the affair and, by extension, so too did British General Montgomery. All of this affected the war in Europe. Eisenhower's burden in all of this caused him to have a mental breakdown to the point he could not even talk and was hastened away to the Riviera in March of 1945. This is an incident never discussed but proven to be true. This occurred just as the secrets of the war held by Germany were ripe for the taking. Eisenhower's actions in regards to the giving away of Berlin to the Russians and ordering Patton to rush to capture the town of Ohrdruf weeks after he received intelligence on the region tend to add to the assertions that Eisenhower was breaking down. They had no idea a labor camp was there, but they knew Nazi secrets were. Information had been sent up the chain of command in March 1945 by Patton's G-2. It was not acted upon until after Ike returned from the Riviera.

General Patton has been reported to have had an ongoing affair with his niece, Jean Gordon, who served as a Red Cross Clubmobile girl in France and Germany during the Third Army's campaigns. Most of this has been speculation based on bits and pieces of a diary written by General Hugh Everett. It has been repeated as settled fact in many books. When examined closely, it is highly fragmentary, and research into the dates mentioned is far more supportive of no affair and refer to dates that the Red Cross Clubmobile girls, as a whole, were traveling and were part of a greater event. In fact, many Red Cross Clubmobile girls knew of the allegations, knew both Patton and Jean Gordon, and work side by side with her in the field and billeted with her. They simply say an affair did not occur. The facts are in the book and readers can judge for themselves.

Recollections of what Patton said were written down by others and many were not published until years after the war. The men closest to Patton (many high-ranking officers) wrote their recollections of him and took their notes from a secret After Action Report to form the backbone of their works. This was because the After Action Report was not de-classified until 1986, so they were careful not to quote from it directly but use it in generalities. The most secret of secrets, the intelligence behind General Patton's decisions, was kept secret by his two top intelligence officers, Col. Oscar Koch and Col. Robert Allen. Col. Allen wrote a book not long after the war called *Lucky Forward*. Col. Koch, perhaps the most loyal of all his men, only wrote in generalities about real dates and places. He gave enough information to help the reader understand the period in which an occurence took place and what was said. General Hobart "Hap" Gay kept the official Third Army daily journal which was not a diary, as it is often referred to. It was a daily log of the comings and goings of those who would meet with General Patton, recording the time and date of the meeting. In some cases, the exact wording of a telegraph, order or telephone conversation was recorded in it. When significant events occurred, a notation was also made. These proved to be most valuable. Many secrets were touched upon but not openly stated. Deputy Assistant G-2 Intelligence Officer Col. Robert Allen kept a very secret personal journal that was highly illegal at the time. This journal was lost to historians and, after his death, it was donated to the Patton Museum at Fort Knox, but was never used by historians. It was lost again until found during my research in Georgia in a forgotten file. For the first time, Ultra secrets and the reasons behind many of the actions taken by others are revealed in this book, by its inclusion. It is quoted by date, verbatim.

After the war, many "yearbooks," or unit histories, were published by the US Army and made available to the veterans of Third Army. Many were limited in printing and are today very rare. Third Army also had its own printing presses and printed everything from Christmas cards to daily menus and Sunday pamphlets of the order of the service. Some of this material has never been quoted because it is so very rare and was printed in very limited quantities.

There is much more that has been hidden and now brought to light. When Ohrdruf, the first Nazi concentration camp found by the allies, was overrun by Patton's forces, they were surprised at the horror they found. Yet what is frequently overlooked was that they were ordered to make their advance there a priority and to get there by April 1st. So why the hurry if they had no idea there was a concentration camp there? It was a labor camp in the middle of Hitler's German State of Thuringia. Why get there in a hurry? They answer to the question was a secret at the time, and still is. The entire region contained secrets that the US wanted to stay secret. Much of it is still secret to this day, but there are now scattered facts surfacing in reports hidden all these years as to just what these secrets were.

As I researched these books, I read as many first hand accounts as I could from those who served on his staff or under his command. There was one thing that stood out about General Patton: They almost all loved him, respected him and would have died for him. Even many who did not like him were proud to have served under him. In fact, many soldiers did die knowing he gave the orders and did their duty knowing it may very well lead to their death. This was true from the top to the bottom and from the ground up. So what else can be written about the life and times of this famous general, this icon of American history. He always pointed to the men he commanded as being the real heroes. He said it was his staff and Third Army that did it all.

Perhaps the most overlooked set of reports was the huge After Action Report that was published by Third Army in 1945 and classified as secret until it was declassified in 1986. There were only 282 copies of it produced and it is a most complete and comprehensive account of what Patton and his Third Army did. It shows the minute details of how the army was formed, operated, fought, lived and died and told what it witnessed. There are detailed maps of every battle and a comprehensive report written by each of the section commanders that commanded elements of the Third Army. It is amazing that all of the books published prior to 1986 have been as accurate as they are without the use of this report. In the research of this book I finally understood why. Many of the earlier books were written by officers who had access to these reports but could not quote them directly because they were still classified. They had to write their recollections from their on notes and, if anything, they were careful not to allude to these after action reports because they were still secret. In fact, most people today don't even know of their existence and very few people have read and studied them. Patton must have thought it ironic and sad that they were classified and the public could not read them.

Ironically, it was Patton who classified them because they showed exactly how the war was prosecuted by Third Army. After the war, there were many enemies of the United States and the cold war would soon dominate the new world. If this report had fallen into the wrong hands, it would have certainly given the enemy a great advantage in understanding the inner workings of an American army at war.

As a student of General Patton and Third Army, one day I saw one of these After Action Reports listed on an online auction site. I knew what it was but had never read it. I had no idea how rare it was. It was not listed very well and the owner was not sure how complete it was. So I bid on it. To my surprise I had the winning bid. This report was huge and weighed over 50 pounds. When it arrived, the first book of two was in disarray and I, too, wondered if it was all there. It took several days and I found it was indeed all there. Then I began to read it. This report takes great study and just reading the tens of thousands of words is not enough. Overwhelmed is not strong enough a word to describe the material included in it. Now, I understood. All the bits and pieces in all of the other books I had read, together with these after action reports, put it all together for me. I was holding in my hands the original source document for the history of the greatest military army in the history of the twentieth century and certainly the history of the generalship and organization of Patton's Third Army. All that I read before suddenly was viewed in a totally different light. Together with this after action report and the many books and periodicals I have sourced, there still remains a story to be told about Patton and his beloved Third Army.

**United States Third Army Headquarters, ETO**

So what did Third Army have that made it such a fierce fighting force that won more battles and moved further and faster than any other army in history? Certainly, General Patton had everything to do with it, but there was much more to it than just him. He was well aware he got the credit for what others did and was keenly aware that his staff and his entire command was unified as a team and that they, as a team, accomplished what would have otherwise been impossible for him to have accomplished on his own. Whenever he could, he pointed out their valor, visited with them, came to see them in the hospitals, and decorated them. He constantly pointed toward their accomplishments and away from his own. He would tell the soldiers that they had worked a great feat in battle but tomorrow the press would say he did it. He would then try to tell the press who really accomplished the deed but, no matter how he tried, it was reported that "Patton's" Third Army did this and that. More often the headlines would only read "Patton Advanced" to some place on the map. This publicity irritated Patton's superiors and it irritated Patton when it did not give credit to his men. General Patton knew, and said on many occasions, that he did not do this or that but that his men had done it. He was particularly proud of what the headquarters of Third Army did. At one point in the war, it numbered close to 4,500 men.

These headquarters units moved over 500,000 men and materials in several different directions at one time. They were divided into corps and the corps into divisions. Patton visited every one of them in the field, as many times as it took. Nearly all of them saw him in the field, where they were fighting. He left his headquarters daily and went to see his commands. He drove, flew, and walked to wherever they were fighting…daily. His headquarters was so efficient, it ran itself. So what exactly was this headquarters of such a fighting force composed of and what did it do? Third Army's 281 days of incessant, victorious combat penetrations advanced further in less time than any other army in history. It fought its way across 24 major rivers and innumerable steams and liberated and conquered more than 82,000 square miles of territory, including 1,500 cities and towns and some 12,000 uninhabited places. The 3rd Army captured in battle 956,000 of the enemy and killed or wounded over 500,000 others. France, Belgium, Luxembourg, Germany, Austria, and Czechoslovakia bear witness to their exploits. There were, from time to time, some six different corps and 42 separate combat divisions that served under Patton in the ETO or were part of Third Army, even if briefly.

One of the greatest accomplishment was the turning of the army 90 degrees, in the middle of the coldest winter on record, and moving elements of it to engage the enemy in less than 48 hours. Even more astounding is that it was planned far ahead of time and the surprise attack known as the Ardennes Offensive was predicted by Patton's staff over a week before it took place. So, how could a General and his headquarters command pull this off? This, in itself, was one of the greatest military feats in history. How could his army move so quickly and so efficiently? When you examine the After Action Reports you see a highly organized headquarters that did what it did with purpose and great forethought and organizational skill. The headquarters organization of Third Army was no accident and was one of the most efficient headquarters commands in the European Theater. This was due to General Patton's skill in finding the best staff members he could find, putting them in charge, telling them what he required, having them trained, and keeping them focused and—most important—allowing them to do their job. They loved him and were fiercely loyal to him and he to them. His method of command has become a model for organizational structuring of business and military headquarters. In fact, it is now known as the "Patton Principals" and has copied throughout the world in one form or another.

General Patton was also a man who believed in God and prayed constantly for divine guidance. He read and followed the principals written within the pages of the Bible, a book he read every day. Today, this almost seems a contradiction to the man known in public since he was prone to outbursts of extreme profanity and his outward bravado tends to lead those who did not know him to believe him anything but a God-fearing man. That belief was more a product of Hollywood than of those who truly knew him. In fact, he referenced the Bible many times when in private and believed strongly that the bible was highly reliable for a multitude of uses in war and organization. He also believed that the Lord was with him and watched over him. Whether others believed this or not, it is important in understanding him and his headquarters because HE believed it.

I was 17 years old when I saw the movie *Patton*. I knew little of him or his headquarters. I did know I wanted to know more about this General who appeared on the screen and told his men, "You know, by God, I actually pity those poor bastards we're going up against. By God, I do. We're not just going to shoot the bastards. We're going to cut out their living guts and use them to grease the treads of our tanks. We're going to murder those lousy Hun bastards by the bushel."

Patton fought his battles on the battlefield front successfully but the fight to get permission to fight was not always as successful. He made his superiors highly uncomfortable and he was far too great a general in the field for them to relieve him. He knew way too much for his own good.

I have included General Patton's complete, unedited diary, as he wrote it, day by day. The diary, in itself, would have derailed many military and political careers had it been known, but when adding into account what others wrote, a more complete story is now told. When you combine and understand what his command knew and what they said, in their own words day by day, what was once hidden in plain sight is now told. In writing this book, I found things hidden in plain sight not because they were missed but because they were not placed in the order they occurred. There are some things you will read in this book that are not in any other books.

…And to General Patton and his Third Army… Sir, it is as it was written, uncovered now and in print.

Denny G. Hair
Hockley, Texas
2018

---

i Ayer 152.

# CHAPTER 1

## THE BATTLE BEFORE THE WAR

Commanding the United States Seventh Army in Sicily, Lieutenant General George S. Patton's second major campaign of the war, was as successful as his first. He'd triumphed in Operation Husky and helped to drive the Germans off of the island. Together with his victories in North Africa, Patton had now proven the formidability of the United States Army and Air Corps, elevating their prestige from an untried to a world class fighting force—one to be reckoned with. His good friend, General Dwight D. Eisenhower, had ridden his coattails along the way. Those few privileged who witnessed the campaigning or were privy to sensitive information knew how Patton's actions elevated Eisenhower. They also knew how this old, authentic friendship had now become strained.

Patton was in line to receive an army group command in the looming invasion of Europe. He may very well have found himself second only to Eisenhower, but now his friend was rising to the vanguard of public praise while he plummeted to the depths of public scorn.

Patton had been in the public eye before … but not like this. His exploits in North Africa and Sicily had made him a household name back home. He'd been revered as one of, if not the most, qualified commanding generals in the United States Army. He knew and had studied more about wars and fighting than any other American military leader. A student of history, he used his vast knowledge of it to predict, with great accuracy, what his enemy would do. He'd studied the German people, their commanders and tactics and used this knowledge to out-think and out-command their military leaders.

He stood 6' 2" and weighed 211 pounds. He was balding, had bad teeth, was prone to colds and, although he was against smoking, like most in his generation, smoked. His passion for cigars had grown while in the combat theater and he smoked them to the point that they were beginning to affect his health … otherwise, he was in great physical shape. He ate properly and exercised regularly. Looking at him, he seemed to tower over others who shared his height. While stateside, Patton had lectured his staff on the benefits of good posture. "In war, as in everything else, a man needs all the brains he can get. Brains come from oxygen (to it) and oxygen comes from the lungs. The oxygen in the air gets into the blood and travels to the brain."[1] He reasoned that by having greater lung capacity, the brain would be healthier, therefore, standing erect facilitated the supply of oxygen to one's brain which in turn increased the ability to think.[2]

In the midst of his great victories and tactical achievements, Patton had visited two field hospitals in Sicily. There, he came across two soldiers he believed were cowards trying to evade fighting by hiding amongst the wounded. He became enraged at the sight of what he viewed as cowards sitting amongst those he considered heroes wounded in battle and his emotions got the better of him. He slapped one, kicked the other, and ordered both to be thrown out of the hospital.

As Patton's commanding officer, Eisenhower had been made aware of these incidents and had Patton apologize for his actions. However, the incidents were given new life when a Washington-based journalist, Drew Pearson, obtained classified information and brought "the slapping incidents," a name quickly adopted by the media, to the attention of the general public. A firestorm of criticism ensued.

The news of "the slapping incidents" had turned the public against him. A previously unblemished record of high achievement was now being doubted. Should such a commander retain his command? Patton's military career, as well as his reputation, teetered on the brink of ruin. Would these events bring a premature and unfortunate end to this brilliant career and once admired hero?

As a proven battlefield commander, Patton had few or no equals. But, this had to be weighed against the public scrutiny of his deeds at the hospitals. In the halls of Washington, D.C., the question was clear: Should the generals and politicians back home attempt to mitigate the public backlash in order to keep their finest battlefield general active; one they would need in order to win the war?

The timing of the publication of the slapping incidents could not have come at a more regrettable moment. U.S. President Franklin D. Roosevelt, Prime Minister of Great Britain, Winston Churchill, and the leader of the Communist Party and absolute ruler of the Soviet Union, Joseph Stalin, were meeting in Tehran, Iran on November 28th to December 1, 1943 to discuss and plan the next phase of the War. Where and when would the next phase of the war in the European Theater begin? What were to be the roles of the United States and Great Britain in the upcoming European invasion? Who would assume the role of a Supreme Commander and command the Western Allied forces? Before the Tehran Conference, Roosevelt and Churchill had met in Cairo on November 26 – 28th to discuss D-Day leadership and issues concerning China.

[Patton]
**November 28, 1943 Sunday**

```
Palermo Sicily
Seventh Army Headquarters


So far as I can see there is nothing for me to do except read the Bible
and trust to destiny. I certainly do not intend to read (any of the dirt
```

published in the papers or broadcast over the radio.) There is no use in giving myself indigestion for nothing.

The day before his 64th birthday, General Kenyon Joyce, an old friend, stopped by to say goodbye.

[Patton]
**November 30, 1943 Tuesday**

He looks fifty. He thought my letter to the Secretary fine.  Had a wire from Hughes[3]  not to send it so concurred, as he is on the ground and knows the score better than I do, and is a sincere friend.

I have done better than I realized.  My command so far has disposed of 177,000 Germans, Italians and French - killed, wounded and prisoners of which they have killed and wounded 21,000.  Our average loss has been one man for 132 of the enemy.  It would be a national calamity to lose an army commander with such a record.

Patton had also recorded his sincere regret of the slapping incident and knew the ramifications could be devastating.  He replayed the sequence of events over and over in his mind.  What could he do to make things right now that things were completely out of his hands?  All he could do was wait.

[Patton]
**December 1, 1943 Wednesday**

General Joyce, whom I talked to on the Drew Pearson 'incident', remarked 'George, tell them the exact truth in these words "I had been dealing with heroes. I saw two men whom I thought were cowards.  Naturally I was not too gentle with them."'

Technically, Patton was still in command of the United States Seventh Army. From his headquarters, he continued to perform his duties.  He wrote reports and conducted business with official visitors. As well, he entertained those who'd come to pay their respects and those who offered words of encouragement.

[Patton]
**December 7, 1943 Tuesday**

Mr. McCloy [the Assistant Secretary of War] came to my office at 1730 and said that he wanted to put me wise to what had gone on at the two conferences.

[McCloy stated] When Churchill and the President first got to Cairo the Chinese were there, and Churchill and Roosevelt committed themselves to an amphibious operation in the Chinese theater. Then Churchill and Roosevelt had a near split (too bad it did not materialize) over the "Overlord" plan. Churchill said that instead of its being Overlord it was becoming "Master." He is still fooling around about small attacks in the Aegean Sea, particularly with a view to the capture of Rhodes. He is actuated in this by political considerations, as he has been attacked at home by the opposition for losing the three islands.

They also quarreled over the appointment of a supreme commander to the British, hedging on the amount of authority he was to have. Things were apparently pretty grim when they went to see Stalin.

Stalin came into the conference and said,

"There are only two things I want to know. When are you going to attack France and when are you going to appoint a Supreme Commander?"

Churchill began talking about the Aegean operation this winter, and Stalin said, "That is nothing. This is the last round of a prize fight and it is not the time to dance around the ring but to go in and slug. I admit that your bombing has removed some enemy air, but what I want taken off my neck is divisions, not bombers. It is time for you to attack both in the north, and also in the south, of France. I have whittled the enemy down to your size." Churchill suggested that a committee be appointed to consider plans and make a report and Stalin said, "If we three can't decide, who can? I don't have to ask my generals to make up my mind for me. I have no time for discussion by juniors. I have to get back to Moscow and win a war and win it fast, so I can reconstitute my country."

Stalin had cut to the heart of the matter.

To put on the attacks in northern and southern France landing boats will be necessary, hence the Chinese operation will have to be canceled; and in addition, landing boats and carriers will have to be withdrawn from the Pacific. Admiral King was agreeable to this when Stalin said that as soon as Germany was wiped up, he would help us in Japan, as he had an old grudge to settle with her.

It has been decided that Marshall will remain as Chief of Staff, but will participate more actively in operations, that Ike will be Supreme Commander in the UK and that when the southern attack gets ashore, that too will come under him. Also that Spaatz will go to UK as chief of all air operations both in UK and Africa.  Churchill kicked on this and so did Portal, but Stalin insisted.  General Sir Henry Maitland Wilson will succeed Ike in Africa.  Churchill picked Wilson over Alexander.  I think there is considerable discontent over lack of drive in Italy.

I asked Mr. McCloy about myself.  He said that he had never let friendship move him, but that he felt that I had in my makeup certain chemicals no other General had; that I was a great fighter and an inspiring leader, though probably not a Moltke[4], and must be used.

That I was not to worry about what was said about me as that would hurt my efficiency.  He also said that I look and act like a general and that no one else we have does.  He asked General Marshall what was to become of me and Marshall had said, "He will have an Army."  I should have a group of armies, but that will come.  I think that my luck is in again.  In a few minutes I leave to see the President and after that I can tell more about it.

Mr. McCloy asked me for a brief account of the "Incident." I told him I could not do better than to read him the letter I had written to Mr. Stimson but not mailed.  When I had read it, he said, "I wish you would give it to me to show Mr. Stimson."  I replied that I would give it if he wanted it but that I was not volunteering anything. He requested me to hand it over.


Though they did not excuse Patton's actions, the U.S. Secretary of War, Henry L. Stimson, and John J. McCoy, Assistant Secretary of War went to bat for him.  They believed that a man of his talent and record could help to win the war.  Yet, this battle was not over.

Kay Summersby was a member of the British Mechanised Transport Corps.  She'd originally been assigned as chauffeur to General Eisenhower because she knew her way around England.  However, she would often accompany Ike to many events and affairs, posing more as a secretary or assistant rather than simply his driver.  On Tuesday, December 7, 1943, she accompanied him to meet President Roosevelt at the airfield in Algiers.  For Roosevelt, Eisenhower's failure of discretion in taking Kay Summersby along confirmed his suspicions that he and Kay were lovers.


[Summersby]

"Child," the President said as I got out of the car to join the other drivers, won't you come back here and have lunch with a dull old man?"

Startled but pleased, I climbed in back and sat down beside him. General Eisenhower remained outside to hand us in delicious chicken sandwiches …"[5]


FDR delighted in gossip and, having met Kay in Algiers, was convinced she and Eisenhower were having an affair.  He confided to his daughter Anna that he'd come to the conclusion that this attractive young British woman was sleeping with General Eisenhower.[6]

[Summersby]

On the way from the airfield, he congratulated Ike on his new appointment. It was definite, he told him.  Ike would be named commander of Overlord. The announcement would be made as soon as the President got back to Washington DC.  And Ike would have a new title: Supreme Allied Commander.[7] The General was so happy I almost thought he would burst, the grin never left his face.[8]

The next morning Roosevelt and Eisenhower flew to Malta.  From there Harry Hopkins, General Smith, General Spaatz[9], Watson, Admiral Leahy and several others accompanied them on a flight to Sicily.[10]

Patton used his diary not only to record the dates and times of events, but, because he knew he could only be perfectly candid with a trusted few, his diary also served to record his innermost thoughts.

[Patton]<br>**December 8, 1943 Wednesday**

Mr. McCloy left at 0715 and on the way out to the field he said, "Another thing about you is that you look like a general. You have color, personality and size.  Men like to follow a man they can respect."

Patton, though somewhat encouraged, still faced strong opposition in Congress and his fate was uncertain.

[Patton]

We got to Castelvetrano at 0930. The President was supposed to arrive at 1015, but due to motor trouble, he did not get in until 1420. General H. H. Arnold got in at 1330, and we had quite a talk.

He substantiated all that Mr. McCloy said about the conference and added that Stalin ran the show, saying to Mr. Churchill, among other things, "What is the matter with you English? You used to be good soldiers; now you don't fight at all and you are afraid of the sight of blood."

Arnold also said that, despite our air efforts, the German air force is getting bigger and now has 8,000 planes.  The three Allies have over 20,000 but are not using them. He thinks Air Marshal Portal is to blame. He feels that the Russians and ourselves are much more of the same mind than the British.


A wire had come from General Alexander, his commanding officer in Sicily.


[Patton]
**December 9, 1943 Thursday**

At supper, got a wire from Alexander congratulating me on being a Companion of the Bath.


The Companion of The Most Honourable Order of the Bath, a title of late medieval origin, remains as one of the highest awards in the British honors system.[11] Appointed an Honorary Companion at the Court of St. James, September 17, 1943, for outstanding leadership and successful operation in Tunisia, the esteem of this grand honor was blunted by his state of uncertainty. As decisions of great import continued to be made, Patton could only await word of his fate.

Still, his dedication to duty demanded that he show no signs of weakness, in himself or in the U.S. military, or to the enemy. There may not have been cities to retake, but there were still strategies to plan.

Accompanied by the Secret Service, Patton visited many of the sites of the city of Jerusalem. He flew to Egypt, visited the Pyramids and met with General Alexander of the British Army, whom he both liked and respected. Patton designed this seemingly innocuous site-seeing tour to keep the Germans guessing as to what he would do next and where he would lead his army.


[Patton]
**December 15, 1943 Wednesday**

Had lunch with General Alexander and six Saudi Arabian princes. The latter spoke no known language did not understand each other very well, but were quite fine looking men who wore European clothes under their robes. They are just back from the United States. Apparently there is some sort of an oil deal on. After lunch visited a factory here the British make dummy airplanes, tanks, guns and even landing craft. The tanks run on truck bodies and the boats float. I was told with great pride that the dummies cost only 1/10 as much as an original.

Personally, I think it is money very much wasted but the people who make them are very enthusiastic. When we had inferiority in the air, in tanks, and landing craft, dummies may have been useful, but now that we have superiority they are utterly useless. Yet there are hundreds, or perhaps thousands of men working on them diligently. Another case of something getting started and never stopped.

There is a very definite effort on the part of all the staff, except General

Wilson, to run Monty down and to try and get me to agree with them, but
needless to say, I did not commit myself.  Apparently the Regular Officers
of the British Army do not like Montgomery at all.


A letter from his good friend and confidant, General Everett S. Hughes, awaited Patton upon his return to Sicily.


[Patton]
**December 20, 1943 Monday**

Had a note from Hughes saying that the Gallup Poll was 77% for me, 19%
against me, and 4% not voting.


Patton's aide-de-camp, Lt. Colonel Charles Codman, knew the unadorned, unembellished Patton. As one of his very few trusted and loyal friends, the General allowed Codman to see the man that very few knew.


[Patton]
**December 24, 1943 Friday**

Went to the Seventh Army officer's party at the hotel.  It was very nice,
with a tree, presents and a movie. Each officer got a handkerchief with
a shoulder patch of the Seventh Army embroidered on it.  Later, Codman
and I went to midnight services at the Episcopal Church where there was
a huge crowd.  We talked over the "incident" until nearly 0300.

Codman has been of great help and has also been most reassuring.  He flew
to Algiers to get the latest dope, getting back this afternoon.


Patton was highly concerned; he had no idea as to his fate. Rumors intertwined with reality and half-truths, yet no clear decisions were offered. This would soon change.


[Patton]
**December 25, 1943 Saturday**

I got a great many presents and some lovely letters.  We had the Navy,
the senior British officer, Colonel Poletti and the heads of all the staff
sections for dinner.  Before that I inspected all that is left of the
Seventh Army and they were all glad to see me.  My men are crazy about
me, and that is what makes me most angry with Drew Pearson. I will live
to see him die.  As a matter of fact, the ability to survive this has had

```
a good effect on America, and on me.  My destiny is sure and I am a fool
and onward ever to have doubted it.  I don't any more.  Some people are
needed to do things and they have to be tempered by adversity as well as
thrilled by success.  I have had both.  Now for some more success.
```

Patton despised Drew Pearson.  Pearson had never set foot in a theater of war as a solider.  He wrote from the comfort and safety of his office in the States, and the political influence of Washington, D.C. was apparent in his writing.

Patton hoped he would again command an army soon.  He believed he would be selected to plan the invasion of Italy, commanding his Seventh Army.

### Drew Pearson and Muckrake Journalism

Andrew Russell "Drew" Pearson was one of the best-known American newspaper and radio journalists of his day.  He is most noted for his syndicated newspaper column "Washington Merry-Go-Round," in which he attacked various public persons.

In his review of Mark Feldstein's "Poisoning the Press: Richard Nixon, Jack Anderson, and the Rise of Washington's Scandal Culture," Jack Shafer, noted journalist, previous editor at large for Slate and current reporter for Reuters referred to Drew Pearson as "one of the scuzziest journalists to ever write a story." (The Journalist as Spy by Jack Shafer, Monday, Sept. 20, 2010)

(Retrieved from http://www.slate.com/articles/news_and_politics/press_box/2010/09/the_journalist_as_spy.html)

Jack Anderson was Pearson's one-time staff assistant, partner in "journalistic investigations" and protégé at Pearson's Washington Merry-Go-Round.  Shafer states that "the late Jack Anderson broke scores of big stories about political scandals, Capitol Hill perfidy, the machinations of American foreign policy, and the abuse of power by the White House, the CIA, the FBI, the Pentagon, and corporations. But he accomplished these deeds with unscrupulous methods … [and] Anderson's moral instructor - Drew Pearson" from whom Anderson also inherited his nationally syndicated "Washington Merry-Go-Round" column after Pearson's death. (Shafer, 2010).

Anderson's 1979 "Confessions of a Muckraker: The Inside Story of Life in Washington during the Truman, Eisenhower, Kennedy and Johnson Administrations." (Random House) affirms Feldstein and Shafer's conclusions, however, presents them from a truly *Pearsonian* perspective.  Here, Anderson explains that Pearson's politics came from his religious beliefs, therefore, the progressive Quaker believed that journalism was a weapon to be used against those who worked against the public interest.  The deficiency in this assessment is that Pearson elected himself as the ultimate arbiter of what was in the public interest and who was working against it, thus, at the expense of accuracy, Pearson adopted a Machiavellian approach to publishing his stories.   Hence, he became "the grand strategist of political muckraking" (Anderson, 1979 p. 6).

Pearson's strategies included payments to domestic, service, and hospitality staff to eavesdrop on persons he'd targeted, soliciting information on politicians from political enemies, bribes to military staff to reveal classified data, and even ordering a subordinate to break into the desk of a prominent Washington attorney.  (Feldstein, Mark: Poisoning the Press, pp. 36–37).

Ernest Cuneo, a senior official of the Office of Strategic Services, the predecessor of the Central Intelligence Agency (CIA) and friend to Pearson, leaked several stories to Pearson including the story of General Patton's slapping of Private Charles H. Kuhl and the exchange with Private Paul G. Bennett (aka kicking) which he'd learned about from others in the War Department (Hirshson, Stanley P., *General Patton: A Soldier's Life*, p. 424).  Thus, Pearson was the first to report the 1943 incident.  Though Allied Headquarters had confirmed that Patton had slapped a soldier with his gloves, and denied that he'd received either an official reprimand or a relief from combat duty, Pearson reported that Patton would heretofore be relieved of combat duty and return home in disgrace. (Farago, Ladislas, *Patton: Ordeal and Triumph*, p. 312). Pearson came into the homes of millions of Americans via his weekly radio broadcast.  His sensationalizing and embellishment of the report for his syndicated Sunday night radio audience was the direct cause of the backlash Patton faced from the general public at home.

[Patton]
**December 27, 1943 Monday**

I woke in the night amazed at the size of the training job which confronts me.  I dreamt first that there were endless miles of beach with soldiers training on them.  I wish that I had just one veteran division and one U.S. Armored Division.  Apparently I will have five French Infantry Divisions, two French Armored Divisions and two U. S. Infantry Divisions, in III Corps.  I wish I could go to Africa and get to work.  There is a lot to do.  The French will have to be wholly retrained, especially their Armor.  I will try to get General I. D. White on a loan.  I also need

some infantry officers --- I may be able to get wounded ones, possibly
Middleton or Terry Allen.  Well, we have quite a lot of time and, if
Hughes stays, he and I can get what we need.  I wish to God Ike would
leave and take Smith with him …


Patton knew this was not to be. There were many who would have him relieved from duty and sent
home.  He would not sleep soundly until a decision was made and the matter finally resolved.

General Hughes was privy to the methods, motives and members of the internal decision-
making machine.  When he learned that Patton would not command Operation Anvil[12] (landings
in Southern France) and that the Seventh Army would be commanded by another, he wrote to
record the news.


[Patton]
**December 31, 1943 Friday**

Another year ended.  I hope I do bigger and better fighting in 1944.
Harkins got back yesterday and I can't make head or tail of the mess.
The Seventh Army Staff is going to Algiers to plan "Anvil" but Hughes
writes that I won't command "Anvil".  He thinks I am going to UK.  I hope
not.  I would hate to play too far down in the team, also if I get to
England, as it seems to be set up, it means I go alone to pick up a new
staff.  I prefer my present one to any I have seen.  They have stuck by
me and I propose to stick by them.

Harkins[13] thinks that Italy is over, and that we will get at least one
Corps from there.  If so they must be pulled out and rested for at least
six weeks.  There is no use worrying or guessing --- soon we will know.
Destiny will keep on floating me down the stream of fate.


Patton kept his spirits up but feared the worst.


**Military Bands**
**Official Mission**

FM 28-5, BASIC FIELD MANUAL
THE BAND
CHANGES
WAR DEPARTMENT
No. 1  WASHINGTON, April 22, 1942.

**March 31, 1941**
**FM 28-5 is changed as follows:**

**Mission**
**Military bands provide a powerful means to commanding officers for stimulating and maintaining the moral of their units. Good bands contribute directly to the  contentment and well-being of the troops. Band personnel may be suitably employed in the performance of those combat duties which, their arms and training fit them. It follows, therefore that bands, as military units, must maintain high standards of military efficiency, and that their musical performance be characterized by its excellence and by its spirit.  Specifically the missions of the band are:**

**a.   To participate in and to furnish the desired music at military formations.**
**b.   To furnish musical entertainment for the command on such occasions as may be prescribed by the commanding officer**
**c.   To perform suitable combat duties as directed by the commander of the unit to which the band is organically assigned or attached.**

In the courtyard of Tandergee Castle in Armagh, Northern Ireland, the final parade of a proud cavalry regiment of the US Army was taking place.  The 6th Cavalry Regiment had been in continuous service since 1862.  Most of its men started their military careers as mounted horse cavalrymen; they were one of the last regular army cavalry regiments to be de-horsed in 1942. Now, the unit had been informed that new army regulations prohibited their band from remaining a part of the 6th Cavalry Group.  Chief Warrant Officer (CWO) Gregorio A. Diaz had conducted the band and these same band members since before the war. Under his able direction, for their final performance, the 6th Cavalry Regiment band played rousing marches.  As he stood and addressed the 6th Cavalry Regiment for the last time, Col. Edward M. Fickett, their commanding officer, was unsure of their future.  On January 1st, they would be incorporated into a mechanized cavalry group.  The sadness of a disbanded regiment lay heavy on their hearts, yet, unbeknownst to them, this would mark the beginning of a fateful 18 months that would see them become part of the most celebrated American army, and, under the command of its most colorful combat leader.[14]

[Patton]
**January 1, 1944 Saturday**

Received an "eyes only" radio from NATOUSA[15] saying that I will be relieved from command of the Seventh Army today and report to Algiers for further instructions; that the Seventh Army staff will plan "Anvil" and that when Clark thinks he should quit Italy, he will notify AFHQ and be assigned to command the Seventh Army.

That no transfers between the staff of the Fifth and Seventh Army will be made without permission of higher authority.  That the Fifth Army will have only the 88th, 85th, 34th and 1st Armored Divisions.  The 3rd, 45th and 36th are coming to the Seventh Army to spearhead the attack at "Anvil".  The training center will be moved from Mostaganem to Italy.

I feel very badly for myself but particularly for the staff and headquarters soldiers who have stood by me all the time in good weather and bad.  I suppose that I am going to England to command another army but if I am sent there to simply train troops which I am not to command I shall resign.  There is no appreciation of the fact that a staff is a living thing, not simply an animated table of organization.  I cannot conceive of anything more stupid than to change staffs on a General, nor can I conceive of anything more inconsiderate than not to notify him where he is going.  It is just one more thing to remember when the time comes to pay my debts.  A Hell of a "Happy New Year."


In public, Patton was a pillar of confidence.  In private, he prayed that his career would not end on such a bitter note.

He had a deep love for the Almighty.  His relationship with God was an active one; he prayed regularly, asked for divine guidance, and studied the Bible as both a book of history and a manual for living.  Like others before him, at times, he could misinterpret scripture, however, demonstrated a keen comprehension of scripture and could recite vast amounts of  the Bible's passages, a feat solely equaled by a few of the clergy under his command.

Patton was deeply dependent on the Lord.  He believed in the power of prayer. Though his faith permeated every aspect of his life, its overt manifestation was often confusing to those who did not know him intimately. Supposedly, after observing a Bible on his nightstand, several reporters had inquired if he had time to read to which Patton purportedly replied "Yes, Every God Damn Day." For a religious man to utter such a profane response seemed hypocritical. Was the story true or a fabrication to illustrate how Patton used profanity as punctuation?  In earnest, Patton loved the reactions he received when he would divide a two-syllable swearword in half and add another in the middle.  He knew he'd gained a reputation as a prolific curser; most people would cringe while listening to the words that came from his high pitched voice that, invariably, included swears rattled off at machine gun speed.  Through his speeches to his soldiers and to war correspondents, he developed swearing into an art form; this subtle mnemonic device had an awkward eloquence; though one would object to the language, they would definitely remember what was said and who said it.

Patton hated self-righteous preachers who failed to understand the Bible. "They even know less about the way God works.  They should read the Bible, not just the part they like.  God never hesitated to kill.  God never hesitated to kill when one man or any race of men needed to be punished.  God helped David kill Goliath didn't He?  How about Noah and the Ark?  All of the rest of the people were killed in the flood. War means that we have to kill people. That is all there is to it.  It is a sin not to kill people if we are serving on God's side.  There is no other way to win.

Wars must be won for God's sake. He has a part in every war." Revenge, however, was God's to do. His study of the Bible taught him that God would take care of that. And he was not afraid of death. In a speech to his troops during the desert training, he'd stated that he hoped he was killed in battle as that was a good way to go: Killed by the last bullet of the last battle. "We know little about heaven. It is supposed to be the best of everything. If so, why should men be scared to die? God can whip the devil any day of the week. Any power that can put this universe together, can do everything. I am amused about those preachers who preach about the glories of heaven, but they are scared of death … Looks like they would welcome a chance to get into heaven and get out of earth. Why do they hesitate? One thing I know, death is going to be something!" He gave his usual smile and continued, "At least death will be different from life. I am sure that death will be exciting because it is only a phase in the cycle of life!"[16]

Still, he awaited orders. Old Blood and Guts, the salty General who'd barked out expletives and slapped a soldier in Sicily because he thought him a coward, was now in the dog house.

Patton knew that, though none doubted his ability, he was not well liked by his peers. Fearing he would not rise to the level of his own standards to meet his own expectations, Patton constantly drove himself and worked extremely hard. In his own eyes, he was never quite good enough, but he knew that his standards were much higher than most. This was often perceived as arrogant by those who only knew him casually. His friends, however, were among the most loyal friends one could have. They understood him and his motives well. They could easily separate his public persona from that of the man they knew privately. They knew the Patton who cried for the loss of his men and the Patton who thanked the Lord that such men had lived. Now, his fate lay in the hands of one who had been one of his oldest and dearest friends.

Dwight "Ike" Eisenhower and Georgie Patton had been the best of friends. They'd studied, played, drank and commanded together as they grew from young men in the 1920's to seasoned military leaders in the 1940's. Georgie was aware that he excelled over Ike. He was senior to Ike and had shared his school notes with him when Ike was admitted into the command school. Their friendship and careers bound them together; no other field commanders or staff officers were closer. Indeed, they knew each other well. They were, however, very different men. While Ike grew up very modestly, Georgie grew up well-off. Ike worked very hard to rise to his level of achievement. He was a quick study and rose to the occasion—some say too much to the occasion—however, was not prepared to deal with the politics of command. Inversely, Georgie, knowing how to play the game of politics within the army, prided himself in the fact that he was, and would always be, a soldier and neither a politician nor a diplomat. World War II sealed their fortunes together in history and strained their friendship to the point of collapse.

[Summersby]

"The most difficult man that Ike had to cope with - always excepting Montgomery, who was in a class by himself - was the flamboyant General George Patton. They were old, old friends, and Ike had great respect for Patton, but that man caused him a lot of grief."[17]

As Patton's superior officer, Eisenhower was commended on all the battles that Patton had won. This elevated Eisenhower's visibility and increased his popularity with the President and the American public alike. Though Eisenhower enjoyed this recognition, he was often reminded that these victories were directly attributable to Patton, a fact Eisenhower grew weary of hearing. Caught in a web of war-time politics, their once close bond had now turned into a love/hate relationship, one founded on mutual respect, an undeniable knowledge and acceptance of their respective talents, skills … and faults. General Eisenhower had made a decision.

Mrs. Beatrice Patton and her husband were in constant written communication while he was overseas. To avoid Army censoring, Patton denoted General Eisenhower as Divine Destiny, referring to the first two letters of Eisenhower's given name. Now Beatrice's turn to write, she drafted and mailed a letter to her husband in Palermo; the exact date of the mailing is unclear.

Working to ensure proper delivery, the Army Postal Service consulted their records and found that General Patton was assigned to command the United States Third Army. They therefore corrected the Army Post Office (APO) address, scratching out the designation of the Seventh Army, and replacing it with APO 403. Having been delivered to the Third Army Headquarters in Fort Sam Houston, Texas, this simple letter between spouses soon found itself in the hands of a Colonel in the Third Army's command staff.

The Third Army Headquarters command had received their orders December 31, 1943: They were being called to duty in the European theater. Their field army had yet to be assembled. Their headquarters were transplanted onto a ship so they could be moved to a new location in England. The Third Army mail accompanied them. En route to their destination, the command staff noted the letter from Beatrice. Once they read to whom the letter was addressed, they knew that General Patton would soon command them in England, information they were under orders to keep to themselves for the duration of the long sea voyage.

Half a world away, Patton knew that he had been relieved of his command of the Seventh Army, but that is all he knew. He had yet to be notified of his new command. Now depressed and weary in spirit, he continued to pray for another chance.

The year 1943 had come to an end. Patton had been asked by Chaplain Gerald Mygatt to contribute to a soldier's and sailor's prayer book. The prayer, though meant to be read by others, was most certainly a prayer offered by Patton. On this final day of the year, Patton composed the prayer:

```
          Those Things in Which I Ask Divine Assistance


                      A Soldiers Prayer

God of our fathers, who by land and sea has ever led us on to victory,
please continue your inspiring guidance in this the greatest of our
conflicts.

Strengthen my soul so that the weakening instinct of self-preservation,
```

which besets all of us in battle, shall not blind me to my duty, to my
manhood, to the glory of my calling, and to my responsibility to my
fellow soldiers.

Grant to our armed forces the disciplined valor and mutual confidence
which insures success in the war.

Let me not mourn for the men who have died fighting, but rather let me
be glad that such heroes have lived.

If it be my lot to die, let me do so with courage and honor in a
manner which will bring the greatest harm to the enemy, and please oh
Lord, protect and guide those I shall leave behind.

Give us the victory Lord.[18]


On December 29, 1943 Eisenhower had sent a communiqué to General Marshall regarding his
planning as Overlord Commander that included an unspecified army level commanding role for
General Patton.  Though Georgie had his faults, General Eisenhower knew that General Patton
had a superior fighting ability; in Ike's mind, there was no better fighting general in the Army.


[Summersby]

"I'm going to stand by Georgie," he told us. "I think we need him." Patton
was not abashed in the least when I talked to him about the incident a
few weeks later. "I always get in trouble with my goddamned mouth," he
said, "but if this sort of thing ever comes up again, I'd do it again."[19]


General Marshall approved all of the planning requests contained in Eisenhower's communiqué.

At the suggestion of General Marshall, Eisenhower left for the States to steel himself for the strains
that would soon accompany his new command.  He visited family and met with Marshall as well as
with President Roosevelt.  Eisenhower would give General Patton an army, but he would keep the
information from Patton … for a while.


[Patton]
**January 2, 1944 Sunday**

Flew to Algiers after church, arriving 1330. Hughes met me and was very
nice. He knows nothing about this "Anvil" plan any more than I do and
agrees with me that it is totally impractical and crazy.


In his diary, Major General Everett S. Hughes wrote that Patton was coming to cry on his shoulder.

Patton indeed did spend part of the day with his long-time confidant lamenting the loss of his trusted staff, for even if he were to receive another command, they would not accompany him. Many of them were with him pre-deployment, since their days of training in the desert in the States. Most were involved in both the North Africa and the Sicily campaigns.[20] They were more than just his staff – the trust between them was strong and reciprocal and they were as loyal to him as he was to them, a very rare thing to create or replicate.

Patton and Hughes discussed the planning of the pending Operation Anvil and both thought it was both impractical and crazy.[21]


[Patton]
**January 3, 1944 Monday**

Went to see Carey Crane, Assistant G-3, but was careful to ask no questions about myself or who conceived this plan.  On the face of it the thing looks like an attempt to save Clark[22] from the onus of his utter failure in Italy.  Probably it was decided to let me relieve him while he got the new job; then someone decided to make Lucas[23] the goat. Called on Hewitt to say goodbye.  He is on his way home for a short visit.  He was most outspoken in his regret that he and I were not to do "Anvil" together.  Saw a copy of a letter by a British general in which he said, "We don't need to worry about being commanded by an American.  Ike is only a political general and cannot command, as he has never had any experience."  I wired Air Vice Marshal Park asking if I could accept his invitation to visit Malta.  He replied yes, and we fly up tomorrow.

I cannot see how any normally intelligent person could inspire this fool change of staffs.  It is unfair and insulting to me, but is heartbreaking for the staff of Seventh Army who have been utterly loyal, and now find that their efforts get them nowhere.  It is damnable.  I hope I find out who did it and then get to a position so that I can really hurt him.  I shall do my best to see that they [the staff] are properly taken care of but they will certainly not be.  I have contemplated asking to be relieved but will stick it [out] at least for the present. Bea gave me "The Duke", a life of Wellington, and he too had many adversities.

His staff was also changed several times. Fate.


[Patton]
**January 4, 1944 Tuesday**

Left Algiers at 1000 and flew to Tebessa.  On the way passed over a rather large Roman ruin with a temple and theater that is not even listed on the map, and took a picture of it.  All the dump areas at Tebessa are cleaned up.  Hunted for, and found, another Roman ruin north of Tebessa ---from the road I saw it in the distance once in March.

Took a picture of Feriana, where we had our headquarters for the attack on Gafsa.  From Feriana we flew down Eesserschmidt Avenue to Gafsa and then over the battlefields. Took a picture of Feriana. It was quite thrilling to fly over Gafsa and El Guettar --- hundreds of memories surged up and all were a success.

I believe had it been possible for me to have looked over the battlefields from an airplane about the end of the first week, after I had got to know the country from the map and from the ground, it would have been a distinct advantage. Certainly had either myself or General Eddy gone up we would not have made the mistake of attacking the wrong half of Djebel Berda.  Also the gum tree road was a far less dangerous avenue of attack than I had thought from a study of the map.

On the other hand, too intimate a knowledge of the terrible difficulties of the mountains might have made me less bold.  In any case El Guettar was a great school, both in regard as to what to do and what not to do, and also as a means of producing self-confidence.  We also flew over Maknassy from the south.  Here I believe that an airplane view would have been an inestimable advantage for Maknassy is not half as strong a defensive position when viewed from the air as when viewed from the ground.

Arrived Malta 1500. Park met me and showed me all around the airfields. His men are the best disciplined and smartest airmen I have ever seen and I told him so. At 1830 we went to the San Lorenzo Palace built in 1620 by the Grand Master.  Field Marshal Lord Gort lives here and Codman, Stiller[24] and I are staying here, as Park is going to Cairo and has packed up his house.  Lord Gort is most charming and quite a man.  He has a V.C., three DSO's[25] and a 70-foot yawl, which he sails himself.  Played ping pong after dinner.  No running water nor heat in the palace.


Patton was well-read on military history.  Throughout his life, he'd had books sent to him and he'd read them cover to cover. It was therefore no surprise that he enjoyed his stay at the San Lorenzo Palace as it afforded him access to the rich history of the area.  He spent the whole of the day visiting the ruins, recalling the dates and times of their use, battles fought, won and lost, the names, field tactics and strategies of opposing commanders, making notes and taking pictures all the while, enhancing the knowledge he'd acquired from the volumes of texts he'd previously absorbed.

[Patton]
**January 5, 1944 Wednesday**

Captain Holland, Lord Gort's aide, took us to see the sights. The forts are artillery stone proof structures, not quite Vauban but pretty good and very well built. They were built between 1400 and 1500 and are artillery stone proof including the roof, although of a pre-Vauban type. They are well built, of local limestone which cuts like butter until it has been exposed to the air. The library was most interesting. I saw a codex of 1420 being the story of St. Anthony from birth to death.

He was continually beset with women, or rather, devils in the shape of women. They all have horns sort of toned in with their headdresses. There was one very interesting picture in this set which showed an armorer's shop with all sorts of armor hanging up for sale. These suits were both mail and plate and ranged from late 1100 to 1400, showing clearly that there must have been a trade in second hand armor, so that one is wrong in thinking of armor as of distinct dates. Every knight had to have 16 crosses of nobility before he could join the Knights of Malta and all these are preserved and are a great genealogical record.

These family trees have been preserved since somewhere around 1200, because when the Knights were driven out of Rhodes by the Turks, they had put up such a great resistance that the Turks gave them the honors of war and let them take out everything, including their library and their money. This collection of genealogical data is probably the oldest and most accurate in the world.

Some of the illuminated manuscripts are beautiful. Even after printing came in, the capitals' were painted in by hand. The knights had to vow poverty, chastity and obedience. They only kept the last vow.

They were not priests. The dock yard was most interesting and shows that air bombing is impotent to destroy a harbor.

[Patton]
**January 6, 1944 Thursday**

Left Malta at 0900. Park came to see me off. This island is densely populated; some 2,000 people to the acre. It is full of walls and houses and churches and is utterly not self-supporting. The people are rather a poor mongrel type, like Sicilians. Reached Palermo at 1030. All the mountains are covered with snow.

I called all the Chiefs of Sections in at 1330 and had Gay read the order relieving me from Seventh Army. I told them not to worry, but to be as loyal to Clark as they have been to me and I thanked them for their loyalty and then choked up and quit. Well, if the Third Cavalry was baptized in blood and fire and came out steel, I have been rolled in the mud and have come out with my faith and a sense of humor.

[Patton]
**January 7, 1944 Friday**

Made out recommendations for the promotions of Gay to Major General, Cummings, Muller, Nixon and Franklin to be Brigadiers. Also had two copies made of recommendations for the DSM[26] for officers of the Seventh Army who have been turned down.  I am taking all these to Italy tomorrow and am going to ask both Clark and Lucas to do what they can to get them approved.  It is the most, and the least, I can do for men who have been utterly loyal to me.

Though the papers and the pundits caricatured him based on the more colorful aspects of his personality, Patton was deeply loving … and loyal.  He looked after his men.  He had known the Commanding General of the Fifth Army, Mark Clark, since he was "in knee pants"[27], and he did not like nor trust him.  History would soon agree with Patton's assessment.  Patton flew to Naples to meet with both Clark and General Gruenther, Clark's Chief of Staff, to personally reinforce his written recommendations, as well as to have the opportunity to see some of his men once more, those who had served so faithfully and so well under his command.

[Patton]
**January 8, 1944 Saturday**

Landed at Naples at 1000. Lt. Colonel Southerland, Aide to Clark met me with two cars and two motorcycles. We drove to Caserta where Clark has his headquarters. The rear echelon occupies the Bourbon Palace, a huge building of 2400 rooms which, with its grounds, served as a model for Versailles. The advance Command Post, in which Clark advertises that he lives with his troops, is some 4,000 yards farther north but still in the palace grounds. He and Gruenther have caravans there and a large wooden hut, with a radio, reading lamp, easy chairs, etc. This dangerous outpost is some three hours hard driving from the nearest front line.

Both Gruenther and Clark were most condescending and treated me like an undertaker treats the family of the deceased. It was rather hard to take, especially as I am certain that they pulled the wires which got me removed from "Anvil", but I had to be nice as I want my men promoted and decorated. I then drove with Codman to see Keyes, whose command post is well up. Keyes met me on the road and we went to see the right side of his front.  I slept in a caravan for the first time and think they are very comfortable.

[Patton]
**January 9, 1944 Sunday**

Keyes, Codman, Lowman[28] and I drove up to see Honk Allen's[29] attack. We climbed a high hill, and in spite of my practice at Palermo, I was quite out of breath.  So were the rest.  Honk had his OP in a house, the only one on the hill. This is a mistake as houses, especially isolated ones, draw fire.  He is doing pretty well but is too far back.  He had taken his objective but the British on his left failed, as usual, to take theirs and are trying to blame Allen, saying that fire from the hill he captured got them enflanked. This is not true. They failed because they only sent in a battalion where a regiment was needed.

In the afternoon we visited General Ryder at the Headquarters 34th Division.  He still has his bum chief of staff, whom I told him to get rid of in Tunisia.  He seemed full of reasons why things cannot be done. I believe that, while he is a brave man, he is not a good soldier.  We then drove down to an artillery Observation Post and climbed up to have a look.  On the way down one of our batteries close by started to fire so I stopped to take a picture.  We then started down again and a salvo of four shells struck, two in the road where we would have been but for the picture, and two on top of the hill where we had done the observing.  It was a nice volley, as they all arrived together and were well grouped.

None of these shells burst more than 30 feet from where we were, yet no one was hit. Codman had some fragments hit his helmet and a piece of a nose of a shell struck within a few inches of my foot but was evidently a ricochet as it did not bury.  At the foot of the hill there was a cave full of ammunition and sleeping men.  One of the bursts lighted the ammunition piled in this cave, which started to go off and I have never seen people move so fast in evacuating. One man turned two somersaults, lit on his feet, and passed me doing a hundred yards in 8 seconds. However, a Lieutenant, whose name I regret I forgot to obtain, and several men, hurried back and went into the cave to see if any of the men had been wounded.  None had been hit.  I gave Keyes my fleece-lined overshoes, as it is very cold.

We spent the night at VI Corps Headquarters south of Caserta.  Lucas was fine but looked worried.  He is in charge of the "Shingle" operation.[30] He does not think he will get the Fifth Army when Clark leaves and thinks that some hometown boy from Washington will get it.  I hope he is wrong and I hope he is successful at "Shingle", but I am not sure that he has sufficient drive.


[Patton]
**January 10, 1944 Monday**

Told Clark goodbye.  He says that, due to the efforts of the Prime Minister, more emphasis is being placed on "Shingle", to such an extent that "Anvil" may not have the troops or the boats to come off. If this is so it may produce trouble with Stalin, as "Anvil" was definitely promised him. Clark and the British Navy between them have changed the date on "Shingle" three times. It is set too soon now. No rehearsal. He changed

the date for "Anvil" three times while I was with him, moving it backward
and forward.

The left corner of Clark's mouth is slightly drawn down as if he had
been paralyzed. He is quite jumpy and so is Gruenther.   Drove to see
3rd Division. Truscott was as usual and we had a long talk on river
crossings.  He has done one.  They are like landings.  I also talked on
rifle fire and heavy weapons.  He has no changes to offer on what I have
written.  Sent for Francis Graves[31] and saw him --- just a child. Could
not locate Jim Totten.[32]  He is supposed to be in Sicily looking for me.
Reached Palermo at 1600.  No news, no Totten.


Patton wrote home to Beatrice of his near miss while observing Honk Allen's attack.


**January 11, 1944 Tuesday**

Mathematically, I should be dead as none of the four craters was more
than 30 feet from me, but I am not dead or even hurt. It gave me great
self-confidence.  The Lord had a perfect cut for me and pulled his punch.[33]


January 12, 1944 Wednesday: Thirteen officers and enlisted men left Fort Sam Houston by train
to Port Hamilton, New York.  There, they boarded the HMS Queen Mary to sail to England.
They were the advanced echelon, chosen to establish the Command Post and secure billeting
for the army which was to follow.  During their voyage, they would accidentally learn who their
Commanding Officer would be, yet, weeks after the approval of the decision, Patton still remained
uninformed.

January 13, 1944 Thursday: Patton flew back to his headquarters and waited impatiently for any
news.  He wrote to his brother-in-law, Frederick Ayer, as he often did when he was distressed.


[Patton]
**January 14, 1944   Friday**

The "incident" has given the stenographers hot bearings so I am typing
this myself.  I have had over two hundred letters from everyone from
Frank Murphy down and only eleven were nasty and these by very ignorant
people.

The Catholic Church has been very much on my side, as have the veterans
and the war mothers.  I think I could run for office on the strength of
my misdeeds.  I am not the first General to catch hell; Wellington had
plenty of it, as did Grant, Sherman, and countless others.

I am quite worried over the reaction after the war.  I have already met several quite intelligent men who say, "Now we will have no more wars," and when you ask them on what they base that forlorn hope since the history of the world is the history of war, they smile and reply, "Things are different now." Yet the avowed purpose of the Treaty of Vienna in 1815 was to see that that was the last war.  Around 1700 B.C. the Hittites, Cretans, and Egyptians had a tri-party treaty to avert wars, and we learned about it when in 1914 some explorers discovered the Hittite capital and in the Library discovered the bricks with the treaty on them - yet before the mud had dried, the Egyptians and the Cretans had ganged up and destroyed the Hittites.

If we again think that wars are over, we will surely have another one and damned quick.  "Man is WAR" and we had better remember that. Also, we had better look out for ourselves and make the rest of the world look out for themselves. If we try to feed the world, we will starve and perhaps destroy America.

Our soldiers are coming to form in a wonderful way.  The men who have been through it have developed a pride and discipline that is magnificent. You can tell a new outfit a mile off by the fact that they lack both pride and discipline, but due to association with the old men, they pick up very fast.

My own officers have been wonderful in their loyalty to me throughout the trouble.  I told some of them that I might be on the skids and that if they wanted to leave me, I would help them to as good a job as I could. Not a man quit.  I had to loan some of them recently and they all begged me to be sure and get them back, and two of them cried. So did I.

Did you read "My Thoughts on Christmas" by Bea? It is swell.

Lots of love and many thanks for your loyal support.[34]


[Patton]
**January 14, 1944 Friday**

Gay had a letter from Colonel Harkins which is quite discouraging.

Clark has sent General Caffey[35] to Algiers to represent him in planning "Anvil".  Caffey is no good, so Clark must think the show is off.  Also we are already pressed for time on the requisitions.  I wish this thing would clear up.


[Patton]
**January 15, 1944 Saturday**

General Gay, Colonel Odom, Maj. Murnane[36], Maj. Stiller and Lt. Busey[37] who speaks Italian, and I left by car for Troina.  Gay's and my car both broke down so we rode in a Command Car and a weapons carrier.  We went on the road just short of San Stefano and reached an elevation of 3900 feet (quite cold) and had a magnificent view of Aetna, of which I took some pictures.  I hope they come out.

On the way to Troina we stopped off to look at the Chateau Cerami, from which place I observed the attack on Troina during the battle. There is very little left of the Chateau which, however, is extremely ancient as it apparently developed from a cave and has now practically returned to its original cavern state.  However, the town is worth seeing as it is the dirtiest of all the filthiest places I have ever been in. It is amazing how animals can live with such dirty people, not how people can live with such dirty animals.  Troina is much less hurt than one could expect when it is remembered that we shelled it with 130 guns for nearly five days and attacked for two days with 70 medium bombers. During this operation, only 240 civilians were hurt.  Roger the Great Count's Castle is now part of the church but is clearly Norman, and I saw some pieces of what I think are Roman brick in the cellar.  The priest knew something of the history, but not much. It was in front of this tower that Roger had his fight with the drunken Saracen, and after his horse was killed, calmly unsaddled him to take the saddle back into the castle in order to show that he had no fear of the Saracens.

I had hoped to get to Enna before dark to see the castle there, which is supposed to have been built on a Roman basilica, but it was too dark.

No news of what will happen to me.

On the way home Gay made a profound remark, which is well to remember in the next operation.  He said that when Bradley stormed Troina it was not necessary, for we had cut it off.  Of course to use the road east, it was necessary to go through the town, but we could have taken it by starvation in a day or two.

General Eisenhower's appointment as Supreme Commander of Allied Forces in Europe put him in command over every British general, and in control their armies.  His arrival in England was not well received.[38]

Eisenhower sent his private B-17 Flying Fortress to fetch his driver, Kay Summersby.  He'd previously sent it to Algiers, in January, to pick her up from Egypt where she'd been touring with him and his son before General Marshall had summoned him back to Washington for his "secret vacation."  Kay was now landing in London.

[Summersby]

I flew to London in General Eisenhower's brand-new B-17. It was a fantastically luxurious plane, with wood paneling and comfortable seats upholstered in blue leather. After hitching rides in cargo planes where you were lucky if there was a bench or a row of bucket seats bolted down (and the toilet facilities were also of the bucket variety), I thought this plane, with its carpeting and bunks and a washroom with a Bush toilet, was like a Claridge's in the sky. This time I was not traveling with Vuitton cases and silken luxuries carefully wrapped in scented paper. All my belongings were easily stuffed into a duffel bag, and I did not feel the least bit underprivileged. I had learned how unimportant possessions are.[39]

Due to heavy fog, Ike could not fly into London. Instead, he boarded *Bayonet*, his private train. They headed for Scotland the evening of January 14th, the day before Kay was to arrive. Late the next night, on the 15th, Kay and Ike were reunited.[40]

[Summersby]

I suppose inevitably, we found ourselves in each other's arms in an unrestrained embrace. Our ties came off. Our jackets came off. Buttons were unbuttoned. It was as if we were frantic.

And we were …[41]

They were unable to go any farther. Ike confessed that the long trip had exhausted him. In the morning he apologized again.[42]

Kay and Ike had been paired a short time after the beginning of the war. In London, they shared "Telegraph Cottage," and during their time together in Algiers, "Sailor's Delight," a well-guarded hideaway thirty miles outside of the main city.

The unique name they chose for "Ike's" dog further suggested an all too familiar relationship between them, thus, added some validity to the rumors about them. The black Scotty was named "Teleck," an abbreviation of the name of the cottage they shared, combined with Kay's first initial. And Kay carried Teleck everywhere.

Years later, Kay would confirm the suspicions and rumors of the affair[43], but, only after President Harry S. Truman made mention of their relationship as lovers.

## Truman Drops a Bombshell

In 1973, President Harry S. Truman was interviewed for a book of oral history, *Plain Speaking, An oral biography of Harry S. Truman.* (Miller, Merle, Berkley Publishing). In it,

Truman stated that, as President, he learned of certain letters between Generals Eisenhower and Marshall that were housed at the Pentagon.  In this exchange, Eisenhower declared his desire to divorce his wife and marry Kay Summersby. Marshall, in turn, informed Eisenhower that if he were to do so, he would make Eisenhower's life miserable, for the rest of his life.

Truman sent for the letters and had them destroyed. (Miller, 1973, pgs 367-369)

*Plain Speaking* became a best seller, which may have been one of the factors that persuaded Summersby to write her own "tell all" book.  She died of cancer shortly thereafter.

The favorable outcome of the War, Eisenhower's prominence as Supreme Allied Commander and his popularity with the general public back home, as well as the urgings of key players in the political machine, placed Eisenhower as a top candidate for the U.S. presidency.  Thus, at War's end, and at Marshall's insistence, Ike severed his relationship with Kay.

[Patton]
**January 16, 1944 Sunday**

General Joyce and two aides came at 1600 and stayed all night. He is apparently on the way out but was very sporting and showed no bitterness.

[Patton]
**January 17, 1944 Monday**

Saw General Joyce off in the morning.  Came to office and am either coming down with some disease or else have "cafard" very badly. I simply don't feel like doing a thing, so am going home.  I do wish something would eventuate about myself.

[Patton]
**January 18, 1944 Tuesday**

Feel all right this morning.  Sergeant Meeks[44]  told me after breakfast that he heard on the radio last night that General Bradley has been made commander of all the ground troops in England. I suppose that this means that he will command the American Army Group.  I had thought that possibly I might get this command. It is another disappointment, but so

far in my life all the disappointments I have had have finally worked out
to my advantage, although at the time it is hard to see how they will.
If I am predestined, as I feel that I am, this too will eventually be to
my advantage.

Bradley is a man of great mediocrity.  At Benning in command, he failed
to get discipline.  At Gafsa, when it looked as though the Germans might
turn our right flank on April 5th and 6th, he suggested that we withdraw
Corps Headquarters to Feriana.  I refused to move. In Sicily, when the
45th Division approached Cefalu, he halted them for fear of a possible
German landing east of Termini.  I had to order him to move and told
him that I would be responsible for his rear, and that his timidity had
lost us one day.  He tried to stop the landing operation east of Cape
D'Orlando because he thought it was dangerous.  I told him I would take
the blame if it failed and that he could have the credit if it was a
success.  Finally, on the night of August 16-17th he asked me to call
off the landing east of Milazzo, for fear our troops might shoot at each
other.  He also failed to get word to all units of the II Corps of the
second paratroop landing.

On the other hand Bradley has many of the attributes which are considered
desirable in a general.  He wears glasses, has a strong jaw, talks
profoundly and says little, and is a shooting companion of the Chief of
Staff.  Also a loyal man.  I consider him among our better generals.

I suppose that all that has happened is calculated to get my morale
so that I will say What the Hell!  Stick it up your ass and I will go
home"; but I won't.  I still believe.[45]

### *Avoir le Cafard?*

There's been some speculation, and more than a few have written about this time in
Patton's life, suggesting that he was unbalanced or paranoid.  However, a comprehensive
examination of the events of that time, as well as an examination of what Patton was
feeling, as documented in his own words in his diary, reflects the spectrum of emotion,
with all its peaks and valleys, that one would expect from anyone faced with similar
circumstances.

To be received at Clark's headquarters as a mourner at one's own funeral when one had
been a highly respected military leader for the duration of one's career would be difficult
for anyone.  For Patton, this was amplified by his assessment of Clark as an ineffective
military leader.  Because Patton's men were now directly under Clark's command,

Patton had to swallow his pride and "play nice" in order to get them promoted and decorated. As their disaffection was mutual, Clark availed himself of this opportunity to talk down to Patton.

Furthermore, the main "cast of characters" involved all had personal, societal and/or military relationships before the war. At this point in Patton's career, his chain of command was a very short one. Patton answered to Eisenhower, who answered to General George Marshall, who answered to President Roosevelt.

Patton and the Secretary of War, Henry Stimson, were good friends who'd first met when Patton was assigned to Fort Benning. Before the war, Patton was often called upon to help with the procurement of materials and support for military matters as the U.S. Army was underfunded and under-resourced at the time. General Marshall and Patton also knew each other very well. Even President Roosevelt knew Patton well. Coming from a wealthy family, Beatrice Patton was well connected in both political and social circles. She'd met the first lady, Eleanor Roosevelt, while riding. The two became friends and would ride and lunch together. And then there was Eisenhower. Having met during their days at the military academy, the Patton and Eisenhower families had befriended one another long before the start of the war. Ike told Georgie that if Georgie were ever to get a command, he wanted to be his executive officer.[46]

In September of 1942, the battles in the African desert were going very badly for the British forces. Prior to the planning of what would become Operation Torch and the invasion of North Africa, Marshall had asked Patton to plan to be sent ahead into Africa to support the British with one American armored division. He ordered Patton to submit a military strategy. Naturally, Patton assumed that he would command the operation. Patton studied the situation, then suggested that two divisions would be better. Marshall sent him back to the Desert Training Center without explanation. Patton suspected that he'd been sent back because he hadn't followed orders without question. He was unaware, and uninformed, that Churchill and Roosevelt had changed the plan to a full-scale invasion (Operation Torch), which was now being organized. Patton, believing he had ruffled General Marshall's feathers, redid his estimates and submitted a revised plan with only one armored division. Patton was unaware that his original plan was reviewed, thought well developed, and that he was picked to command the ground forces in the North African invasion. Perhaps Marshall knew of Patton's tendency to brood over his decisions and revise them to please his superiors. Perhaps both Marshall and Eisenhower knew this would humble Patton and make him more compliant, something they thought should be done for his own good. Regardless of planning or intent, such were the results. The intent and planning of Patton's superiors again comes into question when examining Eisenhower's withholding of information regarding Patton's reassignment and command of Third Army, long after the decision had been made. Was Eisenhower trying to manipulate Patton's mood to make him more obedient?

Eisenhower was a well-schooled diplomat, an attribute that Patton did not possess. Thus, though junior to many of the generals he would latter have to command, Marshall selected Eisenhower as Supreme Allied Commander. Though the content of many of Patton's diary entries and letters home can be perceived as sharp and biting towards Eisenhower, too often they are cultivated to paint a picture of extreme disharmony between the two. Many of Patton's observations were keenly correct but kept to himself or in letters to his wife. Patton also had many friends in high office who were politically influential and was not as politically naive as others have thought. He was good friends with Secretary of War Henry Stimson. Beatrice was good friends and went riding with Eleanor Roosevelt, the first lady. Patton had great political influence as well as did his wife, but Patton was a soldier first. He would not think of holding a political office as he was no politician; he was a soldier.

Patton was often angry with "Ike" and for good reason, but knew his place and vented in private and mostly in his diary. Both Patton's and Eisenhower's actual behavior suggest otherwise; they were friends when they meet in person. Patton respected the chain of command. Ike was now the Supreme Allied Commander in Europe. Thus, Patton demonstrated a military decorum with Eisenhower when the two were in the presence of subordinates. And though Patton was, at times, highly critical of Eisenhower, and Eisenhower unhappy with Patton's "goddamned mouth," they were still friends; the kind of friends that could disagree and argue privately and yet never question or doubt that they could depend on one another at pivotal moments, "When the chips were down." Though stated quite bluntly, many of Patton's observations were keenly correct, however, Eisenhower never knew of them. Patton only shared such thoughts with his wife, in the form of letters, and in his journal, his main vehicle for "blowing off steam."

Whether he was being purposefully manipulated by people who knew him well, Patton himself best explained what it was that he was going through during this time – he had a very bad "cafard." By this, Patton was referring to the abbreviated version of the French idiom *Avoir le cafard*[47], a poetic, thus, much more expressive way of saying that one, as B.B. King would put it, "has the blues," a condition that is a far cry from a clinical state of depression, unbalance or paranoia. As well, he was determined that this chapter in his life would pass and, thus, would not comprise the greater part of his eulogy.

January 19, 1944 Wednesday: General Patton wrote home to his wife that he had nothing to do and no place to do it in. Patton wrote his wife that if he did not believe in fate … he would tell them to all go to hell and put the "When and If"[48] in commission and sail. "[I] am not dead and buried by a long shot."[49]

Patton turned his thoughts to military matters, specifically, to Operation Shingle, the landings at Anzio, Italy.

[Patton]
**January 20, 1944 Thursday**

Captain Carey, of the Navy, came to call. He says that "Shingle" is pretty dubious as the beaches are bad and largely unknown, and that in the event that the LST's[50] can't land they are to be landed by LCVP's[51]. This is always a difficult operation, and if a coastal battery at one end of the beach is not taken out by the Rangers, it will be nearly impossible. At a rehearsal, some nights ago, 40 Dukws[52] were lost. I think that the British 1st Division is using the Dukws. If the thing is a success, Clark will get the credit. If it fails, Lucas will get the blame. It seems inconceivable that the Boche[53] will not guess that we are coming, but he has made so many foolish mistakes that we may get ashore unopposed after all.

January 21, 1944 Friday: General Eisenhower visited with the King of England. Weather permitting, Operation Shingle would be launched on the 22nd of January. The Operation was a top priority of Prime Minister Churchill, thus, a high priority tied to the politics of the day, and of the highest importance for success. It would consist of two divisions, one British and one American, landing on the west coast of Italy at Anzio somewhat ahead of General Mark Clark's Fifth Army. Its purpose was to land behind the enemy's front lines in order to outflank them.

January 22, 1944 Saturday: Troops of VI Corps, Fifth Army led by Commanding General John Porter Lucas landed on the Italian beach near the prewar resort towns of Anzio and Nettuno. The operation was code-named SHINGLE. The flawless landing took the Germans by complete surprise; there was little to no resistant, thus, the Allied forces were able to swiftly advance inland. The next four months, however, would see some of the most savage fighting of the War as German troops gathered to eliminate what Adolf Hitler called the "Anzio abscess."[54] The blame for the bloodbath that ensued did indeed fall on General Lucas.

General Eisenhower had problems of his own. His acceptance as the Allied Supreme Commander was not taken well in some circles of the British military nor among the English people. He was also busy building his staff at his new headquarters in London. Eisenhower, now with a much larger responsibility, had recommended Major General Walter Bedell Smith, his Chief of Staff, for his third star, to elevate him to the rank of Lt. General.[55]

Rank in the Army was two-fold: rank, and date of promotion. Therefore, when soldiers shared a rank, the date of the promotion determined seniority. With few exceptions, in theory and in practice, if all other duties remained equal, the junior officer answered to the senior officer of the same rank.[56] The Chief of Staff, as an agent of the Office of the Supreme Commander, however, spoke for General Eisenhower in his absence. General Smith was keenly aware of the boundaries of his office, and was thus aware that he should only act when Eisenhower delegated him to do so. The constraints of this position made the job an extremely difficult one. As well, though the same rank, it was a completely different job than that of a combat general.  In the field, Smith would have been a decision-maker; however, as Chief of Staff, he served as a trusted diplomat, one who had to execute the decisions of the Supreme Commander.  Loyalty to the Commander was of utmost importance; loyalty to a fault.  Generals Patton and Bedell "Beetle" Smith[57] were like oil and water, and would remain so.


[Patton]
**January 22, 1944 Saturday**

Gay, Codman, Madame Marconi, Odom, Stiller, Murnane and I flew to Castelvetrano where we met the cars and drove to Selonius which is now called Selinute. Until yesterday I had always thought this place was "Sciacca" but I was wrong. This town had a life of only 250 years, but must have been very prosperous and was destroyed in 406 BC by the Carthaginians. On a hill west of the town there are three temples, completely wrecked by an earthquake --- the northern one, that of Apollo, is the largest in Sicily and must have been very magnificent, but it was never finished and only a few of the columns are fluted. The columns are perfectly stupendous. The capitals, which are Doric, must weigh five to ten tons each. We then visited the town where there are several smaller, but older, temples. The wall around the town is very interesting. On the north side, which was the most vulnerable, there is a double wall, the inner one having flanking towers on each side of the gate. There is an open space and a second, in front of which there is a ditch, and, on the near side of the ditch is a hollow way, which was apparently roofed over at one time, with doorways entering the ditch through which the defenders could counter-attack people who had got to the bottom. In front of the ditch is a semi-circular outwork, or barbican, which, in turn, is defended by a ditch with a drawbridge. Unless I am very wrong, this is a more complicated form of defense than was known in 405 B.C., and to me it smells very much of Norman influence. I believe this town must have been refortified by the Normans, yet it is said never to have been occupied since it was destroyed. However, the stonework seems to be Greek.

On the return trip, we flew over Moyta which was once the leading Carthaginian city in Western Sicily, and which is now an island occupied, apparently, by one farm.  Some of the walls are still visible, and from the air you can see, underwater, the causeway which the Greeks built in order to storm the place. We also flew over Erice, which is the original of the present city of Trapani, being situated on top of a high mountain. There is a fairly good Norman castle there.

On reaching Palermo, I received the following telegram:

> To: CG[58]
> Seventh Army, for Patton,
> 22 January 44.
> George S. Patton, Jr. Lieut.
> General, 02605, U. S. Army,
> Orders issued relieving you from assignment this theater

and assigning you to duty in U.K. Request you proceed to
NATOUSA, Algiers for orders. ---CG, NATOUSA.

Looking at it in retrospect to the chain of events this sounds logical,
but on the other hand, why have they been so slow about it and why have
they taken all of my staff? It makes it most difficult for my people and
for me. I wired Devers, who I think is in Italy, asking him whether he
wants me to wait for him here. Radio saying VI Corps landing at mouth of
Tiber is a success, and unopposed.

[Patton]
**January 23, 1944 Sunday**

Went to church and spent the rest of the day doing up my desk and doing
the other things incident to packing.

[Patton]
**January 24, 1944 Monday**

Took off at 1030 with Colonel Cummings, Lt. Colonel Codman and self for
Algiers and we were met by Colonel Harkins. Went to Hughes' office who
knew nothing but that Devers had heard I was at Palermo and had wired War
Department orders for me. When they came they simply told me to proceed
to UK. This was very nice of Devers but not instigated by me.

[Patton]
**January 25, 1944 Tuesday**

Visited the Ecole Normale and told the planning staff of the Seventh Army
goodbye with sincere regret on both sides. Left Algiers at 1200 in a C-54
with 250 pounds of extra luggage (mainly consisting of papers pertaining
to my personal files, and some clothes) and a female secretary belonging
to Ike. Arrived in Marrakech at 1600 and went to Taylor Villa, which
is run by the Air Corps for visiting strangers. There are no charges,
which I think is a mistake, as it wastes good money and people are not
appreciative of what they get free.

Brigadier Dunphie (British), who was with me in Tunisia and who was
wounded the day Major Jenson was killed, happened to be in the house. I
asked him why he was not wearing his Silver Star and he told me he had
never received it. I had recommended him for it on April 1, 1943, but
since he went to the hospital and I left the Corps shortly afterwards,
the paper apparently never reached him. Colonel Codman took off his own
Silver Star Ribbon, and we decorated Dunphie there on the spot. I will
have to see that he gets the citation when I get to England. Left for
Prestwick in a C-54 at 2400.

[Patton]
**January 26, 1944 Wednesday**

Arrived Prestwick at 0945 after a perfect trip, save for the last hour, when there was no visibility. Colonel Henry, AC, met us and was most obliging. I shaved and we had a good breakfast. Left Prestwick at 1100 in a C-47 --- pea soup all the way --- could not land at the point we meant to. General John C. H. Lee and Commander Butcher met me. Lee put Codman and myself up at his flat. Called on Ike at office and found I am to command Third Army. All novices and in support of Bradley's First Army --- not such a good job but better than nothing. Ike asked me to dinner … As far as I can remember this is my twenty-seventh start from zero since entering the U. S. Army. Each time I have made a success of it, and this one must be the biggest.

When Georgie arrived for his dinner with Ike, he found that Ike had planned to bifurcate their evening into formal and informal, thus, after General Eisenhower had given General Patton "a severe bawling out"[59] for failure to follow his previous instructions of counting to ten before issuing an order or taking any abrupt action, Ike changed hats and invited his old friend to dine. Patton had been most contrite. Though holding a position of confidence, Eisenhower's U.S. naval aide, Captain Harry C. Butcher kept a secret diary which he published after the war. Not understanding the complicated nature of the deep friendship between Ike and Georgie, as well as not fully appreciating the tenuous position that Patton found himself in as he was still on probation, Butcher's impression of Patton was colored by the pre-dinner exchange.

[Butcher]

He is master of flattery and succeeds in turning any difference of views with Ike into a deferential acquiescence to the views of the Supreme Commander. For instance he told Ike during a lively discussion of history that anyone would be foolish to contest the rightness of the Supreme Commander's views, particularly as he is now - in Patton's words - "The most powerful person in the world." Ike glumly and noncommittally passes off flattery. General Patton is to command the Third Army, headquarters of which are now assembling. While censorship has been imposed on Patton's arrival, Ike said that he does not intend to keep him under a blanket for more than a few days. When Patton's name is released he will probably get critical reaction from the press, not only from the US but from the UK because of his new assignment. According to General McClure, the British press had keenly resented Patton's action in Sicily. Some American correspondents had thought the incident would ruin Ike. Of course he was made supreme commander after disclosure of Patton's rash actions. Incidentally, Patton said that hereafter he certainly would be more careful as to the place he had his tantrum and certainly will not choose a hospital.[60]

In his diary, Patton chronicled the events of the evening as well, stating, "Kay Summersby, Capt. Harry C. Butcher USNR, Navel aide, diarist and confident to General Eisenhower, a British aide-de-camp and a WAC captain were present." Patton reflected that Ike was very nasty and a show off, "he always is when Kay is present and criticizes General John Lee for his flamboyance which he, Ike, would give a million to possess."

Georgie did not begrudge Ike the company of Miss Summersby. Out of respect for their long-time friendship, Georgie felt obligated to hold his tongue; and Georgie's knowledge of the relationship was a factor that Ike was constantly aware of.

However, even if this were solely a wartime fling, it was an affair with a man who was presently one of the most powerful men in the world. Even if they were truly in love, this love affair, which had been exposed to influential forces in powerful circles, was unwise as it presented real threats to security, as well as the opportunities for blackmail and undue influence. Having an affair with a married man who kept the most highly guarded secrets of the Allied forces may have been exciting, but it was also extremely dangerous … for everyone.

Patton had always felt that Kay was part of the reason for Eisenhower's undue allegiance to the British. He felt that she and Churchill had Ike's ear on what should have been military decisions. He believed that Churchill had surrounded Eisenhower with an over-abundance of British officers. And though, officially, Kay Summersby was *just* Ike's driver, Kay had access to all of Eisenhower's mail, and had served as his hostess at numerous dinner parties. Patton believed that Kay obtained military and personal information through the intimate relationship she and Ike shared, and that she continuously relayed this information to Churchill. Patton remarked that through Kay, "Churchill knew when Eisenhower talked in his sleep."[61]

"Kay [Summersby] was an attractive 30 year old model and was a both shrewd and knowledgeable woman."[62] Though many knew of this relationship, few suspected, as Patton did, that Kay was a British agent. The evidence, when inconclusive. However, if Kay was indeed a spy for Churchill, she would have been a perfect one as she had specialized access to important information, files, and Ike.[63]

Patton also believed that knowledge of the Eisenhower/Summersby relationship was exploited by General Bernard Montgomery. He'd remarked to close staff members that this was indeed one of the reasons that Montgomery seemed to get his way when tactical and strategical considerations were against him.[64] Yet, clarity regarding the existence of this influences or its extent was not known with certainty.

Though Patton had a fear that Ike could relieve him of his duties at any point during the war, their friendship, as well as their intimate knowledge of each other's secrets, restrained their actions. With that said, Patton was in the process of writing his book, *War as I Knew It*, when tragedy struck and lead to his untimely demise. After his death, the book was heavily redacted by his wife before publication as she feared her children would be targeted for retribution being that both daughters were married to career military men. Had Patton defiantly detailed Eisenhower's infidelity during the war, Ike's presidential bid would have been derailed.

Patton was always courteous to Kay, and Kay had a high opinion of Patton. They first met on August 6, 1942 when Patton came to London for a conference with Eisenhower. On several occasions during this time, at Ike's insistence, Patton acquiesced to Kay driving him around London to show the sights of the city.

[Summersby]

I had met General Patton in London and driven him about occasionally.
I'll never forget my first meeting with him. Ike had suggested that I
give him "the dock tour" - the same tour I had given Ike and Mark Clark
when they first visited London. General Patton reacted very emotionally
as I drove him around the East End dock area and showed him site after
site that had been a grammar school, a warehouse, a cinema, a tenement
or whatever and now was a heap of rubble. He would burst out with
"The bastards! The dirty mother-fucking bastards!" He would apologize
immediately. "Excuse me, Miss Summersby. I beg your pardon. My tongue ran
away with me." Seconds later he would be at it again. "The sonsabitches!
The bloody sonsabitches!" he would curse - and then apologize.

Despite his profanity, he was by no means coarse or crude. He was a
gentleman, terribly courteous and very proper, with great respect for
and consideration of women. I am not saying that the legendary "blood
and guts" George Patton did not exist. He most definitely did. But there
was another side to the man, a rather sweet and affectionate side. He was
very strange - and very endearing. He loved the Army. He loved pomp and
spit and polish. He was always ramrod stiff, whether standing or sitting,
and always a military fashion plate. I had never seen as many decorations
as he used to wear. They stretched from armpit to armpit. He should have
been a general in the time of the Romans when he could ride around in a
chariot. And he had the world's most unfortunate voice, a high-pitched
womanish squeak.

Georgie was amazingly childlike in some ways. One day he pulled out one of
his guns and waved it under my nose. "Look at that," he commanded. "It's
very handsome," I commented, wondering why he was showing it to me. "People
always talk about my pearl-handled revolvers," he complained. "That's
not pearl. That's ivory. Good solid ivory," he said with satisfaction.
"From an elephant," he added a few seconds later… it was typical George
Patton.

You never knew what was coming next.  Unfortunately… after dinner, when
the men started swapping off-color stories, Patton would always shoo me
out of the room as if I were his daughter, saying, "Kay, it's time for
you to leave. You tell one of those handsome aides of mine to play Ping-
Pong with you." Ike would wink. I'd excuse myself and off I'd go. I always
appreciated his thoughtfulness. Georgie was really quite prudish. He
could be very charming, and I liked him.[65]


Kay further mused …


Unlike Ike, General Patton believed in nothing less than the very best
for himself. He was living in a palace that had once belonged to the King

of Sicily. It suited Georgie's grandiose style very well. After lunch, he took us on the promised sight-seeing trip. He was an enthusiastic and well-informed guide. Our final stop was a medieval church just outside Palermo. He gave Ruth and me a short lecture on medieval architecture and then sank to his knees and prayed aloud for the success of his troops, for the health and happiness of his family and for a safe flight back for Ruth and me. He was completely unself-conscious and did not care who listened in on his prayers.

When I told Ike about our day, he smiled and shook his head. "Georgie is one of the best generals I have," he said, "but he's just like a time bomb.  You never know when he's going to go off.  All you can be sure of is that it will probably be in the wrong place at the wrong time …" But he never did learn to keep his "goddamned mouth" shut.  And he caused Ike a lot of grief.[66]

Ironically, in the fall of 1945, Patton summoned now Captain Kay Summersby, Women's Auxiliary Corps, United States Army into his office to dismiss her.  The unpleasant task came as a direct order in the form of a coded message from General Eisenhower - "her services were no longer required."[67]  Patton later told Beatrice that he felt it was an ungentlemanly command, and he was equally appalled by Captain Summersby's reaction to it; her language and her final remarks sent "shivers up his spine."[68]

"Who the hell does he think he is … [h]e can't treat me like this, I'll get him, if it's the last thing I do, even over my dead body."[69]

[Patton]
**January 27, 1944 Thursday**

Had a talk with Lee and his Chief of Staff to orient myself on the setup in England. Went to see Bedell Smith, who was in rare form --- s.o.b., --- has just been made a Lieutenant General, and is looking better than I have ever seen him. I also called on Tedder who seemed genuinely glad to see me. After lunch, went to see Bradley's plans, which I consider bad; the landings are so close that an attack against one affects the whole thing. As it is now set up, Bradley with the First Army of six infantry and two armored divisions, lands on a two division front. The British to his left, east, land on a three division front. After the British have got the port of _______ the Third Army comes ashore at the port. We take Normandy and Brittany, then countermarch and come up on the right of the First Army. While all this is going on, two other U. S. Armies land. A hell of a lot of things can happen before that time.

Got Smith to approve a list of fifteen Seventh Army officers for transfer here. Both Ike and Smith strongly advise me to get rid of Gay, but I am not doing it. Bradley and Smith rate Truscott, Middleton, Gillem ahead of Keyes; I don't see why. Well, I am off to a bad start but am on my way. In addition to the general "Overlord" plan, there is a plan called "Rankin A and B and C" to be put into effect should the Boche cave. In addition to the plan for the assault and the plan in case Germany breaks down, I feel there should be a third plan to be put into effect in the not too unlikely event that the initial landing of the leading armies [First U. S. Army and First British Army] gets boxed. In that case I believe that what troops are left should be landed in the vicinity of Calais, following an air bombardment of the nature used at Pantelleria; that is, land at the narrowest place by day, under all the air we can get, and simply blow a hole. We may well have to do this. I have talked to Spaatz on this subject and he agrees with me. Got to Lee's special train "Alive" at 1600. Colonel Heriz-Smith, Chief British Liaison Officer with SOS and Colonel Vaughn, U.S. Commanding Officer of the WBS were on the train. Train too fine. Dined and drank.

Patton then went to see the newly promoted Lieutenant General Bedell Smith. Patton kept his dislike of Bedell Smith to himself, mostly. He'd come to distrust Beetle on every level, however, had to deal with him as Beetle handled, with little interference, all of General Eisenhower's staff and appointments to command. Both Eisenhower and Bedell Smith had previously denied Patton's request for the transfer of fifteen men from his 7th Army staff to Third Army.[70] Many of the 7th Army staff in Sicily had been with Patton since North Africa; a few had even come with him from the States. All were loyal and efficient. Their transfer would allow for a smooth continuation of operations. More so, Patton trusted these men; they were as loyal to him as he was to them. Patton was keenly aware that a new staff may not be as loyal and, knowing what he knew or believed he knew of some of Eisenhower's staff, he was even more cautious regarding to whom he should bestow his trust. Lastly, and most importantly, soldiers' lives depended on the decisions made by Army staff echelons, so Patton had no time for incompetency.

While Patton was at the Command headquarters, he met briefly with British General Tedder whom seemed glad to see him.[71]

Generals John C. H. Lee and Patton had been classmates at West Point. Lee was now Chief of Services and Supply and a deputy to General Eisenhower at the European Theater of Operations United States Army (ETOUSA). As such, Lee was extremely well connected and was in charge of all the supplies and provisions for the whole of ETOUSA's ground, and most of ETOUSA's air forces. Lee, therefore, lived well above most generals as he had the ability to utilize or assign any ETOUSA provision. A perk he often availed himself of was the use of his "personal train." As he and Patton were friends, he'd arranged for General Patton to use this train, enabling Patton to meet and transport his command staff when they arrived by ship from the States. This allowed Patton to keep his identity as the commander of the Third Army secret. Secrecy of his new post was part of the Allied strategy to keep the German High Command misinformed. Thus, while he secretly built up the United States Third Army and planned for the real invasion, public reports assigned Patton as the Commanding General of the First United States Army (FUSA) whose mission would be to invade the shores of Calais.

**January 28, 1944 Friday**

Arrived at Gourock, which is near Newcastle, at 0700. Was met by Colonel Crothers, Commanding Officer of the 26th District SOS. We inspected the Quartermaster and Air Force depots and General Hospital 50. We started after lunch to board the "Ile de France" with a view to making an inspection, but the weather was too rough, particularly since they were trying to land with the wharf to leeward in a high wind. Lt. General Sir William Thomson and Major General Sir Eric Goowood, British Army, both retired, Air Commander Hawes and Admiral Hill, the Naval Commander in this region, all came to tea on the train. After dinner we boarded the Queen Mary to welcome the advance party of the Third Army under Colonel Williams. General Thomson asked me to make a talk to all the officers which I did, first telling them that I was still a secret and not to be mentioned.

"I am your new commanding officer, I am glad to see you. I hope it is mutual. There is a lot of work to be done and there is little time to do it. There is a special train on the dock to take you to your CP and we will leave in an hour." On the train they were ordered not to write or say anything about their new commanding general.[72]

We took Williams and his party of 13 officers and 26 enlisted men on our train and left for Knutsford about midnight.

The same day, Lt. General Omar N. Bradley was officially designated as Commanding General of the First United States Army.[73]


**January 29, 1944 Saturday**

Colonel Jacobs met us and took us to headquarters, Third Army, at Peover Hall and Toft Hall camp. I was not too pleased with proposed arrangements of Headquarters at Toft Hall so decided to move Advanced Echelon to Peover Hall. Work done by SOS was excellent and remarkably quick. In the afternoon visited the Board of Ship Canal Company and met Mr. R. D. Brown, the manager, and members of his staff. The visit seemed futile to me. Went to Red Cross Club in Manchester, which is run by Miss Hendrickson, Mr. Cassidy and Lady Leese, wife of Sir Oliver Leese, commanding General Eighth Army. Later they all came to dinner on the train. All seemed very nice. The station master, who is one of the two in England who wears a silk hat, called to have a drink. He puts on a good show, but I feel that he is too ostentatious. Train left for Cheltenham during the night. When we came out of the club, there was a crowd of

several hundred, or perhaps a thousand people waiting, so when I got on
the train I had Colonel Harry Smith call up the censor's office in London
to see that there was no statement about me.


The men proceeded to Peover[74] camp, about three miles from Knutsford, Cheshire, England. Peover
camp and Toft Camp were approximately two miles away from each other and were former British
camps.[75] Colonel Brenton C. Wallace had been assigned as liaison officer to General Patton and his
staff.  He assisted in identifying the locations for the Third Army headquarters and orientated the
men to their new surroundings as he'd been in England many months prior to their arrival.  Colonel
Charles Codman, Patton's aide-de-camp, asked Wallace if there was an appropriate place for the
General to attend church the following morning. Wallace informed Codman of the chapel attached
to Peover hall. The General extended an invitation to Wallace to join him, thus, the two attended
services together that Sunday.


[Wallace]

The Headquarters was located in the large, old and very interesting
manor house called Peover Hall, dating back to the fourteenth century.
The grounds of the estate had remained in possession of one family, the
Manwarings, for about 800 years. The Manwarings were closely related to
the famous Peel family. For countless years fox hunters started the chase
from this old hall, and Old John Peel, about whom was written the famous
hunting song "John Peel", probably hunted there.

When the first Sunday arrived, the General's senior aide, Colonel Charles
R. Codman, asked me if I knew anything about the churches in the
neighborhood. He said he had looked over several in the town, but thought
the General would be better pleased with something simpler. I asked
Colonel Codman if he had looked at the private chapel on the estate. He
said he did not know there was one, so I took him back and showed him.

This chapel was one of the most interesting and beautiful I have ever
seen. For hundreds of years it had been the private place of worship
for the Manwaring and Peel families and also the families of those who
worked on the estate. The interior was lined with tombs of knights and
their ladies, and on top of each tomb, or recessed within the walls,
were life-size figures of the dead. Each knight's head rested on the neck
of his horse and his feet against the body of his favorite dog, all in
lifelike marble.

Colonel Codman thought the General would like the chapel and asked me to
join them for the service. It was a bitterly cold January day and about
as cold inside the chapel as out. We could see our breaths and kept our
trench coats on.

The service was extremely simple, and the rector himself came down and
gave us hymnals. It was Communion Sunday and when it came our turn,

General Patton rose and went forward. We followed and all knelt at the altar and took Communion.

Soon after the service I asked Colonel Codman if the General had been displeased by anything about the service. He replied, not in the least, that the General had enjoyed its simple sincerity. From that day on he was a regular attendant at the services until we moved on in June.
After we moved, General Patton had a simple bronze tablet made and presented it to the chapel, along with an American flag. The tablet, now embedded in the chapel wall, bears only these words: "Presented by Headquarters, Third U. S. Army, January-June, 1944."[76]


General Patton's vehicle and those of his staff were released from Palermo and transported to the United Kingdom.

> Subject: Movement of Vehicles from NATOUSA.
> Action: We cabled NATOUSA, our SOSTC 4840, dated 27 January,1944, that the following vehicles are to be moved from their existing locations to the U.K. :
>
> Col. Cumming's -Plymouth or Buick
> Gen. Gay's -Plymouth
> Gen. Patton's -Packard
> Two – Peeps (jeeps)
> One - Scout Car
> Two - C & R Cars.
> Two - Caravans (now at Oran)
> Balance of vehicles at Palermo.
>
> Transportation should also be arranged for the EM
> drivers of the above cars and T/Sgt. John L. Mims, 6399787
> who drives General Patton's car (Packard) . We requested
> an acknowledgement and advice as to what shipping arrangements are being made.[77]

For historians, this confirms that General Patton had two Caravan trucks assigned to him. These two Shop Vans, CCKW's would be converted to mobile command posts and sleeping quarters for General Patton. Patton also had a Scout Car, two Command and Reconnaissance three-quarter ton Dodge trucks and two peeps.[78] Though General Patton had his black Packard scout car that he used in North Africa and Sicily shipped to England, this is the last account of its mention as Patton replaced it with an M20 Armored Scout Car.[79]

[Patton]
**January 30, 1944 Sunday**

We arrived at Cheltenham, the field headquarters of the SOS, for breakfast. Lee's Deputy in the SOS, General T.D.W. Weaver, gave me the set up. I later talked to Colonel Laymon who heads the replacement system of the SOS. Drove to Little Compton Manor for lunch with Major and Lady Alexander Metcalf. He was the Duke of Windsor's aide-de-camp and she is the youngest daughter of Lord Curzon. Her sister married Oswald Mosley, just released from jail for being a Nazi. Miss Mosley came to lunch; a big fine looking girl with a tragic face. On the way home, drove through Cottswolds and inspected Prisoner of War.

Dinner for the SOS Staff, where I made a speech and again warned that I am incognito.

[Patton]
**January 31, 1944 Monday**

Attended SOS weekly staff conference. I made a speech, which was good and alive, but warned them that I am a myth.

Reached London at 1530 and went to see Bedell Smith. We were both charming. The nurse who takes care of him, Miss Teston, was present, and I had the opportunity of letting him advertise himself. I let him do all the talking and played him up. Washed mouth out later.

General Patton spent the day at General Wood's 4th Armored Division Headquarters.[80]

[Patton]
**February 1, 1944 Tuesday**

Left by car at 0800 to visit 4th Armored Division, Major General "P." (John S.) Wood, near Badminton, the Duke of Beaufort's place, where the game was invented and all the hunting took place. Lovely drive. Passed huge Dolmen supposed to have been thrown up by Merlin. He must have been very ill as it covers 16 acres and is several hundred feet high. Charles II is alleged to have climbed up it. He must have thrown a curb, or his horse did. "P." was delighted to see me. We inspected troops all afternoon and found them in fine shape, except the 46th Medical Battalion, Lt. Colonel R.E Maillord, which was dirty. P. is a good leader. He wants to get the 988th Treadway Bridge Company, which used to belong to his engineer battalion. He should also have nine mine detectors. I found that there were not enough in the division and asked for more. Senior officers came to dinner.

[Patton]
**February 2, 1944 Wednesday**

Talked to all officers of the 4th Armored Division and inspected the remaining units which I failed to see yesterday. The Division is superior. In the afternoon called on Mr. Fred Darling, who trains the King's horses. He and I agreed on need of length from point to hip to point of buttocks, so we are true friends. Also looked at druid ruins.

General Patton and his aide-de-camp, Codman, were driven to London by MSgt John L. Mims for a secret meeting with General Patch, who was just in from overseas and would be commanding 7th Army in North Africa. They were to discuss staff changes and met at a new Mount Street flat at 4 p.m. Upon arrival, Patton and Codman were met by a Supply Of Service (SOS) Corporal. When they reached the second floor landing, their senses were assaulted by the décor that consisted of exotic wall prints, thick carpet, soft indirect lighting, and a period sitting room, making the atmosphere more boudoir than salon. Patton questioned the SOS corporal, wanting to know "Who the hell had picked this place." The corporal responded that it was General Lee himself. Patton then asked to see his room. When the door opened, a white bear rug, pink walls, curtains, a matching pink brocade, and a triptych-mirror dressing table greeted them. The glint of nickel finishes and two tone sea foam tile could be seen through an open door. Patton's eyes then "caught the reflection in the mirror on the ceiling of the enormous bed lying low and lascivious under its embroidered silk coverlet, the silence was broken by a single highly charged exclamation…Jesus!"[81]

**Artistic License**

Though the 1970 movie "Patton", directed by Franklin J. Schaffner, adapted for the screen by Francis Ford Coppola and Edmund H. North, and starring George C. Scott in the lead role, introduced many audiences to General George Smith Patton, Jr. Being an artistic endeavor, it also distorted facts and altered timelines, wording and locations for dramatic effect.

*Patton*, the movie, won seven Academy Awards, including Best Picture. The opening monologue, delivered by George C. Scott as General Patton with an enormous American flag behind him, remains an iconic and often quoted image in film. The film was a success and has become an American classic. In 2003, Patton was selected for preservation in the United States National Film Registry by the Library of Congress as being "culturally, historically, or aesthetically significant".

Yet, the Patton depicted in the movie bearing his name was more of a caricature of the true man and, being adapted from the books *Patton: Ordeal and Triumph* by Ladislas Farago and Omar Bradley's memoir *A Soldier's Story*, it contained the subtle and blatant biases of the authors. The aggregate of personal accounts, official reports, and Patton's own words in his diaries, as well as his correspondences expose the *onional* layering of a complex character. At his core, Patton was a deeply loving and loyal man who looked after others far more than anybody knew. He had no aspirations for a political career.

The meeting in the "bordello-like" setting of the movie differs greatly from reality in content as well as context.  In the movie, this setting was used as a backdrop to a fabricated encounter where General Smith gave Patton a severe scolding.  In reality, Patton was meeting with General Patch; a meeting that required the utmost secrecy, thus, one can surmise that General Lee chose such a location as it would probably be the last place one would expect to be found for such a meeting.

After Patch arrived and settled into his own room, Patton and Patch convened.  Patton pleaded with Patch to convince Eisenhower to release the fifteen staff members he'd requested for transfer to Third Army, staff members that Patch had now inherited as the Commander of Seventh Army.

[Codman]

```
This morning at SHAEF, General Patch was saying Beetle claimed that
particular matter was high level stuff. He said I would get instruction
in due course. Patton responded saying, "The whole headquarters was
Goddamn high level you have to carry an oxygen tank to live there."
General Patton's voice rose, "To Hell with Beetle, see Ike himself."
General Patch's serious face lit up when he smiled, "I'll keep that in
mind George," he said.⁸²
```

Neither Beedle Smith nor Eisenhower liked General Hobart Gay, Patton's Chief of Staff, and did not want him to reprise this role with Patton in Europe.

After a few drinks Patton declared, "Look Sandy, I'd rather be shot than sitting around this Anglican bordello. How about it, Codman." There was a play in town that night and Codman knew its stars, Alfred and Lynn Lunts, so Codman arranged for the generals to attend the performance. As their meeting was in secrecy, they entered through the fire escape. Patton and Patch were also escorted backstage to meet the Lunts after the performance. The shared experience helped to form a bond between the men, and Patch intervened on Patton's behalf.⁸³

[Patton]

```
Went to a play in London by the Lunts, "There Shall Be No More Night",
and after the play we met them. It is well acted, but badly written. Miss
Marian Hall of the Red Cross and General Donovan⁸⁴ (Wild Bill) called
at 2100.
```

It stands to reason that General Patch understood that if the loyalty of the staff of the 7th Army laid with Patton, they would not have served him well. Additionally, as a matter of course, most generals choose their own staff. Soon after the Patton/Patch meeting, General Smith approved the staff transfer.

A command staff of an army has several integral parts. The aide-de-camps serve as a general's hands and eyes, thus, must have the complete confidence of their general. As it was next to impossible for one person to do all that was needed to be done at the level of detail required, Patton had two aide-de-camps. Major Alexander C. Stiller had been with General Patton since the invasion of North Africa, and Lt. Colonel Charles R. Codman joined the staff after Patton's other aide was killed in North Africa. Master Sergeant John L. Mims was Patton's driver, and Sergeant George Meeks, who had been with the General since his Fort Riley days, was his trusted orderly. General Hobart R. Gay had been with General Patton since the desert training in the States and stayed with him throughout the war as his Chief of Staff. As second in command, it would be Gay's duty to take over as Commanding General if Patton were killed or relieved of duty. Other staff that came for 7th Army included Colonel Oscar Koch, G-2, Colonel Muller, G-4, Colonel Cummings, Adjutant, Colonel Paul D. Harkins, the Deputy Chief of Staff, Colonel Charles B. Odom, MD, Patton's physician, and nine enlisted men.[85]

Sergeant Thue P. Lee, who had been with Patton since the North African campaign, was the General Patton's personal cook. Lee was a native-born American of Chinese descent and Patton considered him the best cook in the army. As part of a memorial tribute to General Patton, General Lucian Truscott published an account of how Lee and Patton first met.

[Truscott]

Operation Torch found Patton in French Morocco and on the evening of the invasion General Patton was ashore inspecting the beachhead.  In typical fashion, Patton wanted a presence with his men and for them to know he was in charge and with them all the way. So he had the first password or challenge words to be "George" and the countersign response, to be to be "Patton."  On this night Patton himself captured a member of his staff.  General Patton was touring the beach late after dark and heard the sentry say, "Who's there?" He then repeated himself and said, "Who's there … George?" He heard this, "Me no George. Me Sergeant Lee, the best damn cook in the US Army." Before the sentry could reply, General Patton himself shouted, "Sentry, grab that man. If he is the best damn cook in the US Army, I want him. He is cooking for me from here on out." The new cook was California born Chinese, Sergeant Wong Lee.  Patton loved good food and Lee loved to cook it. The combination proved very felicitous for the both of them. Patton's staff soon came to know him and love his cooking. They would sneak over and mooch into Lee's cook shack for a tasty smack of toasted chicken, apple pie and coffee. Lee's roasts, steaks, and pies were famed in the higher echelons throughout the ETO. No top commander had a cook as accomplished and resourceful. Generals would drive 100 miles out of their way to revel of one of Lee's recipes. For as the dashing little commander of the gallant French Armored Division, which served with Patton, rhapsodically expressed it after ecstasizing through one of Lee's omelets, "Your cook, General, he makes the egg sing ze grand opera."[86]

England had an extensive market for finely tailored uniforms. Now that they were finally in a place where he could get clothing made, General Patton was anxious to do some shopping for some uniforms.

[Patton]
**February 3, 1944 Thursday**

Bought two pairs of boots from Faulkner, one high and one low, and an overcoat, a pair of trousers, a combat coat and a blouse from Weatherill.[87]

Had a long talk with Bradley and met General J. L. (Joe) Collins, Wilkie's younger brother, who commanded a corps in the South Pacific. He will command the VII Corps in this operation. I had known him in the Tennessee Maneuvers, where he was Chief of Staff of the IV Corps, and was not much impressed with him, but they say he is a good fighter. Called on General Spaatz and told him that he and I may have to pull the chestnuts out of the landing operation if the attack of the First Army bitches by putting an attack across the Channel at Calais. He agreed with me and said that if I could give him five days, he could blast a hole five miles long and about the same depth into which I could land even without landing craft. Speaking of the British influence, which is very apparent, he made a profound and regrettably true statement. He said, "He had paid a hell of a price for the Supreme command." We have. We both feel that, instead of "Overlord", we should have shot the works on Toulon and in Italy, where we were already ashore and had much better fighter protection than we can get here. I am sure that if I had commanded there we would have had Rome by now, and would have been towards the Alps. However, I did not command, so there is no use arguing.

Went to a farce, "While the Sun Shines," then to dinner with Maria Hall. At dinner at Miss Hall's I met Lady Cavendish, who was Miss Adele Astaire, sister of the dancer, Fred Astaire, and who is the most profane person I have ever seen or heard; otherwise not attractive. Colonel Johnny Castle was there and made big talk about how he wanted to get with me. When we started "Torch", I offered him a job and he declined it because he expected to be made Armored Force G-2. He can stew in his own juice now as far as I am concerned. Air raid came on but no one was disturbed it lasted all night.

[Patton]
**February 4, 1944 Friday**

Drove to Knutsford via Banbury, Chelsea, Birmingham and Stratford. At the latter place we had lunch at the William and Mary Hotel. Bea and I stopped there in a room named "Two Gentlemen of Verona" in 1910 almost 34 years ago but it seems shorter. Coming the way we did, and not knowing the road, it took us six hours.

[Patton]
**February 5, 1944 Saturday**

Wired to expedite the arrival of the rest of the Third Army staff. Also asked for Colonel Koch as G-2. To keep Hodges from being reduced, I have to be attached to the Third Army till he is made a Lieutenant General --- now he is only a Lt. General by virtue of commanding the Third Army. General Williams and I had a badminton court set up and played a game. John Peel used to own this house. Monty's aide-de-camp phoned last night asking me to see him at 1000 on February 11th. I will go to Ireland on Monday to inspect the XV Corps under General Haislip.

[Patton]
**February 6, 1944 Sunday**

Went to the Peover Chapel this morning and was put in the Master of the Hall's place. Right next to me was a very fine effigy of a recumbent knight and his lady. The armor seemed late 1300. There is another effigy near the altar of an earlier period --- I would think about 1200, and a third in a side chapel of a very modern armor, probably late 1400 or 1500. Called on Major and Mrs. Leicester-Warren, who are the parents of Lady Leese, General Sir Oliver Leese's wife. They live in a very large house dating from Tudor times. The family was De Warren and apparently crossed with the Leicesters and then the nobility died out. They have a huge place with a brick wall entirely around it. They seem quite real. Wrote up some notes for future exhortations to units. The more I see of this fool thing of swapping staffs, "the more I thank whatever Gods may be for my unconquerable soul."

Patton mentioned the father in law, Major Leicester-Warren, in a letter home to Beatrice, stating, "Has a little place of a thousand acres completely surrounded by a brick all ... They are very nice people."[88]

Lady Leese was a wonderful host to Patton's staff and his Third Army headquarters. She was dignified but loving to the troops. She saw that they had parties and that they were given a home away from home. Thus, she was very well respected and appreciated by Patton and all who met her.[89]

---

**For My Unconquerable Soul**

Invictus
by William Ernest Henley


Out of the night that covers me,
Black as the Pit from pole to pole,
I thank whatever gods may be
For my unconquerable soul.

In the fell clutch of circumstance
I have not winced nor cried aloud.
Under the bludgeonings of chance
My head is bloody, but unbowed.

Beyond this place of wrath and tears
Looms but the Horror of the shade,
And yet the menace of the years
Finds, and shall find, me unafraid.

It matters not how strait the gate,
How charged with punishments the scroll,
I am the master of my fate:
I am the captain of my soul.


Academy of American Poets, Retrieved from
http://www.poets.org/viewmedia.php/prmMID/21242

---

[Patton]
**February 7, 1944 Monday**

Drove to the headquarters of the Western Base Section, SOS, at Chester, where I was received with a guard of honor and guided to the airport, where I boarded a De Haviland Rapide, a wooden two-motored bi-plane built many years ago with a ground speed, under the best conditions, of not over a hundred miles an hour. We started at 1000 and had a heavy head wind so did not arrive at the Headquarters XV Corps at Lurgan until 1200.

In the afternoon I inspected the 2nd Division at Armagh. It is commanded by General W.M. Robertson with General C.A. Martin as Assistant Commander. Robertson was in Italy. I was quite impressed with the neatness and general good appearance of the Division. I was accompanied on the inspection by Colonel C.V. Allen, Corps G-3. In my opinion, General Martin talks too much and has an excuse for everything. General G.P. Hayes[90] is the artilleryman. We then drove to the Mourne Mountain area to inspect the 5th Division under General S. Leroy Irwin. General Allen D. Warnock is Assistant Division Commander. Harold C. Vanderveer, who used to be artillery instructor at Riley, is the Artilleryman. This Division has been in Iceland for two years and is alleged not to be up to the others, but, in my opinion, it is a very fine division. General Irwin was Chief of Artillery in the 9th Division in Tunisia with me, and did a very good job. I was responsible for having him made a Major General. On returning to the Headquarters, I was told that General Eisenhower had phoned. He wanted me to come and to see him about Hughes, who he feels is getting a rough deal at the hands of Devers. He may want me to take Hughes in the Third Army. I will do anything for Hughes, and, of course, anything Ike wants, but should prefer to keep General Gay as Chief of Staff, although Gay would work perfectly satisfactorily with Hughes if I had to take him. General Haislip is in Italy, so while here I have been trying to do a little missionary work with Colonel Lovett of the Engineers, Chief of Staff. In my opinion, he is a very intelligent officer.

[Patton]
**February 8, 1944 Tuesday**

Colonel Allen and Colonel Person Menoher and I drove to Onagh Area to see the 8th Division, General W.C. McMahon is at the front. It struck me as a good division. I gave a talk to all senior officers, first warning them that I was a secret. Later, I talked briefly to various units. General Nelson Walker is the Assistant Division Commander, and General James A. Pickering, Artillery Commander. Haislip is back. He was a little on the patronizing side but I don't think it was intentional. Talked to the remaining senior officers and Generals of the Corps. Warned them that I was a myth.

[Patton]
**February 9, 1944 Wednesday**

Haislip, Allen and I inspected the 6th Cavalry, Mechanized, at Landragee. They made a very fine impression. Corps Engineers seemed good. Made talks. Gay, Cummings, Odom are here and will see them in London in the morning. Feel like I have a disease. The officers of the 6th Cavalry are billeted in the castle of my old friend, the Duke of Manchester, whom I called "Mr. Grace" in 1917. We also visited the engineers and made a short talk to each group of troops we passed. After lunch we flew back in extremely bad weather, so bad in fact that we had to make a detour to the south to avoid running into the Isle of Man, because there was no visibility which would permit our seeing it.

Patton had given many speeches, variations of his standard speech. He continued his visit, making three more speeches to the troops.  It was getting very cold, and the combination of falling temperatures and vocal exertion had begun to affect his voice.[91]

[Patton]
**February 11, 1944 Friday**

Brad and I went to Monty's headquarters at 1000. DeGuingand, Chief of staff and the Commanding General of the Second British Army were there. General Quartermaster Staff, Monty, Bradley and myself. Monty who is an actor but not a fool -- made the wise decision to cut out a great many gadgets which the British were trying to induce into the landing operations, including the rocket boats and some tanks with the engines removed, which would have been about as useful as a fifth wheel. He also outlined the general plan of campaign and in some things I think him too optimistic, in others too cautious. One division followed by the rest of one corps, Third Army, goes in with Bradley. Possibly the two armored divisions via the same route. These will start in on D plus 10, the rest in the Third Army on D plus 25. It is not a very critical job for me but things can develop almost any way at any time.  One can make his own job. In Sicily, I was destined to cover the rear of the Eighth Army but I did not. Littlejohn told me that it was Brigadier Sugden who said, "Patton is such a thruster that soon he will have Monty surrounded."

Patton was shrewd enough to tell Harry C. Butcher, Eisenhower's naval aide that, "Ike is on the threshhold of becoming the greatest general of all time, including Napoleon," as he was leaving the office. He knew full well that he would relay this to Ike.  Butcher later quoted Patton in his unauthorized book about his time with Eisenhower:[92]

> Called on Ike at his house, as he asked me to. He said that he was
> rather reluctant to bring up the question, about what did I think

about taking Hughes as Chief of Staff, as Devers had declared Hughes surplus. Ike said he was not making the suggestion due to lack of confidence in Gay, but because, in his opinion, Gay does not impress others sufficiently, and that he wants to do something for Hughes. I said that I would take Hughes and felt sure Gay would understand. I had already guessed this move and had spoken to General Gay who had, of course, stated that he would be very glad to be Deputy. He is a perfectly unselfish man. This will not be too easy for any of us but I doubt if it lasts.

General Kenner had us in for a drink. He brought two letters, one from Bea Jr.[93] and one from Ruth Ellen. He is now chief medical inspector under General Eisenhower.


Author's Note:

There is far more to the Chief of Staff issue than is being said. Eisenhower had held a bad opinion of Gay, based on his Chief of Staff, General Walter Bedell "Beetle" Smith, that originated in Sicily. There was no love lost between Smith and Patton and Eisenhower was always obliged to take Smith's advice. In some cases, Smith even acted in Eisenhower's name, without the knowledge of Eisenhower.

In 1981, General Gay was asked in an oral interview why he was, at first, Chief of Staff, and then demoted to Assistant Chief of Staff of Third Army. General Gay said that Eisenhower's Chief of Staff [Smith] had said he had "done wrong" in Sicily. He said, "This was in Sicily and I had gone forward, we were just stalling around there. The Seventh Army was on the left. General Bradley's Army was on the right and they were just sitting, they would not or could not just drive ahead. I went up to see General Gaffey, who had been Patton's Chief of Staff, and then in command of this armored division, and he said to me, "Hap, if you give me authority, I'll break out of here and go clear up to the sea, and I'll turn right, and I'll be right behind the enemy and we'll end this damn thing." I said, "My friend, I give you the orders. The responsibility is mine." Well, it ended the war in Sicily was practically over before anybody realized what had happened. They relieved me as Patton's Chief of Staff because Eisenhower's Chief of Staff said that I had done wrong." General Patton was aware of this and many other instances where Smith had acted with a calculated viciousness. Eisenhower even held up Gay's promotion to Major General based on Smith's recommendation. It would be well over a year before Eisenhower would change his mind on the promotion and this time based on what his Assistant Chief of Staff recommended after finding out the truth. Gay stated, "But, later, I was then kept as the Chief of Staff, and later Eisenhower sent for me. He said, "I just wanted to tell you, you were right and my staff was dead wrong. I'm going to see that you're promoted." And, that's the story on that. Because, it saved thousands of lives and I'm glad I did it, even if they had to bust me to a private, I'd still do it over again." [94]


[Patton]
**February 12, 1944 Saturday**

Went to see Bradley in the morning to get a joint note we are writing on the question of one extra colonel per division to replace casualties among regimental commanders. Haislip and Irwin suggested it in Ireland and I got Bradley to come in, and Ike said that, if Brad and I would write a note, he would put it over. Later saw Ike in his office and asked him for General Gar Davidson. He sent a wire for him to General Marshall. I hope it does not make Jake Devers mad and cause him to hold up Harkins and the rest of my staff. Ike says that Devers is .22 caliber and I rather concur, but some others are not over .32 caliber themselves. Ike said of me, "You are fundamentally honest on the larger issues but are too fanatical in your friendships." It is a good thing that someone is.

Drove to Peover in 4 hours.

The beachhead south of Rome is apt to be lost. Monty told us that, on the 10th, we had already evacuated 4,000 vehicles. If we lose that beach it will be bad, but so much sloth, or timidity, was shown at the start that the thing was doomed. Only 8 miles in 12 days. I would have been in Rome. I hope I don't have to go back and straighten things out.

The Combined Chiefs of Staff issued a directive to General Eisenhower on his duties as Supreme Allied Commander, Expeditionary Force. He would invade the European Continent to destroy the German armed forces. The target date was set for May 1944.[95]

[Patton]
**February 13, 1944 Sunday**

Gay, Codman, Cummings, Murnane, Odom and self went to church at Peover Chapel. Codman and I went to lunch with the Leicester-Warrens at a most beautiful house and picture gallery, in Knutsford. General Sir William Bromley-Davenport, the Lord Lieutenant of Cheshire, and his wife were present. The Leicester-Warrens are a run-out noble family, but must have been hot numbers at one time. General Sir William Bromley Davenport told me that Knutsford means "Canute's Ford" and that King Canute crossed some kind of a stream here when he was visiting this part or the country around 900. There is a great deal of talk about gas warfare from the British, and also from some of our own people. In my opinion the Germans will not use it. As an offensive weapon to win a war gas is O.K., but as a means of deferring the losing of a war, its use is foolish.

[Patton]
**February 14, 1944 Monday**

Lt. General E. C. A. Schreiber, commanding the Western Defense command, called at 1000. We had a Military Police Guard of Honor and a band from the 360th Service Engineer Regiment, which played the ruffles, but not the flourishes. Walked for 40 minutes and played badminton for 45 more. Ongoing into Peover Chapel yesterday I found a pasteboard plaque which states, as I remember, "To the Glory of God and the Honor of the Manwaring Family," who supported this Chapel for 800 years. The Manwaring

Family finally died out in 1924 when the Hall was taken over by the John Peel family, who went broke this year. It is now owned by a junk dealer in Manchester.


[Patton]
**February 15, 1944 Tuesday**

Gave a talk to all officers and men of the Third Army now in this vicinity. Notes for talk as follows: Discipline - smart, best; Letters - censorship; Why Fight - honor, joy in battle; Mental Attitude - eager, fierce, without fear; Prisoners or War - search---don't trust; Dig or Die - hit dirt, shoot; Surrender; Mines - AA and air; Repeat, Best Troops; Congratulations. Think this is a good sequence. All men paid close attention. Time 25 minutes.


[Patton]
**February 16, 1944 Wednesday**

At 0130 Codman had a telephone call from Commander Butcher for me to report to General Eisenhower at once. Codman said we would start at once, but that it would take 4 1/2 to 5 hours. Butcher then said we should report prior to 1200 hours. We started at 0600 in the pitch dark and arrived at 20 Grosvenor Square at 1045. When I went in Ike said, "I am afraid you'll have to eat crow again for a little while," and I said, "What have I done now?" He replied, "You may have to take command of the beachhead in Italy and straighten things out." I replied that this was not eating crow but a great compliment because I would be willing to command anything from a platoon up' in order to fight. He then gave me a radio from General Alexander to the Combined Chiefs of Staff, or the Prime Minister, (I'm not sure which) in which Alexander said in effect that there was no drive in the VI Corps, that the British had sustained most of the losses (I doubt this) and, "If you cannot send me a thruster like George Patton, I recommend putting a British officer in command. I have already sent a British Major General to the Headquarters of the VI Corps to spur them on a little."

Ike said he would never consent to letting the British have the command, but he would loan me for a month, as the only fighting general in the army. He also made certain remarks about Devers, wondering why the hell he hadn't gotten into the fight, saying, "As he was doing nothing anyway." Ike and the Prime Minister sent a telegram offering to let me go for one month. This telegram was addressed to Alexander, Wilson, Devers, and Clark. They will consider it and reply. In the meantime one C-54 and one B-25 are waiting at the airport in London, warmed up, ready to take me to Italy, and I have telephoned for Stiller, and Sergeant Meeks, and my fighting equipment. I told Ike that I was anxious to go, but that I must be backed up by him, as otherwise I would have my throat cut. He said he would back me up and would report the whole thing to General Marshall by special messenger. I suppose I am the only person in the world who would be elated at a chance to commit personal and official suicide, but I am tickled to death and will make a go of it.

Patton telephoned Stiller and Sergeant Meeks to get his fighting gear together. At midnight, Colonel Odom was also instructed to get his gear together and be prepared to move. Patton knew he would be among generals who did not like him and would try to cut his throat politically. He relayed this to Ike so Ike would agree to back his plays. Ike agreed and promised to relay the matter to General Marshall.

Patton was confident he could rectify the situation. He was proud of the confidence and support he had from Generals Alexander, Eisenhower and Marshall; this illustrated that both his superiors and his peers thought him to be the most formidable fighting general of the war. However, he also knew that the other generals would have their careers on the line if he could accomplish this solely; And that they would be quick to hang him out to dry if he failed.

### A Mutual Regard

Sergeant William George Meeks is often solely noted as General Patton's orderly or striker, however, in truth, he was a part of Patton's intimate personal staff and a trusted friend.

When Patton was assigned to Fort Riley in 1937, Vergie, an African-American domestic who had previously worked for Lt. Col. John Waters, the Pattons' son-in-law, was hired by Beatrice Patton as a cook. Vergie, therefore, moved into the maid's quarters at the Patton household. Private George Meeks, an African-American cavalryman, and Vergie's love interest, had accompanied her in this move as they'd been living together.

Beatrice had always prepared her husband's uniforms. However, one day, she found Private Meeks engaged in this process. He made the brass look like gold and the boots were so highly polished you could see your face in them. He'd devised the secret of making uniforms match perfectly. He would use a bleach-based solution to fade a new Khaki woven belt to match the patina of a worn khaki uniform. Patton's uniforms were immaculate. Beatrice realized that this man of few words, who could neither read nor write, and could barely scribe his name, rank and serial number when required, had demonstrated a mastery of pristine and impeccable uniform preparation. From that moment on, Meeks took care of Patton as only he could. He saw to it that General Patton always looked his best, which, by all accounts of Patton's attire and dress, was near perfect. More so, Meeks became a trusted friend to the Pattons; indeed, he became a part of the family.

Patton took care of Meeks as well.  Meeks had been in the army for a very long time and had not risen above the rank of private.  No one knew just how old he was; he'd shave his head to keep his grey hair from showing.  He'd been carried on the army roles as a cook.   Now, as Patton's personal aide, whenever Patton was promoted, Meeks earned a stripe.  Patton also had Meeks paid above the army regulation pay scale.  Though his duties had changed, Meeks was still on the army roles as a mess sergeant, thus, could not justify the amounts he sent home through army service channels as they were in excess of the official salary for this position.  Patton therefore sent these funds to the States in his name, through his brother-in-law, Frederick Ayer, an accountant.  Ayer would then transfer the funds to Meek's account.  By war's end, with the help he received from General Patton and Frederick Ayer, George Meeks had accumulated a healthy sum on which to retire. (Totten 289-290); (G. S. Patton, Patton Papers; Finances, Letters to Frederick Ayer, May 1945)

Meeks served under Patton for the entire length of the war.  Upon General Patton's death, Sgt. Meeks was summoned to the hospital to bring Patton's personal four star flag.  When he arrived, he tearfully handed the flag to Dr. Hill who gently placed it over the General's body. (Hair, Denny.  The 64th Anniversary of General Patton's Death, Heidelberg Germany, U.S. Army Medical Department (MSAMH). Patton Third Army, Living Historians retrieved at http://www.pattonthirdarmy.com/HeidelbergTrip.html )

[Patton]
**February 17 1944 Thursday**

Went to Middlesex Hospital at 0945 to have a spot on my lip treated with x-ray. While there Lt. Colonel Lee, an aide, phoned to say that Ike said I could return to Knutsford. Nothing more. He did not even think it worthwhile to tell me what had happened. Gaffey reported at 1245, ready to go as Chief of Staff of the expedition. I was also going to take I. D. White as G-3, and Colonel Williams as Artillery Officer. I could not take Gay as he has to stay and keep the Third Army in shape. Gay came down to see me off and warned me to get rid of the Fifth Army staff for fear that they would cut my throat. He was working on the assumption that I was to relieve Clark and take over the whole show. This is an excellent example of how much forethought and loyalty he has for me. We were all very sorry that the show was called off. It would have been very risky, but much honor could have been gained. No man can live forever.

General A. C. Wedemeyer called at 1400 to see me.  He told me Truscott is to relieve Lucas in the Italian beachhead. He also told me that when he was in India, he got some clipping about the Drew Pearson incident and had written a letter to General Marshall praising me. He sent me a copy of this letter. He said, that on his own initiative, Admiral Mountbatten also wrote General Marshall to the same effect.

### The Battle Uniform

Though many officers had tailor made dress uniforms, modified from regulation uniforms, they were made with standard cloth and regulation army buttons. General Patton was a notable exception. Patton was very particular in what he wore as he knew the image he portrayed was as important to the impression he made on his troops, and the enemy, as his combat proficiency as a General.

Customized from the standard "Ike" jacket issued to the American enlisted man, Patton's new "Battle Jacket" was designed by Patton as a garment that was uniquely his own. As issued, the standard "Ike" jacket was designed to conceal the buttons. Patton's "Battle Jacket" featured officers' brass buttons placed on the outside where they could be seen and traveled the length of the garment.

Patton had his current service stripes as well as his "V" shaped WWI service stripes sewn onto the left sleeve in proper chronological order. Three bullion (gold) stars were sewn onto each epaulet (chevron) and a bullion "U.S." graced each lapel.

Along the edges, towards the bottom of the jacket, four metal hooks were sewn. These were designed to catch his holster and pistol belt as well as to provide the weight necessary to keep his gig line (the line formed by the shirt, belt buckle, and the fly of one's pants) constant. This also kept his gun belt from sagging to one side due to the weight of the revolver.

His belt buckle, a brass "U.S." taken from a WWI belt; his holster, made by the El Paso Saddlery company, Texas, carried his single action army colt .45. The two notches carved into the ivory grips represented two of Poncho Villa's men he'd killed during the Poncho Villa expedition in 1916. A left-handed holster could also be affixed to the pistol belt; in 1935, he'd acquired a Smith and Wesson .357 Magnum to carry in that holster. Though no pictures have been found of Patton wearing both pistols simultaneously during his time in Europe, a small number of pictures have been found of him wearing them both during his time in Sicily. A 12 round ammunition loop comprised the back of the pistol belt and a first aid leather pouch and compass case were located on either side of the belt buckle.

His matching trousers or his riding breeches, suspenders attached to buttons on either choice of pant, his "tanker boots", riding boots - the type of boots we commonly refer to today as "buckle boots"- he had cut down to two straps with buckets rather than three (much like the style of the enlisted riding boots of 1938, but half size), and a tie (Patton always wore a tie and required the wearing of a tie throughout his command) completed his uniform.  It became his favorite uniform.  Adorned with his service ribbons, he wore it into battle, as well as on occasion for the remainder of his life.

Patton was seldom seen or photographed in public without his blouse (Battle Jacket). The first color photos taken of him in this uniform were taken when he posed for pictures after landing in France.  At his desk, he often took off his coat and wore a standard issue shoulder holster with a M1911 semi-automatic .45 caliber ACP. Colt Pistol. Patton also carried a backup .32 caliber government issue Colt pocket pistol in his pants, between his waist belt and his underwear.

General Patton's uniforms were fitted to portray an image of strength and resolve. He was an impressive figure, stood upright and straight as an arrow. His uniform and demeanor worked together to allow him to stand out in a crowd. (Blumenson, Martin. *The Patton Papers*. Vol.1, 412).

[Patton]
**February 18, 1944 Friday**

Went to see Bradley at 0900 and told him that we should be prepared to land the Third Army at Calais if the First Army and the British get boxed up, as is highly possible. The thought had never occurred to him but he thought well of it, and said that if it comes off he would trade an amphibiously trained division from the First Army with one of mine, not so trained. I feel that there is much merit in the plan, as it would disperse the German Reserves and give room for maneuver. At the moment there are 52 German Divisions in Holland, Belgium and France, 40 of which can oppose us. I hope the strength of the opposition does not bluff us out at the last minute. I still feel that the British do not have their heart in it. Had a long talk with Butcher yesterday, in which he told me that post-war divergence of aim is already causing friction between us and the British and is also coloring military operations. Alex is certainly trying to suggest that failure in Italy is due to us. Called on Ike to say goodbye. He was very cavalier and told me of a General Corlett who had captured a Pacific Island in a "nearly perfect" maneuver. (He did not have to fight until after he got ashore). Ike is going to get him for a Corps Commander (XIX Corps). I told him that we had also done pretty well in landings. This made him mad. He has an unfortunate habit of under-rating all Americans who come under him and overrating all British and all Americans who have served elsewhere. I wish to God he was more of a soldier and less of a politician. Called on Beadle Smith to bootlick him.

Though Bootlicking is commonly regarded as a derogatory term as it refers to under- or over-flattering to gain favor, as Patton had no respect for Beetle's abilities to get things done and, as well, knew that this strategy would keep Beetle from deliberately constructing obstacles to injure him, his men and his career. Patton knew he had to maintain this façade.

Saw General Hull and we had a long, pleasant talk. He agrees with me that both Clark and Monty are timid and probably more afraid of losing a battle than anxious to win one. He told me that General Marshall said, "I wish Patton was commanding at the Beachhead." He also said that Middleton and an unnamed Colonel (probably Rooks) told him that I had captured Sicily in spite of Monty, and while I had driven them further than they thought men could endure, they would love to fight under me any time. Hull is going to Italy to find out why Rome was not taken. Later, there was quite a big air raid, and we could hear the planes and machineguns.

He wrote to Beatrice that he also looked in on Bedell.

[Patton]
**February 19, 1944 Saturday**

Left for Peover at 0904, having stopped to tell General Lee goodbye. About 5 or 6 blocks from Grosvenor Square[96] we came on several blocks in which all the glass had been smashed last night. We also saw some houses on side streets that were flat. It snowed and rained all the way back. Went to dinner with Mr. and Mrs. Frank Stockdale at Alderly Edge, Cheshire. There is not much left of him. He lost an ear, most of an arm, and a shoulder and lung in the last war. She is really pretty and nice. We have been struck with how few pretty women or girls there are in England.

[Patton]
**February 20, 1944 Sunday**

Called on Mr. R. D. Brown, Chief Engineer, Manchester Ship Canal. He is not much.

Third Army's headquarter staff, still in the states, arrived by train to Camp Shank, New York. It had installations in and around Orangeburg in the Town of Orangetown, New York. Situated near the juncture of the Erie Railroad and the Hudson River, it served as a point of embarkation for troops departing overseas during World War II. Dubbed "Last Stop USA," the camp housed about 50,000 troops spread over 2,040 acres (8.3 km2) and was the largest World War II Army embarkation camp, processing 1.3 million service personnel including 75% of those participating in the D-Day invasion.[97]

"It was a beautiful day, clear and cold with ice on the ground."[98] The train was unloaded and the men marched with full pack for several blocks up a steep hill with full packs. In the afternoon they had their firearms inspected and afterward stood in line for more medical check-ups and another shot. Because of what it was, censorship did not allow the mention of where they were when they wrote home. They could only say they arrived at camp. Many of the men had no way to take care of any personal hygiene and bathed for the first time in five days.

"No passes are granted for the first 48 hours…"[99]

Patton wrote home to Beatrice that he was seriously considering getting a dog. He said that Kay Summersby and Lady Leese were searching for one for him.[100]

[Patton]
**February 21, 1944 Monday**

Worked on a letter of instructions for corps, divisions and separate unit commanders.

[Patton]
**February 22, 1944 Tuesday**

The Red Cross had a grand opening of a Red Cross Officer's Club in Manchester. The Lord Mayor of Lanchester and several other Mayors were present, all with their chains of office on. Also there was American who knew the Merrills. Lord Derby was there.  He is very old and drooly, with a collar far too big for him, but quite a personality just the same. Lady Leese seemed to be running the show and introduced me to everyone from Lord Derby to the cook. Lord Derby asked me to visit him if I ever go to Liverpool. Lt. General E. C. A. Schrieber of the Western Defense Command asked Gay, Codman and myself to lunch at Chester. We were met by a motorcycle escort and had a guard of honor made up of men not to exceed 2 months service. However they are extremely soldierly and well set up. The British are better at doing this than we are. It is one of the few advantages over us that I ever admit.

Colonel Oscar W. Koch was in Bouzareah, a suburb of Algiers when he received orders to proceed to a command in the European theater. Since he had been General Patton's G-2 Intelligence officer in North Africa and Sicily, thus, had been part of the Seventh Army planning of "Operation Anvil", Koch had a good idea that Patton had a hand in these orders.  The orders also authorized Koch to bring his driver, Tech. Third Class Carmen DeJohn.[101]

[Patton]
**February 23, 1944 Wednesday**

Colonel Myles Brewster, of the Amphibious Training Command, came to dinner. He commanded E Battery at Myer at one time. He gives me the impression that there is a lot of useless fear of pillboxes, mines, and wire among the officers at the training center. The officers doing the training have never been in a landing, yet we have many available in Africa who have participated in at least two landings. The trouble is theater jealousy. Devers refused to let any of his officers go as observers to Sicily, and never secured any experienced officers from there. We will suffer very much from lack of command. No one is running the show. Certainly Africa, Italy and UK should be under one commander, so he could exert pressure where, and as, he chose. Ike has no conception of physical command, as he has never exercised it.

[Patton]
**February 24, 1944 Thursday**

Played golf for the first time in over 40 years. Did very badly but it is an easy and fairly amusing means of getting exercise.

Training continued for the body of Third as they waited to leave Camp Shank. They took an eight-mile hike in full pack and gear.[102]

[Patton]
**February 25, 1944 Friday**

Captain Murnane (aide-de-camp to General Gay) got me two golf sticks and some balls and I practiced in a pasture, and did better as he coached me. Codman, who had not had one in his hand since he was eight, hit some good balls. Fear I am bitten by the golf bug.

[Patton]
**February 26, 1944 Saturday**

Bradley called up to ask if I would come to London on Tuesday to discuss what could be done to the new type armored division to improve it without really reorganizing it. General Walker and all Armored Division Commanders will be present. When we were in Tunisia last year General McCreery, then Chief of Staff to Alexander, was loud in his idea that the 1st Armored Division should be cut down to more nearly the British model. General Ward and some of the 1st Armored people also favored this. Ike sent General Harmon up to investigate and make a report. Harmon and

I talked it over and agreed that the original division was O.K. but should have another infantry battalion and more reconnaissance. I wrote General McNair to the same effect and also wrote Jake Devers. Apparently no one paid any attention to us, but changed to a modified British model. I don't think the difference is too great, but it is a curious added evidence of the mania to trust anyone but Americans. Some weeks ago, when I was talking to Spaatz he remarked, "We are paying too high a price for Supreme Commander." We are, especially when we don't exercise it, and are just pawns. I fear that, after we get landed in France we will be boxed in a beachhead, due to timidity and lack of drive, which is latent in Montgomery.  I hope I am wrong.


February 27, 1944 Sunday: The men of the 301st Operation Signal Battalion marched in the rain from their transports to board troop ship number 542, formally the USS *George Washington*. They were met by donut girls of the Red Cross with hot coffee and donuts. The 301st was trained to be the main signal battalion assigned to Army Headquarters. They would become its communication network, responsible for all radio and wire communications in and out of headquarters.[103]


[Patton]

Had the Parson for lunch, then lunched with the Leicester-Warrens at Tabley house. Lord Edgerton of Totten was there. He is a portly, deaf little man, whose property we are using. Also Major Becke, Chief Constable, and his wife were there. They are all real people. Koch and Hammond arrived from Africa and were delighted to be here. Mr. Stockdale told me that he had never met such loyal and enthusiastic supporters as my staff. He knows most of them.


Each day, the men of Third Army think that that day will be their last State-side.  The officers are given training that is substantially similar to that of the enlisted men.


[Lt. Col. C. Cabanne Smith]

There had been an early formation, a march to breakfast was from 0730 to 0830, at 0830 another formation. There were lectures and training each day and some included climbing of cargo nets. Lunch was 1200 to 13:00 hours then a march with full equipment. After the march, passes were given to go into town. Since the men thought they would be shipping out any day, they would go into town. Orders were relaxed enough to allow the men no curfew time but they had to be ready for formation the next day. Many would not get back to early in the am. It is very cold and it freezes at night and thaws some during the day.[104]

[Patton]
**February 28, 1944 Monday**

Called Bradley to suggest that he have a chart of the two types of divisions arranged, so that when we are discussing them we can see the differences more readily. He said that he had already thought of doing that.

[Patton]
**February 29, 1944 Tuesday**

Left Peover at 0300. Very cold with a heavy mist, so that for the first two hours there was not over 100 yards visibility. Got to meeting at 1335, five minutes late, found Bradley, Ike, Watson (3d Armored Division), Gaffey (2d Armored Division), Wood (4th Armored Division), Oliver (5th Armored Division) and Grow (6th Armored Division), also Walker, XX Corps, all present. After a brief discussion it was decided to leave the 2d and 3d Divisions, which are organized along American lines, and to correct the other divisions as follows:

1. Add a signal section by utilizing the 15% overhead.
2. To increase organic transportation by 10 2ton trucks, 10 trailers, and 10 peeps.
3. That the proposed new table for artillery headquarters solved the problem when it was put into effect.
4. To add one quartermaster service company platoon to each division from those allotted to the Army. The shortage in trucks can be made up by allotting quartermaster truck battalions if and when needed.

General Eisenhower also stated that in so far as possible, anti-aircraft and anti-tank battalions would be permanently attached to the divisions. He further suggested that regiments be given names of dead soldiers.

General Courtney Hodges was also present. He seemed quite depressed. Called on Hughes, who has just arrived and is not to be Chief of Staff of my Army, as his job is to be personal representative of the Commander in Chief. In other words, his eye. On the day Hughes went in to report to General Eisenhower, he met Brigadier General McClure, of the press relations, just coming out. Ike told Hughes that McClure had expressed the opinion that I should command an army, due to my reputation, and that Hughes is to investigate.

Devers certainly treated Hughes in a nasty way. He must be a very small caliber man, although he has always been very decent to me and even lately has released a lot of former Seventh Army officers I have asked for. As I was walking home from Hughes' place, there was an air raid but nothing happened.

61

[Patton]
**March 1, 1944 Wednesday**

Called on Mrs. Horace Hutchinson, who is the sister-in-law of my Godfather, Captain Arthur John Lindsay Hutchinson, now dead. She must be seventy, but is a very active old lady and goes around in the middle of the night putting out lights for people who have run off during an air raid and failed to extinguish their lights. She says she feels that she should have a tin hat, but has not been able to get one. Her husband was amateur golf champion of England around 1890.

Went to Middlesex hospital about my lip. Professor Wyndham says it is coming along fine. He has treated three British Lt. Generals for the same thing, and it is always the result of a blond being exposed to too much sunlight. I took Mrs. Prismall and Hughes to lunch at Claridges, then we went dog hunting and got one to be sent up on approval. Then I took Hughes to the hospital as he has the flu. Ike sent for me. I waited one and one-quarter hours to see him but he was busy, so made time with Kay to good effect. He told me that while he would not definitely order me to replace Gay, he certainly wanted me to do so, as he felt that while Gay was an extremely efficient chief of staff, he did not have the presence to represent me at other headquarters, nor to take over should I get killed.

Keyes has always felt the same way. Of course I was originally selected for "Torch" through the direct action of Ike and therefore I owe him a good deal. On the other hand, I have paid my way ever since. I am very reluctant to supersede Gay, but it looks to me and to Hughes, and others with whom I have talked, that if I don't, I will be persuaded myself, so I will have to make the change. The two people I have in mind are either Gaffey or Troy Middleton. I would prefer Gaffey as I know him better, as I had him in the desert and also in Tunisia. Of course if something should happen to make Keyes available I will take him like a shot.

Ike and I dined alone and had a very pleasant time. He is drinking too much but is terribly lonely. I really feel sorry for him. I think that in his heart he knows he is not really commanding anything.

[Patton]
**March 2, 1944 Thursday**

Waited till 1100 to get the dog but he did not come. While waiting I visited with Hughes who feels like I should comply with Ike's views on the Chief of Staff. I also went to see Beetle Smith to keep things greased, and saw Lee, who is making a fool of himself over the colored question. I fear that what he is doing is going to cause a great deal of unnecessary suffering and killing when we get back to the States. Called on First Army Group to butter up Leven Allen. After all the ass kissing I have to do, no wonder I have a sore lip. Ike told me he had not decided which of us three, Hodges, Bradley or I, should command the First Army Group. Brad will. Ike's version or the McClure incident was quite different from what he told Hughes. He told me he kicked McClure out for being a fool. Beetle Smith offered McClure to me as Chief of Staff. Oh, God I suppose that he did not know what McClure had said about me to Ike?

Shortly after Koch had arrived in England, Patton called Koch in to see him. By this time, Patton thought of Col. Koch, his G2 Intelligence Chief, as the finest intelligence officer in the army. Koch was a highly intelligent, quiet, soft spoken man who'd been with the General since North Africa. He and Koch bent over a map against an inner wall.

[Koch]

His elbows and forearms were resting on a spread Michelin road map of France, the type automobile clubs provided the world over for their members. Glancing sideways, the general straightened up and asked me to join him at the table. His finger continued to rest on the map.

"Koch," he said, "I want all of your G-2 planning directed to here." I bi-focaled my glasses and looked. General Patton's finger rested deep in France. On Metz! Then, starting at Nantes on the Atlantic coast and sweeping his finger along the Loire River toward the east, the commander continued, "I do not intend to go south of the Loire unless it is necessary to avoid a right-angled turn."

In broadest terms, Patton had just stated his EEIs - Essential Elements of Information - for the planned Third Army offensive on the European continent. Although I didn't know it then, he had just concluded what was to be his only personally-expressed intelligence directive, not only for the cross-channel invasion in Operation "Overlord," but for the rest of the Third Army's operations in Europe until the war's end.

The task facing my intelligence staff was now clear. Anything which might affect the Third Army mission, from the coast of France all the way to Metz by way of a circuitous route through Brittany, was now of critical concern. Initially, the commander would want to know what to expect upon arrival on the Continent in terms of enemy opposition, the terrain, and the weather. From then on he would want to be kept abreast of the details of these and other factors, well in advance, as operations proceeded. [105]

Patton's only personally-expressed intelligence directive was profound. Koch recognized that Patton had perceived exactly how the war should be fought long before his superiors had even drawn any plans or conceived any ideas. Patton knew where he wanted to go and how he wanted to do it. Koch knew exactly how to provide the information to allow Patton to plan … and he did.

[Patton]
**March 3, 1944 Friday**

Drove back to Peover leaving London at 1130. I feel very bad over this damn chief of staff business. I must do it in a way not to hurt Gay's feelings for I truly consider him the best chief of staff in Europe, Italy, or Africa. The only two I can think of are Gaffey or Middleton. Gaffey is probably as good, or better, than Gay, but I do not know him as well. Middleton is a brilliant man but I know him very little.

March 4, 1944 Saturday: Patton purchased a scrawny, malnourished little English bull terrier.[106]

  Patton loved dogs and had missed not having one around him. He liked bull terriers as he was familiar with the breed and had owned several including one he had bought for his daughters in the 1920's named appropriately "Tank".

[Patton]
**March 5, 1944 Sunday**

Church. Lunch at Stockdale's. Had a movie in the evening. Dog arrived, named Punch.

### What's in a Name?

General Patton told several people, including his aide-de-camp, Alexander Stiller, Kay Summersby, and Lady Leese, wife of the British Eighth Army Commander, who he was looking for a suitable bull terrier. Patton finally obtained a white bull terrier named "Punch" that had previously been owned by a RAF pilot who was killed in action. The dog is believed to have been secured or purchased from a British home for dogs located at 4 Battersea Park Road, London. Patton was told that the dog had been on 6 bombing missions over Berlin. Patton renamed the terrier Willie. By March 6th, Patton and his new pet were getting along very well.[107]

Unlike the origin story depicted in the movie *Patton*, Willie was not named after William the Conqueror. When Patton first saw this loveable little runt, "Punch" was small and undernourished. Patton wrote to Beatrice "My bull pup took to food like a duck on water. He is 15 months old, pure white except for a little lemon on his tail which to a cursory glance would seem to indicate that he had not used toilet paper."[108]

Patton's youngest daughter, Ruth Ellen Patton Totten, wrote a very different account of how Willie came to be named. In 1935, her father held a barbeque. He'd invited many of the young unmarried troopers from Fort Myer.  It was a custom for debutantes (unmarried young ladies), of whom Ruth Ellen was one, to be introduced at such functions. Patton was looking after all the details including the barbequing of a whole steer and two sheep. This was an enormously significant social event; many prominent guests were invited, among them, several Generals.

*It was at a barbeque that Georgie's famous Bull terrier, as yet unborn, was named … Georgie was checking on everything he saw and saw a little colored boy writhing on the ground under a tree making loud sounds.*

*Georgie was afraid the youngster had eaten something bad, or had appendicitis, or something had bit him.  When he got close enough to hear the sounds, he heard: 'Lil Willy Whiffle, you belly full for the first time in your life-you got a full belly-boy didn't it feel good! Lil Willy Whiffle, you got all the ribs and racks you kin hol' an' that big white man done done fo you, an' he don' even know yo name, but you name is L'il Willy Whiffle an' you is happy an you is full as a TICK!'[109]*

Did the sight of the undernourished pup remind Patton of this young boy who for the first time in his life had a full belly?  Nevertheless, the name "Willie" became very popular for English bull terriers.

[Patton]
**March 6, 1944 Monday**

Went for a walk with Punch and got lost --- must have walked six miles and did a little running too. Feel fine. He is extremely cute. Had a long talk with Cummings on what to do about Gay telling him, so I did. It was most distasteful. I really believe I would retain more self-respect if I resigned, but I am not quite that big hearted. Gay was fine --- could not have been better. I told him the exact truth, that Ike ordered me to do it. Leaving for London in the morning to see a movie of new equipment. People there don't realize what a long trip it is from here.

Now that Patton had a dog for a companion he still had to go about the business of building a good staff. Patton also had to secure his chief of staff as it was evident he could not keep General Hobart Gay in that position. He met with Troy Middleton and went to General Bradley's headquarters to ask him to transfer General Hugh Gaffey from command of the 2nd Armored Division. He had already asked General Gaffey if he would accept the position if he could get it done. Bradley had the 2nd Armored Division under his command and agreed to the transfer.

[Patton]
**March 7, 1944 Tuesday**

The lecture, given by an ordnance colonel who had never heard a gun go off in anger, was a farce. He began by telling Ike, Bradley, myself and a number of others, that we wasted ammunition, didn't understand tactics, and were generally useless. Of course it is evident that the speech had been written to inform people in the United States who had not been in action; but it was evident that a man, who was in the presence of people with a reputation of having been in action and who could not change his speech, was a fool. Middleton and I went to see Hughes at the 16th Station Hospital on Hartley Street. Mrs. Prismall was there and I asked her to dinner.

Took Middleton home and went to 22 Mount Street. Gaffey was there, as I had wired him to meet me and discuss the question of complying with Ike's order to get a more senior chief of staff than Gay. The two men I had in mind had been Middleton and Gaffey. Since Middleton was sent over by General Marshall to command a Corps, he is out. Gaffey said that, while he did not wish to give up the 2d Armored Division, he felt that, since he owed me so much he would do it, if I can get Bradley to turn him loose, and I think I can. That will be a good solution because when Gaffey quit being chief of staff in the desert he recommended Gay, and they are therefore good friends. Mrs. Prismall and I went to supper at Claridges'. It was expensive and bad except for the wine.

The bulk of the Third Army was still at Camp Shanks. The cold weather, with occasional snow flurries, was beginning to take its toll; many had minor sore throats and colds. The majority of the time, the weather was below freezing. The full pack marches continued.[110]

[Patton]
**March 8, 1944 Wednesday**

Middleton and I called on Bradley and we arranged to ask Ike to cable for a new commander for the 2nd Armored Division. Our order of priority being —

1). Newgarden, 2). Leonard, 3). Prichard, and 4). Brooks, to replace Gaffey.

Middleton will take the VIII Corps and I will get all the corps troops now attached to that corps, which has been a housekeeping corps assigned to the Third Army, and then re-assign them to their proper corps. When the 90th, 79th and 80th Divisions arrive, they will go to the VIII Corps, and when the XII Corps arrives, or perhaps it may be the IV, I will use it to take up the new arrivals. I also got the 5th and 6th Armored Divisions assigned to the Third Army and put them in the Corps. I arranged to call on Ike, with Bradley, to get all of this approved.

I then went to see Lee, and he informed me he had phoned Beedle Smith, recommending Middleton for my chief of staff, on the alleged grounds that since General Marshall had great confidence in Middleton, it would strengthen my position. I told Lee I was quite able to take care of myself and that for the future he would not meddle. He is either a conscientious doer of good deeds or has some ulterior motive. I am rather inclined to the latter belief.

I hurried back to see Bradley and asked him to come with me to see Ike. I saw Middleton, who said he would prefer a corps. We went out to Widewing to see Ike.[111]

He was talking on the phone and said, "Now, listen, Arthur (Tedder), I am tired of dealing with a lot of prima donnas. By God, you tell that bunch that if they can't get together and stop quarreling like children, I will tell the Prime Minister to get someone else to run this damn war. I'll quit." This is as near as I can remember. He talked for some time longer, and repeated that he would "ask to be relieved and sent home" unless Tedder could get the British and American Air, and the two Navies, to agree. I was quite impressed, as he showed more assurance than I have ever seen him display. But he should have had the warring factions in and jumped them himself, and not left it to his Deputy, Tedder. After he got through, he approved all our requests, including a 15 over-strength for the Third Army, and told me to stop by and tell Lee to get the orders out. However, it is always depressing to me to see how completely Ike is under the influence of the British. He even prefers steel to rubber tracks on tanks because Monty does.

As my car was getting a new pump, I drove down to Chisledon with Gaffey to visit the 5th Armored Division, General L. P. Oliver. General Walker, commanding the XX Corps was there, as was Gene Regnier, who commands a combat command in the 5th Armored Division. Regnier looked exceptionally dirty in the new type of field jacket, which I told him never to wear again. I gave them a few thoughts, and then we inspected the artillery, which is distinctly bad in that it was distinctly not good. Late supper there.

Patton called on Brigadier General Thomas B. Hurley, who referred him to Colonel Clell B. Perkins in regards to taking care of the needed shots for Willie. Though assigned to the medical section to take care of the troops, they were also part of a group of four who were also veterinarians. Patton's valet and friend, Sergeant George Meeks, took care of Willie as part of his duties.[112]

[Patton]
**March 9, 1944 Thursday**

I inspected the units near headquarters. The uniforms were bad and dirty. There was no attempt to have all the men dress alike. The men were very negligent, and the condition of the quarter, kitchens and latrines was bad. At 1000 I made a thirty-five minute speech to all the officers and seemed to get a good result. Tupper Cole, who commands the other combat command, as a colonel, was the best officer I have seen in the division. I get the impression that the Division will fight diligently but not brilliantly as it lacks finish, class, and polish---in a word it lacks a good leader.

Left at 1400 to visit the 6th Armored Division, under General R. C. Grow, at Morteon-on-Marsh. I addressed all the officers at 1600. The show was very well put on, and had a finish entirely lacking in the troops of the 5th Division. Inspected troops till dark and had dinner with division staff and Lord and Lady Dulverton, who live in the house with Grow. He is "Wills," the British tobacco king. Grow was utterly bemused by being with a lord of and frequently addressed him just that way. The effects of titles on even the most rugged Americans is disgusting.

[Patton]
**March 10, 1944 Friday**

Inspected the rest of 6th Armored Division and found it in superior shape.  I will have General Walker inspect it and take General Oliver with him to note, as painlessly as possible, the difference.

Reached Peover about 1750 and found that Willie, my new dog, had been run over by a car and the skin taken off his leg.  He feels very sorry for himself but is not really hurt at all.

[Patton]
**March 11, 1944 Saturday**

Colonel Oscar Solbert (changed from Sohlberg by Act of Congress) and Captain Wallace, son of the Vice President, arrived to sell me a scheme for evaluating morale by questioning the enlisted men; some of the questions being, "Do you feel that this war is worth fighting?" Another, "Are you ready to fight the Germans?" Another, "Are you anxious, willing, or reluctant to fight the Germans?" I told them that it smelled to me very much of the Russian political commissars whom Stalin had to remove before he had an army. It is an absurd idea and will simply remove the self-confidence of the soldiers.

At Camp Shanks, Third Army headquarters command was about to ship out.  It was about this time that Lt. Colonel Coy Eklund retrieved the mail from the APO.  Beatrice Patton had been writing and receiving mail from her Georgie throughout the war.  As Third Army was activated while still in New York, it served as their official location, and the mail was directed to them there. Beatrice's letter to her husband, therefore, found an indirect route to England, via NY.  Oddly enough, though Patton's command of the Third Army was a secret of the highest order, the army's postal service apparently did not get that memo.  When Col. Eklund looked at the address to determine the intended recipient for delivery, he took note of the name.

[Eklund]

I was the first to know we had a new army commander.  His wife would not have been writing him at APO 403 unless she knew that was his proper address.  I gave this letter to our boss and he ran over to our Chief of Staff, Brigadier General [George] Davis. Davis turned white, as you can imagine, as he knew his days were numbered.[113]

The 301st Signal Operation Battalion dis-embarked from their ship after landing in Liverpool, England and was met by a British band as they walked down the plank. They boarded a train and were taken to Mobberly in Cheshire and Company A proceeded to Knutsfort, England to "Thorny Holme" which would serve as their home while in England.  It was soon announced that they would be assigned the operation of forward echelon, under General Patton at his Army headquarters. Work began immediately as equipment arrived.[114]

[Patton]
**March 12, 1944 Sunday**

Codman and I went to lunch with the Leicester-Warren's, and at 1330 we invited all to come to a movie.  Mrs. Bromley-Davenport, Jr., an American from Philadelphia, and Mrs. Becke and another woman came.  The movie was very good.

Third Army's headquarters staff left Camp Shanks and proceeded to the New York port and loaded on the ship, *Ile De France*[115] When they loaded the ship, they saw why they had been delayed some two months. *The Queen Mary*, originally scheduled to carry them had been damaged by a huge storm on her return voyage from France.  She was still in port in New York being worked on from stem to stern.[116]

[Patton]
**March 13, 1944 Monday**

Had lunch at Manchester Midlands Hotel with Sir Eugene Ramsden, Mr.

Stockdale and General Leroy Collins. I think he is off his nut. He sticks his head down and rotates his chin, and his eyes are funny. Codman and Muller were with me.  Ramsden is president of the Jute industry of England, and Mr. Stockdale, under an English title, is really the general manager.[117]

Third Army sailed from New York at 0830 hours.[118] The SS *Ile de France* had quite a sendoff with Third Army aboard.

[Lt. Col. C. Cabanne Smith]

The Embarkation was quite thrilling with a WAC band alongside the ship and volunteer Red Cross workers giving us hot coffee and donuts as we marched up the gangplanks. We were all exhausted when we got aboard after marching with full packs and carrying our very full and heavy val-a-pacs. You can have no conception as to how crowded these troop transports are now, until you actually get on board one, movies give you no real conception; they are like a vast and very busy ant hill. My cabin is one of the best. It would normally be a nice cabin for two, there are seven other colonels in with me. The captains and majors are twenty to a state room.  The enlisted men hardly have room to stand and their bunks are triple decker whereas ours are only double.  We eat only twice a day. My schedule is breakfast at 9 am and dinner at 7 p.m. It is now almost 5 p.m. and I am plenty hungry. There is quite a storm blowing and the ship is getting pretty active.  Writing is getting very difficult but if it was not for the storm, I would have never had a place to write as the one officer's lounge is normally packed. The storm has already taken a toll on the less hardy voyagers. … There are all types of troops and quite a lot of nurses aboard.  I cannot tell you much about the ship but it is pretty big and we will rely on our speed and not be convoyed."[119]

---

**A Wartime Conversion**

A Grande Dame of the seas, the SS *Ile de France* was a French ocean liner built in Saint-Nazaire, France for the Compagnie Générale Transatlantique (CGT). Often considered the most beautifully built ship by CGT, the *Ile de France* boasted many firsts: the first major ocean liner built after WWI, the first ship ever equipped with refrigeration, and the first ocean liner decorated entirely in the Art Deco style. (ILE DE FRANCE, Portal of the French Cheese Community, retrieved at http:// iledefrancecheese.com/index.php/History.php.)

When war broke out in September of 1939, she remained docked in New York's

Staten Island pier until the following September when she was loaned to the British Admiralty.  Preparing for her wartime duties as a troop carrier, the *Ile de France* was stripped of her famed interiors.  She was refitted with 9,706 berths (compartments), loaded with 12,000 tons of water materials, submarine oil, tanks, shells and several uncrated bombers which were stowed on the open aft decks.  Now serving Allied interests, and under the management of Cunard, the international cruise line, the *Ile de France* was veiled in gray and black, and departed for Europe in May of 1940.  Following the fall of France, she was officially seized by the British in Singapore, her destination after her European landing.

Still under Cunard management, the *Ile de France* reverted to French control five years later, in 1945, at the end of the war.  After serving an additional year as a troop and repatriation ship, in February of 1946, she returned to the French luxury cruise line. [McBee, Scott. (n.d.) The SS *Ile de France*, as published on NewYorkSocialDiary. com, (David Patrick Columbia & Jeffrey Hirsch, New York), retrieved at http://www. newyorksocialdiary.com/node/192455/print.]

Some years after the war, when the Italian ocean liner *Andrea Doria* and the Swedish ocean liner *Stockholm* collided on July 25, 1956 off the island of Nantucket Island due to heavy Atlantic fog, arriving within 3 hours of the collision, the *Ile de France* took charge of the rescue effort, thus, played a major role in the greatest civilian maritime rescue in history where 1,660 lives were saved. (History Channel Online, This Day in History, retrieved at http://www.history.com/this-day-in-history/ships-collide-off-nantucket.)

[Patton]
**March 14, 1944 Tuesday**

I sent Gay, Harkins, Maddox, and Muller to London to get straightened out on planning with the First Army Group. This outfit is not very clever. They plan too minutely on some things and not minutely enough on others. They suffer from not having anyone in command. For example, after the First Army has captured Saint Nazaire and Nantes, if they do, we are take the Brittany peninsula. I think that, if Nantes falls, the peninsula falls too, as it is cut off.

I have just read the First Army Group (FUSAG) Plan again.  It says that the object of "Overlord" is to "secure a lodgment on the Continent from which further offensive operations can be developed."  The words "further offensive operations" indicate to me the intention of halting on a phase line, --- this is clearly wrong.  After we land we must keep driving, as we did in Sicily.  I am very much afraid this operation is going to be conducted in a timid manner. If so, it will not succeed.

On or near this date, "Patton had a meeting with famed historian and one of Britain's foremost writers, Basil Liddell Hart, on military tactics, authority of armor and history. Patton had read many of his writings and the two "got along" quite nicely. Patton listened to the mutual ideas on armor that Liddell Hart expressed to him. The idea of lightning fast moves in the field, bypassing enemy positions and hitting the objective in force without getting bogged down on the way. The meeting was pleasant for the both of them and Patton held him in high regard."[120]

Patton had dinner with his staff at Peover Hall, Knutsford. Willie was quite active and as a young Bull Terrier and had a noticeable sense of humor.

On one occasion he grabbed Patton's holster belt and pistol and started to run off with them. Sgt. Meeks went after him and caught him before any harm was done. It was not uncommon for Willie to grab things from Patton's desk. He even ate one of Patton's cigars and became quite sick over it but recovered.[121]

[Patton]
**March 15, 1944 Wednesday**

Erected a flagpole in front of Peover Hall. General C. D. Palmer, Chief of Artillery at ETOUSA, spent the night. He is stupid and opinionated. He told me that Condor, who fought so well for me with the 5th Armored Artillery Group in Tunisia and Sicily, is still a lieutenant colonel, and I asked him to get Condor promoted.

Today England was now awash with soldiers. They arrived daily on transport ships. Many of the officers and enlisted men were waiting for the invasion and training daily. Major James H. Polk[122], of the 106th Cavalry wrote home explaining that they were issued, "seven packages of cigarettes, one bar of soap, two bars of candy, two razor blades and one package of gum."[123]

[Patton]
**March 16, 1944 Thursday**

In going over some papers with a view to writing a new Letter of Instruction on tactics, I found the following, dated August 5, 1943, Palermo:

Memorandum:
To Corps, Division, and Separate Unit Commanders.

It has come to my attention that a very small number of soldiers are going to the hospital on the pretext that they are nervously incapable of combat. Such men are cowards and bring discredit on the army and disgrace to their comrades, whom they heartlessly leave to endure the dangers of battle while they, themselves, use the hospital as a means of escape. You will take measures to see that such cases are not sent to the hospital but are dealt with in their units. Those who

are not willing to fight will be tried by Court-Martial for cowardice
in the face of the enemy.

/s/ G. S. PATTON, JR.,
Lieut. General, U. S. Army,
Commanding


This order was gotten out immediately after the first "incident" at a
time when no reports on it existed.  It exactly expresses my feelings
then and now.

The bronze plate which I had put in the British church at Palermo was
made by the Navy out of a broken propeller. I paid the sailors who did
the job $25.00, which they did not wish to accept, but finally consented.
The engraving read as follows:

TO THE GLORY OF GOD

In Memory of the heroic Americans of the Seventh Army and of the
supporting units of the Navy and Air Force who gave their lives for
victory in the Sicilian Campaign, July 10 --August 17, 1943.

From their General.


Officers of the Medical Section began a series of conferences and inspections which were to involve
almost daily contact with higher headquarters and with the many Medical units of the Army.


[Patton]
**March 17, 1944 Friday**

I drove to London with Codman to attend a reception given by General
Eisenhower at Claridges. All the high British and Americans were there
except Field Marshal Lord Brooke and General Montgomery. Some people
were unkind enough to say that Montgomery was absent, as he could not
bear to be second fiddle. Sir Andrew Cunningham took special trouble to
look me up, also Air Marshal Conyngham and a lot of others. General
Doolittle was there and we had a nice talk. All the military elements of
the numerous governments in exile were there too. The pleasure was not
worth the long drive but one had to go.


[Patton]
**March 18, 1944 Saturday**

Saw Bradley, Hodges, Joe Collins, and Corlett. The two latter told me a
lot about fighting Japanese. They consider them vicious but not skillful

fighters. The American method in the South Pacific, of using tanks against pillboxes, will not work when anti-tank guns are present.


[Patton]
**March 19, 1944 Sunday**

Campanale, Stiller, and I went to lunch with Sir Eugene Ramsden and the Stockdales at a place some forty-five miles from here. To get there we drove through Manchester and over the Moors. Every few miles we would come on a large city hidden in the valley. Leeds is one of the cities so situated.


[Patton]
**March 20, 1944 Monday**

Worked hard most of the day on Letter of Instruction No. 2, covering tactics.  Gaffey and Gay arrived at 1900.  I was glad to see both of them.


[Patton]
**March 21, 1944 Tuesday**

Had in all the staff of Seventh Army and Colonel E.T. Williams, of the Third Army, and told them that the Third Army staff was carefully selected and of long experience, and that those present are not to jump at the conclusion that all we did was right and all they did was wrong. Both staffs have good methods, and what we must do is to evolve still a better method embodying the good points of each of the old staffs.


Third Army arrived at the Firth of Clyde, Greenook, Scotland.  They were told to remain onboard until the following day. General Patton was not there to meet them, but his orders were.  He'd relieved the Third Army Chief of Staff and, with one exception, all of the general staff officers.


March 22, 1944 Wednesday:The Third Army headquarters staff, less the relieved high command, disembarked.  They were met by the Highland Bagpipers boarding a train for Central England. The men passed them by and left the ship by Ferry to load on a waiting train as they were to proceed immediately to their new training camp in Peover.[124]

The train was equipped with blackout shades and traveled under blackout conditions. There was no light whatsoever in or outside of the train. The officers rode in first class, six officers per compartment. The train traveled all night. They arrived at Chelsford, where they left the train and boarded army trucks for the ride to Knutsford.[125]

`[Allen]`

Third Army's headquarters men arrived in Knutsford on the 23rd. About 1000 men of Third army arrived and General Patton had them form in ranks in front of Peover Hall.[126]

---



[1] Williamson, Porter B. *I Remember General Patton's Principles* 59-60.

[2] *Ibid.*

[3] In 1943, army General Everett Strait Hughes was the Deputy Theater Commander, North African Theater of Operations; in 1944, the Special Assistant to Commander in Chief, European Theater of Operations; and in 1945 Inspector General, European Theater of Operations.

[4] Count Helmuth James Graf von Moltke, was a high ranking German, devout Christian (Lutheran) and member of the conscience-based German resistance in WWII who managed to use position and influence to help German Jews and to publicly oppose Hitler. For more on Count von Moltke, *see*, Balfour, Michael. *Helmuth Von Moltke: A Leader Against Hitler.* Macmillan, London Ltd., October 19, 1972.

[5] Summersby, Kay. *Eisenhower was my Boss* 89.

[6] D'Este, Eisenhower, *A Soldier's Life* 389.

[7] As Supreme Commander of the Allied forces in Western Europe during World War II, General Dwight D. Eisenhower led the massive invasion of Nazi-occupied Europe that began by storming the beaches of Normandy, France on June 6, 1944, "D-Day". The codename for the operation – Operation Overlord. History Channel Online, retrieved at http://www.history.com/topics/d-day.

[8] Summersby, *Past Forgetting, My Love Affair with Dwight D. Eisenhower* 163-164.

[9] General Carl Andrew "Tooey" Spaatz was the commander of the United States Air Forces in Europe, thus directed the American segment of the strategic bombing campaign against Germany which included the Eighth Air Force, commanded by Lieutenant General Jimmy Doolittle, based in England, and the Fifteenth Air Force, commanded by Lieutenant General Nathan Twining, based in Italy. (Codman, *Drive* 197).

[10] Summersby, *Eisenhower was my Boss* 100.

[11] The Royal Household.

[12] Though one of the most successful campaigns in WWII, first code-named ANVIL, later changed to DRAGOON, this controversial operation for an invasion of southern France has largely been ignored as it fell both geographically and chronologically, August 15th – September 14th, 1944, between two much larger Allied campaigns in France and Italy. Originally planned as a simultaneous complement, ANVIL took place over two months after OVERLORD, aka D-Day. U.S. Army Center Of Military History, a Directorate within the Office of the Administrative Assistant to the Secretary of the Army. Retrieved at http://www.history.army.mil/brochures/sfrance/sfrance.htmugh.

[13] Col. Paul Harkins, Patton's Deputy Chief of Staff, was a good friend and a fellow cavalry man of the regular army.

[14] Diaz.

[15] NATOUSA stands for North African Theater of Operations, United States Army.

[16] Williamson, *I Remember General Patton's Principles* 147-151.

[17] Summersby, *Past Forgetting, My Love Affair with Dwight D. Eisenhower* 141-145.

[18] Blumenson, *The Patton Papers*, Vol. 2, 393-394.

[19] Summersby, *Past Forgetting, My Love Affair with Dwight D. Eisenhower* 141-145.

[20] Blumenson, *The Patton Papers*, Vol. 2, 394-395.

[21] Hirshson 431.

[22] Fifth Army was the most international army that fought in Europe during WWII. General Mark W. Clark was in command during most of its campaigns. The Fifth Army was initially composed of General Patton's Western Task Force and Major General Lloyd Fredendall's Center Task Force with the 1st Armored Corps located in French Morocco; the II Army Corps in Algeria; and the XII Air Support Command. Clark, Mark W. *Calculated Risk.* New York, Harper 1950, 145.

[23] General John Porter Lucas was Commanding General of VI Corps, U.S. 5th Army. *Also see*, Operation "Shingle"

at endnote.

[24] Patton was accompanied by both of his aide-de-camps, Charles Codman and Alexander Stillman.

[25] The Victoria Cross and the Distinguished Service Order are Military decorations in the United Kingdom.

[26] Distinguished Service Medal.

[27] Clark, *Calculated Risk* 125.

[28] Captain Lowman was General Keye's aide.

[29] Brig. Gen. F. A. Allen Jr.

[30] For more on operation Shingle, *see* U.S. Army Center for Military History, a Directorate within the Office of the Administrative Assistant to the Secretary of the Army. Retrieved at http://www.history.army.mil/brochures/anzio/72-19.htm.

[31] Frances Graves was the son of a cousin of Ms. Patton; he later served as one of General Patton's aides in Europe.

[32] James W. Totten married Patton's youngest daughter Ruth Ellen, thus, was one of General Patton's son-in-laws.

[33] Blumenson, *The Patton Papers* Vol. 2, 397.

[34] G. S. Patton, Letter to Frederick Ayer, Jan. 14, 1944.

[35] Brigadier General Benjamin Caffey commanded the 39th Infantry during WWII.

[36] Maj. George Murnane served as an aide to General Gay.

[37] Lt. D.G. Busely G-2 Sec 7th Army.

[38] O. N. Bradley & Blair 215-216.

[39] Summersby, *Past Forgetting, My Love Affair with Dwight D. Eisenhower* 168.

[40] *Ibid*, 169.

[41] *Ibid*, 171-172.

[42] *Ibid*.

[43] *Ibid*.

[44] Sgt. George Meeks was Patton's orderly; *also see* A Mutual Regard, Newspaper clipping, Patton Papars Library of Congress

[45] Library of Congress, Patton Papers; Patton Diary

[46] Library of Congress, Patton Papers; Patton Diary

[47] Collins Language. *French Expressions: Cats, Cockroaches and Buttered Spinach*. Collins, 2012, retrieved at http://www.collinsdictionary.com/words-and-language/learning-languages/learning-french/french-expressions-cats-cockroaches-and-buttered-spinach,20,HCB.html.

[48] The "When and If" was the name of Patton's yacht.

[49] Blumenson. *The Patton Papers*. Vol. I, 400.

[50] LST's (landing ships, tank) U.S. Army Center of Military History, a Directorate within the Office of the Administrative Assistant to the Secretary of the Army Retrieved at http://www.history.army.mil/books/Vietnam/riverine/chapter2.htm; for additional pictures of LST's *see* "The Normandy Invasion, The Story in Pictures" at http://www.history.army.mil/html/reference/Normandy/pictures.html

[51] Landing Craft, Vehicle, Personnel. *SALERNO, American Operations From the Beaches to the Volturno 9 September - 6 October 1943*. U.S. Army Center Of Military History, a Directorate within the Office of the Administrative Assistant to the Secretary of the Army, 1990. Retrieved at http://www.history.army.mil/books/wwii/salerno/sal-dday.htm.

[52] A 21-ton, 6 x 6 amphibian truck used for short runs from ship to shore in WWII. MacDonald, Charles B. *The Siegfried Line Campaign*. U.S. Army Center Of Military History, a Directorate within the Office of the Administrative Assistant to the Secretary of the Army, 1990. Retrieved at http://www.history.army.mil/books/wwii/Siegfried/Siegfried%20Line/siegfried-glossary.htm

[53] Derogatory slang for a German, especially a German Soldier in WW's I &II. *See*, http://www.thefreedictionary.com/Boche

[54] U.S. Army Center Of Military History. "Anzio, 1944." CMH Pub 72-19. The Office of the Administrative Assistant to the Secretary of the Army. Retrieved at http://www.history.army.mil/brochures/anzio/72-19.htm.

[55] Butcher 478-479.

[56] For more information regarding rank in the Army, *see* "U.S. Army Ranks." The Official Homepage of the United States Army. http://www.army.mil/symbols/officerDescription2.html.

[57] General Walter Bedell Smith served as General Eisenhower's Chief of Staff during World War II. Known as Eisenhower's hatchet man, "Beetle" as he was called by contemporaries, had the temperament of a pit bull which

counterbalanced Eisenhower's affable nature.  As Eisenhower's representative, he negotiated and signed the terms of surrender with Italy in 1943, and Germany in 1945.  Beevor, Antony. *Eisenhower's Pit Bull*. October 23, 2010, as reported in *The Wall Street Journal*, Bookshelf, a review of Crosswell, D.K.R. *Beetle: The Life of General Walter Bedell Smith*. University Press of Kentucky, 2010. retrieved from http://online.wsj.com/article/SB100014240527023045107045755620734153638844.html

[58] Commanding General.

[59] Butcher 480-481.

[60] *Ibid.*

[61] C. B. Odom 23-30; Charles B. Odom, M.D., Patton's close friend, personal physician, surgical consultant to Third Army was also Colonel Codman's roommate/tent companion throughout most of the European campaign.

[62] *Ibid.*

[63] *Ibid.*

[64] *Ibid.*

[65] Summersby, *Past Forgetting, My Love Affair with Dwight D. Eisenhower* 141-145.

[66] *Ibid.*

[67] Totten 348

[68] *Ibid.*

[69] *Ibid.*

[70] Blumenson, *The Patton Papers* Vol.2, 402.

[71] *Ibid.*

[72] Blumenson, *The Patton Papers* 410; Allen 16.

[73] M. C. Williams 166.

[74] Pronounced "Pee-ver."

[75] *Third Army, Planning in the United Kingdom* Vol.1, 9.

[76] Wallace, Brenton G. Col. 213

[77] Officer of Transportation.

[78] The proper reference term for a peep, the common slang term used at the time for a jeep, would be ¼ ton truck, however, this term was seldom used.

[79] *Ibid.*

[80] Codman, *Drive* 137.

[81] Codman, *Drive* 138.

[82] *Ibid.*

[83] Codman, *Drive* 139.

[84] General Donavan was the head of the OSS and was good friends with General Patton. He was a Medal of Honor winner in WWI.

[85] C. B. Odom 34.

[86] Reprinted in part from "In Memoriam, General George Patton, Jr. General, US Army", by Third Army Headquarters, Lt. General L.K. Truscott, Jr.; Commanding Bad Totz, Germany March 1946.

[87] For more on General Patton's dress and attire, *see* The Battle Uniform *and* A Mutual Regard herein.

[88] Blumenson, *The Patton Papers* Vol.1, 412-413.

[89] *Ibid.*

[90] George Price Hays was a Medal of Honor Winner, WWI.

[91] Blumenson, *The Patton Papers* Vol.1, 410.

[92] Butcher 490.

[93] Named after her mother, Patton's wife, Bea Jr. was Patton's eldest daughter. She was married to Col. John Waters, who was captured by the Germans in North Africa.  His ultimate fate remains unknown.

[94] US Army Military History Institute, Senior Officers Oral History Program, Project 81-G. Hobart Raymond Gay, Lieutenant General, USA Retired, Interview by Willard Wallace, Colonel, USAR 1981 Pages 27-30

[95] M. C. Williams 172.

[96] The entire square, 20 Grosvenor Square, was comprised of government offices dedicated to the war effort.  This was also the location of the former London headquarters of General Eisenhower.

[97] C. C. Smith, *My War Years, 1940-46: Service on Gen. Patton's Third Army Staff* 24.

98 *Ibid.*

99 *Ibid.*

100 Blumenson, *The Patton Papers* Vol.1, 417.

101 Koch 67-68.

102 C. C. Smith, *My War Years, 1940-46: Service on Gen. Patton's Third Army Staff* 25.

103 301st Signal Battalion 20,29.

104 C. C. Smith, *My War Years, 1940-46: Service on Gen. Patton's Third Army Staff* 26.

105 Koch 68-69.

106 Blumenson, *The Patton Papers* Vol.1, 419; R. J. Stillman & M.F. Riggs 8.

107 R. J. Stillman 9

108 D'Este, *Patton: A Genius for War* 580.

109 Totten 244.

110 C. C. Smith, *My War Years, 1940-46: Service on Gen. Patton's Third Army Staff* 29-30.

111 Eisenhower felt it unsafe to have the Allied Headquarters located in the center of London where it would make a good target for bombings, thus, had it moved to Brushy Creek Park in Widewing. (Butcher 499).

112 R. J. Stillman & Riggs, M.F. 16.

113 Lande 97.

114 301st Signal Corp Battalion 30.

115 Eklund 1.

116 Lande 101.

117 G. S. Patton, George S. Patton Papers, Patton Diary 1943-1945 BOX 3 Annotated transcripts Diary entry March 13, 1944.

118 Eklund 1.

119 C. C. Smith, *My War Years, 1940-46: Service on Gen. Patton's Third Army Staff* 31

120 Hirshson 448-449.

121 R. J. Stillman & Riggs, M.F. 17.

122 Major Polk would go on to command several Cavalry units under General Patton, live through the war, attain the rank of full Colonel as commander of the 3rd Cavalry Group before the war's end and be highly decorated for bravery. He retired as a four star General as he ended his career as the Commander in Chief US Army Europe and Central Army Group, NATO.

123 Polk III 26.

124 Allen 16.

125 Eklund 2; C. C. Smith, *My War Years, 1940-46: Service on Gen. Patton's Third Army Staff* 33.

126 Allen 17.

# CHAPTER 2

## ATTEN...HUT!

The United States Third Army headquarters reports for Duty

"All officers and enlisted men were assembled on the large terrace in front of Peover. It was a raw, gloomy, early spring day. Patton stood on the wide stone steps facing the Staff.  On his left was his CoS, Brigadier General "Hap" Gay, and on the right, Willie, Patton's pugnacious-looking, white English bull terrier. On the portal over Patton's head was a weather-beaten stone shield bearing the date 1536. But there was nothing medieval about the General."[1]

[Patton]
**March 24, 1944 Friday**

General George A. Davis, former Chief of Staff of the Third Army, whom I had asked not to have sent to U.K., came anyhow; either ETOUSA failed to send the wire or it was not delivered by the Adjutant General.  At 0100 I had all the officers and men form in front of Peover Hall, and I gave them a talk. The men then marched off and I talked to all the officers. Finally, we had all the chiefs of sections and assistants in the office. Talks went over in good shape.[2]

While listening to Patton speak, Colonel Richard Stillman observed the striking impression the General made, from his highly polished boots and immaculate dress, to his tall and erect posture. His Chief of Staff, Brigadier General Hobart Gay, stood beside him and was also garbed in perfect military attire.  At Patton's right and equally impressive was the General's dog, the "homeliest dog that I had ever seen. Although he was as neat and clean as his boss. His name was Willie and he remained quietly by the General's side. Throughout the speech, Willie gazed imperiously at us as if he were our Commanding General."[3]

Patton was attired in a superbly tailored, form-fitting, brass-buttoned battle jacket, studded with four rows of campaign ribbons and decorations, pink whipcord riding breeches, and gleaming, high-topped cavalry boots with spurs. Around his waist was a hand-tooled, wide leather belt with a large, embossed, shiny brass buckle.  In his hand was a long riding crop; on his shoulders, shirt collar, and helmet, fifteen large stars.[4]  Patton wore three rings, his West Point graduation ring on his left hand and two rings on his right; one of which, according to the inside inscription, was given to him on the occasion of the birth of his first child, Beatrice.[5] After the General's death in 1945, Beatrice Patton gave the ring to her grandson George Patton Waters, the son of Colonel, later General John Waters who was captured in North Africa and liberated in April of 1945 in Germany.[6]

Characteristically, Patton didn't talk long; he was always trenchant and to the point.


[Patton]

I have been given command of Third Army, for reasons which will become clear later on. You made an outstanding record as an able and hard-working staff under my predecessor. I have no doubt you will do the same for me. We now have two staffs merging into one, each with its own procedures. By working harmoniously and intelligently together, a third staff will be developed with a third procedure, which should be better than either of the other two.

I am here because of the confidence of two men: the President of the United States and the Theater Commander. They have confidence in me because they don't believe a lot of goddamned lies that have been printed about me and also because they know I mean business when I fight. I don't fight for fun and I won't tolerate anyone on my Staff who does.

You are here to fight. This is an active Theater of War. Ahead of you lies battle. That means just one thing. You can't afford to be a goddamned fool, because in battle fools mean dead men. It is inevitable for men to be killed and wounded in battle. But there is no reason why such losses should be increased because of the incompetence and carelessness of some stupid son-of-a-bitch. I don't tolerate such men on my staff.

There are three reasons why we are fighting this war. The first is because we are determined to preserve our traditional liberties. Some crazy German bastards decided they were supermen and that it was their holy mission to rule the world. They've been pushing people around all over the world, looting, killing, and abusing millions of innocent men, women, and children. They were getting set to do the same thing to us. We had to fight to prevent being subjugated.
The second reason we are fighting is to defeat and wipe out the Nazis

who started all this goddamned son-of-bitchery. They didn't think we
could or would fight, and they weren't the only ones who thought that,
either. There are certain people back home who had the same idea. Both
were wrong.

The third reason we are fighting is because men like to fight. They always
have and they always will. Some sophists and other crackpots deny that.
They don't know what they're talking about. They are either goddamned
fools or cowards, or both. Men like to fight, and if they don't, they're
not real men.

If you don't like to fight, I don't want you around. You'd better get out
before I kick you out. But there is one thing to remember. In war, it
takes more than the desire to fight to win. You've got to have more than
guts to lick the enemy. You must also have brains. It takes brains and
guts to win wars. A man with guts but no brains is only half a soldier.
We licked the Germans in Africa and Sicily because we had brains as well
as guts. We're going to lick them in Europe for the same reason.

That's all, and good luck.[7]

General Patton was part of a ruse designed to fool the Germans into thinking that he would be commanding FUSAG (First United States Army Group) which would lead the cross channel attack at Pas-de-Calais. Patton therefore instructed his new command that both he, and they, were secret. They were not to speak of him or Third Army to anyone. As a result, Patton did not wear the patch of the Third Army.

### The Origin of "Old Blood and Guts" and the Famous Patton Speeches

General Patton had several "stock" speeches that he used, built upon and "tweaked" to address different ranks and to elicit different effects. The famous speech in front of Peover Hall in England was the one that he typically used when he addressed soldiers. It had been developed over the previous four years. Colonel Codman, a Patton aide, made it a practice to carry this "standard speech" in his briefcase. Patton would remember and build upon key words that would cause very little variation in content. As there'd been some controversy over this speech in Sicily, Patton made slight modifications before he arrived in England.

Patton rehearsed his speeches to present a theatrical spectacle that affected a purpose; thus, though the speeches themselves were, at times, only slightly adjusted, Patton famously delivered all of his speeches in his uniquely uniform Patton fashion.

The vast majority of General Patton's official and personal correspondences were transcribed by his personal secretary Master Sergeant Joseph D. Rosveich who'd been with Patton since 1942.


                                                  [Rosveich]

I was assigned to Patton's personal staff early in February,
1942, only a few weeks after Pearl Harbor. He was then still at
Fort Benning, Georgia. At that time his name was practically
unknown in the United States. But at Benning he was already
called Old-Blood-and-Guts, although not by the men of his own
units. It was in the knowledge of this epithet and of what
it stood for that I approached him on the first day of my new
assignment on his staff. But the man to whom I was introduced as
his "new secretary" didn't look blood-and-gutsy to me.

At first I don't know why he reminded me of Woodrow Wilson. Later,
I thought he looked like the president of an old, distinguished
university. He sat behind his simple desk, in shirt sleeves and
slippers, with pince-nez over his eyes, smoking an expensive
cigar. The only accessory that even remotely indicated his
alleged flamboyance was a pair of red, white and blue suspenders.

General Patton greeted me with a quiet, "Good morning." He
showed me where he wanted me to sit during dictation. It became
a vantage point at his side which I retained on three continents
for three years and five months. I was at his side at the time of
his greatest triumphs and in moments of greatest humiliation.
I was a private when I first joined him and only a non-com when
I left him after the war, shortly before his tragic  death
in Germany. But this wasn't a relationship with which rank
mattered. My official title was "confidential secretary to the
commanding general" and I enjoyed his confidence in full, in both
professional and private matters. It was to me that he dictated
his general orders, combat narratives, reports to Eisenhower,
comments on men and events, and his private correspondence.
And it was to my shorthand books that he confided his
personal diary.

This long and intimate association with the most colorful and
controversial general of the U. S. Army, qualifies me, I feel,
to help correct the distorted picture of the General and to

describe the Patton nobody knows. But I am conscious of my confidential relationship to him and will be careful to draw only on my personal observations and recollections, and not to trespass on that confidence.

On my very first day as Patton's secretary, I had occasion to see that I was serving two men rather than one. General Patton was the fusion of two men who lived in different worlds. One was his own world of calm efficiency, discipline and order. The other was the world of his immediate environment--our world of extreme tension and nervous strain. My introduction to his two worlds was abrupt enough. It came with the first dictation. Patton leaned back in his upholstered swivel chair, puffed on his cigar, and looked at a few notes he had made. Then he started to dictate. For a while I was too preoccupied with my own good fortune (or misfortune, I didn't know) that elevated me to this enviable (or unenviable) position. I wasn't actually aware of the meaning of his words. I was just taking them down mechanically in my shorthand book. But gradually it dawned on me that the General was dictating to me a draft of one of his widely quoted fire-eating speeches which earned him the nickname "Old-Blood-and-Guts."

You would never have recognized it as such from the way Patton dictated it. He spoke in a voice that was fit for the pulpit. But what he said was hardly printable. He spoke of the two most important elements in battle: the need of "guts" and "the desire to spill the enemy's blood." But not once did he raise his voice while he dictated these words. He said: "Rip your bayonets into the bloody bowels of the enemy" in the same even voice in which he dictated his letters to his friends or members of his family.

I was completely dazed by the contrast between the rip-roaring contents of the speech and the cultured, quiet poise of the man who created it. However, I soon was pulled out of my daze. As soon as I returned to his office with a transcribed copy of the speech, he called in a couple of his aides to rehearse it in front of an audience. He worked up to a fury. Those purple passages erupted like hot lava from a volcano. I was standing there, watching the spectacle in speechless awe. Then he came to the end of the speech, without the slightest pause or warning, Patton made a complete reconversion to his calm self. He sat down and, in almost scientific terms, explained the theory behind his speech to us.

He said that the performance we had just watched was exactly that: merely a performance, a put-up show, a calculated and rehearsed act of bravado. He was convinced, he said, that the young men of America needed such a toughening because they had grown soft and careless in the good life.

"For the last twenty years," he said, "our boys have been subjected to a steady diet of pacifist talk and doctrine. Now all of a sudden these 'pacifists' have to be turned into soldiers thirsting to kill the skilled, battle-tested soldiers of a shrewd enemy. The whole situation is perfectly ridiculous. You cannot change the mental habits of these boys overnight. You have to shock them out of their ordinary habits and thinking with the kind of language you've just heard in the speech.

"Here," he said, "where I said: 'Rip your bayonets into the bloody bowels of the enemy.' This is one of the best! I used it again and again. It's intended for its shock effect. It's a somewhat boisterous method of training and commanding men. But it's sure to pay dividends in ground gained and blood saved."

It was during the rehearsal of the speech that I heard Patton's famous high-pitched voice raised for the first time. I didn't hear it raised again until June, 1942 when we moved west into the California desert to train for our impending assignment overseas.[8]

At the conclusion of Patton's speech, the men were divided and moved out by assignment. The enlisted men and company grade officers were assigned to the camp; the field grade officers were billeted in private homes in Knutsford. Upon its arrival at Peover, the Forward Echelon, consisting of the Engineer section, consisted of twenty-eight officers, one warrant officer, and forty-three enlisted men, organized under T/O 5-200-1, dated 15 July 1942.[9] This section, which Lt. Col. C. Cabanne Smith was assigned to, was housed in prefabricated huts.

Patton's Third Army Headquarters and his Army were starting to take shape.

## The Organization of a Field Army Headquarters Division and Function of Staff

To understand how an army functions, one must comprehend how its headquarters is organized.  Staff is divided into four principle "General Staff Sections."

> G-1 - Personnel
> G-2 - Military Intelligence
> G-3 - Operations and Training
> G-4 - Supply and Evacuation

In armies with a large headquarters, there is a G-5 in charge of Civilian Affairs, Displaced Persons and the like.

Additionally, a special staff group consists of specialists and heads of service. These include: Air Officer, Adjutant General, Anti-Aircraft, Artillery, Chaplain, Chemical, Engineer, Finance, Headquarters Commandant, Inspector General, Judge Advocate, Liaison, Ordnance, Provost Marshal, Quartermaster, Signal and Surgeon.

The headquarters "Staff" assists the commander in the exercise of command, collects information, makes plans, arranges details and makes recommendations.[10] Of course, this is an over-simplification of the organization of a field army headquarters and the job they do, which is absolutely essential to overall operations and directly affects the entire army's combat effectiveness.

Third Army headquarters was bifurcated into a forward echelon and a rear echelon. Though their structures were duplicated, they served different functions.

## The Commanding General

In times of War, the Supreme Commander had authority to make temporary promotions by approval of higher authority.  Permanent ranks had to be approved by the Congress.

The Army commander's rank reflects a type of job function. The Commanding General directs the movement of the corps commanders. Having come up the chain of command, the general, though fully informed regarding all specifics, leaves the details of operational planning to the section responsible.

Patton carried the rank of Lieutenant General (Three Stars) and had under him a Chief of Staff at the rank of Major General (Two Stars) and a Deputy Chief of Staff, a Brigadier General (One Star).

A period of intensive planning had begun; troop phasing and bridge requirements were planned; computation of all engineer supply requirements up to D plus 90; terrain analyses and road studies were conducted; and river crossing sites and traffic circulation plans were examined. Strategic terrain analyses were prepared from a study of all available data on the region of Northwest France, north of the Loire River and west of the Seine River and, later, the area south of the Loire. These same regions were studied and analyzed to assess their suitability for tank warfare. The combination of this information would assist the G-2 in the development of their target area analyses.[11]

The families of high ranking British officers would occasionally hold social events to temporarily distract their American counterparts from the pains of homesickness. while they awaited activation into the war zone.

That evening, Lady Leese, wife of Sir Oliver Leese, commander of the British Eighth Army, held a dinner party for Third Army's headquarters staff at her parents' estate. General Patton's personal staff: Col. Codman, Aide-De-Camp, Col. Charles Odom, General Patton's personal physician, and Col. Nicholas W. Campanile, Civilian Affairs Assistant Chief of Staff, agreed to serve as ushers for the event. The occasion also provided an opportunity for the Headquarters staff who'd just arrived from the States to get acquainted with other staffers.

Thereafter, General Patton invited Col. Codman and Col. Odom to his quarters. The old home was very cold, and though an alpine light[12] provided illumination and heat, their laughter warmed their spirits as the friends entertained one another with jokes.

Few of his thousand plus newly-arrived men had ever been away from home before, let alone traveled to this country which most had only read about or seen in newsreels and movies. After a week at Thorneyholme, evening passes were issued, thus began their exploration and initiation into English nightlife. A gin-mill was now a pub; the movies, a cinema, with the most expensive bookings in the rear of the house. Vehicles travelled on the left side of the road; one ate with his fork in his left hand; and when one asked a civilian for directions, the response was invariably "at the next left turning, then straight ahead, you can't miss it." The children's thumbs up gesture was now one of palms out, accompanied by the plea, "Any gum, Chum?" Tuppence, sixpence and shilling took the place of nickels, dimes and quarters; the intricacies of this new system had already been solved in the crap games of the preceding week. Where formerly the men had wandered unhindered in the lighted streets of American cities, they now crept gingerly through the pitch darkness of strict blackout.

Naturally, the first objective was the pubs. There weren't many Toms and Joes behind the bar as women took their places and the men were introduced to the novelty of barmaids ... although the modifier "maid" turned out to be a misnomer that sometimes carried things a bit too far.

Here, beer was, for the most part, the staple beverage. No longer did beer flow from a tap but was pumped up from regions below by a gadget that was amazingly primitive. There was mild, bitter ale and stout and possibly other local names for the beer, but in the pinch of wartime, they were divided into two general classifications: good and bad. Although at times unpalatable, and too often containing the whole grain either from the barrel or the barn floor, it at least had the desired effect on one's head, and a most urgent reaction on the kidneys ... which instituted the next bit of pioneering in the realm of European plumbing.

The first door in the maze leading to the men's room was unblushingly marked "Toilet" or just plain "W.C." (Water Closet). This door opened onto a series of blacked-out hallways and then finally to an alley out in the open. By the time one reached this stage of the game, urgency demanded any differentiation between "the men's and ladies' room" irrelevant. The maze invariably led to a wall and usually, after their eyes had become used to the darkness, the men would be agreeably surprised to find that they were using the correct wall. If, however, instinct failed and no amount of careful groping revealed a wall, nature dictated relief to be found in the middle of nowhere. Unfortuantely, on occasion, there was an irate remark from in front or something warm from behind that revealed the presence of another "mazed" bar patron. It probably was not until the institution of British Double Summer Time that the men could find their way to relieving themselves in confidence.[13]

[Patton]
**March 25, 1944 Saturday**

We got a very amusing report on the Italian Campaign, signed by Barr, Devers' Chief of Staff, but written, I think, by Clark or Gruenther. It spent most of the opening pages saying how much higher the mountains in Italy were, how much bigger and meaner the Germans in Italy were, and how much heavier Clark's losses have been. Clark seems to take great pride in the number of men he gets killed, and he is always boasting to me and making comparisons with the number I lost. I see no use in paying unnecessary casualties for victory. Finally, and to prove their superiority, they say that while we won a campaign in 38 days, they hadn't yet won theirs, which seemed to me a rather amusing method of self-laudation.

The Leicester-Warren dance was a great success and we all had a fine time. Sunday I am going to inspect the Royal Naval College at Eton, near Chester, have lunch there, and then fly to London so as to be on hand to be decorated with the C.B. Commander of the Bath on Monday afternoon.

That day, under the command of Col. Oscar Koch, the new G-2 intelligence staff assembled for the first time. The word came down that the Third Army would be utilized as a secondary force, after the initial invasion where First Army would secure the beaches and the ports. Therefore, all planning was to be phased accordingly with a 30 day lag behind the landing. There was, however, no indication as to the day the landing would take place. A decision was made; the G-2 planning would be worked out on the assumption that they had ninety days in which to complete the work.[14] Lt. Col. Robert Allen was placed in charge of the highly secret Third Army War room; two MPs were stationed at the door twenty four hours a day. What was to become "Operation Cobra" had been planned early on; Allen was now informed of the operation. Additionally, G-2 intelligence was informed of the planning and alternate planning for the Normandy Invasion. General Bradley would be commanding the ground forces of the First US Army (FUSA). The British and American forces would make simultaneous landings at two different locations.[15]

[Patton]
**March 26, 1944 Sunday**

Captain B. H. Warner, Royal Navy, Commandant of the Royal Naval College, Eton, Cheshire, asked me three weeks ago to come down and inspect the college today. Captain Stiller and I arrived at 1000. I saw the Colors taken over by the guard. They use a special march at half-time which is very impressive. One of the color bearers had a fever of 102 but refused to go on sick report until he had had the honor of carrying the colors. I then inspected the guard and 48 WRENS[16] who do the clerical work at the college; then the different companies of cadets, ranging in age from 14 to nearly eighteen. Eton Hall, where the College is temporarily situated, is the home of the Duke of Westminster, who is said to be one of the richest people in England. Most of this money comes from property in the vicinity of Westminster, which is owned by the family. The Captain told me, apparently in all seriousness, that the Duke is not a high-class nobleman, as he has only been a Duke for 300 years, and before that, had been nothing but a Marquis. It is said that his taxes are so great that he has to pay 21 Shillings on every pound he gets; in other words, it costs him a pound and a shilling every time he gets a pound. The grounds of the place are very beautiful. In peacetime 120 gardeners were employed. At the present moment there seem to be none. Flew to London, arriving at 1700 and called on Hughes. Lucas was with him. As a result of my talk with Lucas, I think that he was timid at the Anzio beachhead. He said he did not feel justified in expending a corps. He did not expend it because he did not try. Had he taken the high ground he might have been cut off, but again he might not have been. Without the high ground in his possession, the landing was useless. Our losses to date, in the beachhead, are in excess of 18,000, which is more than a division and a half, so he made the expenditure without any justifiable gain. Both Alexander and Clark were present on the shore on D-Day, and as Lucas said, "Kept breathing down his neck," but neither of them had the guts to order Lucas forward. I feel very sorry for Lucas as I think he knows he did wrong, yet thinks he did his duty.

[Patton]
**March 27, 1944 Monday**

Went to Widewing, Supreme Invasion Headquarters, at 1050, and found that I was not expected to lunch. In fact, with the exception of McClure, the Public Relations Officer, none of the American officers to be decorated were expected for lunch, which was for the benefit of the British. I had lunch with Butcher, Kay, Briggs and several other WACs.

At 1400 there was a two-company guard, one American and one British. Field Marshal Sir Allen Brooke, Chief of the Imperial Staff, represented the King and pinned on the ribbons. General Eddy and I got G.B.'s, Holmes and McClure O.B.E.'s (Order of the British Empire), and others got lesser medals. Sir Andrew Cunningham was there, and very nice as usual. Brooke said, "Don't wince, Patton, I shan't kiss you"[17]. He also said that I had earned the decoration more than any other American. He probably said the same thing to each one; he is of the clerical type. Ike said, "I wish the Americans could be as smart as the British." I also chatted with Mr. William Phillips, political advisor to Ike. Mr. P. was terribly worried about how to prevent fraternization between Germans and Americans during the first seven months of our occupation. I told him he was crossing a bridge before he got to it and that, anyway, nothing could stop fraternization. I learned from Lucas that, in the initial landing, the British, as usual, failed to land until evening --- 14 hours late.

Lt. Col. Robert Allen had been living in town with a British family, as most officers were allowed to do; however, this was no luxury. His British hosts had no hot water, no toilet and no heat. He soon moved to a hut on the Peover property which was closer to his office and, as well, where he could get a hot shower. That night, he was joined by several others for an evening service at the small church attached to the main hall. They'd spent all day preparing for the staff conference that would be held the next day, Monday, the 27th, the official opening of the "War Room" headquarters.[18]

Tasked to complete the overall plan for Third Army's role in Operation Overlord, masses of Top Secret material was pouring into the War Room from T.I.S. (Theater Intelligence Service), First US Army ETO and the British. Third Army's role would entail breaking from the bocage country into southern France. They were informed that their target area was Normandy and the Brittany Peninsula from Honfleur to Nantes. The following codenames were designated:

| | |
|---|---|
| "Overlord" | The Invasion of the continent. |
| "Neptune" | The 21st Army group consisting of the 1st US army and the 2nd British Army. |
| "FUSAG" | First U.S. Army Group, presumably comprised of the 1st and 3rd US Armys |
| "SHAEF" | Supreme Headquarters Allied Expeditionary Force, Commanded by Eisenhower |
| "ETOUSA" | European Theater of Operation United States Army commanded by Lee[19] |

To ensure success, every objective needed to be effusively detailed. All planning was centered around mapping. Many areas in Europe had bad maps, old maps, and in many cases no maps. Creating a precise map was a laborious task. Third Army engineers were given this task, and performed admirably.

Colonel Oscar Koch was responsible for the assembly of the requisite elements that would allow for a comprehensive mapping of the area. This entailed studying photographs of the topography of the intended fields of battle and plotting all areas of possible movement to relay this information to the Army commander. Hundreds of maps were assembled and thousands of maps were updated and printed as part of intelligence reports that displayed enemy positions.

Topographical maps were generated for every sector. Roads suitable for tank travel were identified. Detailed maps of all the cities and towns were obtained and studied. Marsh lands, rivers and lakes were clearly marked. Once the terrain models were constructed in detail, photographs were taken in the form of half tone model mosaics. When photo mosaics became available in areas that units were to cover in battle, they were shipped to the various units for pre-invasion training. A 1:250,000 scale terrain model of the entire operational area in France was fabricated.[20] Though terrain models worked well, in some cases, three dimensional topographical views were employed. This form of 3D photography, vectography, a stereoscopic process, involves two superimposed images, embedded in a plastic sheet, polarized at 90° to each other, and viewed through polarizing glasses, producing a three-dimensional image. To this end, a plant was charged with the production of some 75,000 vectographs monthly. Though initially thought promising, the use of vectographs proved to be impractical as the factory was located near High Wycombe, England, hence, field use on the European Continent would have been inexpedient.

Two topographical reproduction units were formed; one in Third Army's rear echelon, "Lucky Rear," for reproduction and printing, and one in the forward echelon that functioned as a quick mobile unit for emergency applications. For the mobile unit, a reproduction detachment was established consisting of one commandeered press trailer, a Harris 20 x 22½ lithographic press, a camera and a 2 ½ ton truck, one officer and nine enlisted men.

The entire printing operation was dependent on electricity, so generators, as well as lighting, desks, drafting supplies and tables were all mobile. During field operations, emergency map requests were not uncommon. Within 24 hours, photographs and film had to be taken, dropped from planes, developed, given to the topoghraphical map makers for the creation and completion of maps, and flown back. As the army moved quickly, this thoroughly modern undertaking would be duplicated several times over the course of the war. In normal working conditions, this function was part of Lucky Rear's responsibilities. Addtionally, as part of the Army Survey Center, they also assisted the Engineer Construction Company with bridges and airfield construction. Though the XIX Tactical Air Command had many camera-equipped planes and took useful photographs of all its bombing missions, Lucky Rear developed, and in some cases, took the actual photographs that were used by the intelligence sections. As the war would progress, German maps would be captured, updated and converted for use in the field. The survey section would survey areas to set up radar that would enable precision bombing through radar-controlled signals. Though the whole of the battalion was self-sufficient in the field, expendable commodities were often in short supply; gasoline and water consumption would cause logistical challenges as supplies could be limited.

[The 652 Engineer Topographic Battalion]

General Patton wants maps fast. The first step was aerial photography. Then operations prepares the work order. They then take the photos and orientate them to existing maps. The photo-spread of the area is placed

on a table in a mosaic to determine the coverage of the intended map. Then
a stereocomparagraph is made by comparing the photographs and drawing
them to scale on an existing map. On a plan table a final check is made to
insure accuracy and scale. The blue line board color separation is made.
Then a complete sheet is edited to add or remove components to bring it
up to date. Then a completed sheet is then approved. The operation dead
line pace is calculated. Then a negative is shot of the map. The negative
is then developed and put on a lay out and registered. A plate is made
of the map. Once the plate is made, the map is then printed in a large
printing machine. Map distribution is set up and then sent out.[22]

---

**Patton's Personal Security Map**

Constructed in leather, affixed with three stars denoting his rank, and monogrammed
with his name in gold, General Patton's personal security map case contained Patton's
daily map.

[Col. Koch]

[It was] uniquely folded, covered and water-proofed and about
10 by 20 inches in size; it accompanied him on all travels.
Scaled in about 8 miles to the inch, it contained more
important towns and a cross roads with secret identification
numbers. By referring to these, he could keep his headquarters
staff informed as to where he was or what he wanted done. Four
identical copies were always made - one for General Patton,
one for his chief of staff, one for the signal officer, and
for me.[23]

Exhibiting his lighter side, when one of the young G-2 staffers brought Patton his
personal map in the early days of the planning for Operation Overlord, Patton carefully
studied the map, and with the soon familiar twinkle in his eye, said, "That's fine, but it
only goes as far as east of Paris. I am going to Berlin."[24]

---

[Patton]
**March 28, 1944 Tuesday**

At noon, Beedle Smith phoned me about my letter to Lee asking for 15%
over-strength in the Third Army. He stated that General Bradley and
General Allen were excited because I was trying to rob them. He said I
should have come to him after General Eisenhower gave me permission to
ask for the overhead, because General Eisenhower really knew very little

about what was going on, and it was up to him, Smith, to fix things up.
He said, "Ike often makes mistakes unless I see to it." Since Eisenhower
gave me this permission in the presence of Bradley on March 8, it seems
to me that Smith is very much off base. I think he is dying of a swelled
head as the result of being promoted. I told him that I had carried
out the exact instructions I had received from the Commander-in-Chief.
I also stated that in fifteen days, from March 8 to March 23, when Lee
phoned me asking me to confirm the order in writing, nothing had been
done by Lee or himself, Smith. Smith replied that when I knew Lee better
I would not be surprised that it took him fifteen days to do nothing.
We are very unfortunate to have Lee occupying both positions of Deputy
Commander-in-Chief and Service of Supply. He is one of the starry-eyed
boys and too pro-British, while Smith simply yearns for safe power, which
he can exercise under the shadow of a real man.

Patton's plans also called for complete religious services, thus, he appointed James Hugh O'Neil to
the Third Army Staff as his head of the Chaplain Service. O'Neil was a US Army Chaplain for
twenty-six years, which included his service in World War II.[25]

[Patton]
**March 29, 1944 Wednesday**

Hughes, who came back with me on the 27th, and I waited all day for the
weather to clear so we could fly to Ireland but it did not clear.

G-2 intelligence received top secret information from Capt. Dups of TIS. Lt. Col. Robert Allen was
informed that the printer in Amsterdam who produced all of the maps for the Germans, as well as
their order of battle slips - which show hierarchical and command structure, strength, disposition
of personnel, equipment of units, and army formations - sends a copy of these materials each week
to TIS. Allen was also informed that TIS had a regular plane service between France and England.
Capt. Dups was very confident there were no leaks but Lt. Col. Allen had some doubts.[26]

A reorganization of duties and personnel at 3rd Army HQ gave the G-2, G-3, and G-4 the
"cream" of special staff personnel. As a result, the three G's were greatly expanded.[27]

[Patton]
**March 30, 1944 Thursday**

At the moment, 0900, it looks as though we could get off soon. We took
off at 1330 and landed at 1440. General Haislip met us and we arrived to
the Headquarters of the 5th Division commanded by General L.R.C. Irwin,
who was Artillery Officer of the 9th Division in Tunisia, and whom I
got promoted. Brigadier General Allen Warnock is the Assistant Division
Commander and Brigadier General H C Vandeveer is Artillery. He was
Artillery Instructor at Riley when I was there in '38. The whole division

was arranged en masse and looked superior. I have never seen a better turn out, and having done it many times in all grades from Major to Major General I know the amount of care and effort put into it. The junior officers must be good. My talk was a little too long but I praised them for their two years in Iceland of which they are proud, and on which no one has commended them. We then saw an attack against a fortified position using all types of live ammunition.

It was very well done. They will fight.

Lt. Col. Allen put on a practice brief for Col. Koch so Koch would be aware of the Situation room's capabilities.[28]

[Patton]<br>
March 31, 1944 Friday

Made a talk to the 8th Division, Major General H.C. McMahon; Brig General M.N. Walker. Walker is #2 and General J. A. Pickering, my old Chief of Staff, Artillery. The division was massed and looked as well, or better, than the 5th. It was a most inspiring sight. After lunch they put on a battalion, reinforced, in an attack on a hostilely occupied position. It was the best thing of its sort I have ever seen. They used marching fire and two men were hurt, one in the fleshy part of the right shoulder, the other in the calf of the leg. Nothing serious. The man hit in the shoulder kept on and even threw grenades. It showed a very fine spirit. The man who will do that in maneuvers will go a long way in battle. After this maneuver I called the battalion together and told them about this. The Colonel commanding the battalion is a reserve officer named Jones, who was a very famous football coach in the south. The same qualities which made him a great coach make him a great battalion commander … a natural leader. I asked General McMahon to see that the soldier shot through the arm got the Soldier's medal. This division will fight.

Patton walked downstairs. In one corner, Lt. Col. Manly was sitting with several junior officers. Manly, a regular Army officer NCO, got a reserve commission and was Lt. Col. in AG section. He saw Patton but did not get up. Patton walked through twice. The third time, he wheeled suddenly, walking over to Manly. "I should think that an officer who has been in the Army long enough to be a Lt. Col, would know enough to get on his feet when his commanding General enters the room." Patton then turned and walked away.[29]

Battle preparations continued. The headquarters of western Base Section was consulted in connection with water supply, sanitation, and venereal disease control among troops in the United Kingdom. Investigation of medical units revealed that no major personnel shortages existed, as most units had arrived at the full table of organizational strength. However, in order to provide maximum efficiency, a number of medical officers were shifted, resulting in better balanced professional staffs in the hospital units. Medical personnel attended department schools on a quota basis and nurses were placed on temporary duty with Services of Supply hospitals for practical experience. Formal training inspections were commenced for all units to determine their ability to perform in the field. Conferences were held with the Office of the Chief Surgeon, European Theater of Operations, Headquarters First U.S. Army Group, Advance Section Communications Zone, and the European Theater of Operations Blood Bank, regarding the availability and distribution of whole blood during the coming operation.

In a report to General Patton, G-1 declared Third Army's strength at 134,200 men.

The men were now used to the night life in England. When regulations finally allowed passes of longer duration and transportation as well, the men poured into the nearby towns: Mobberly, Wilmslow, Alderly Edge, Altringham, Sale and, last but not least, Manchester. It did not take very long to transplant their philandering ways from Indianapolis to Manchester. It is stretching it a point to liken the Long Bar in the Gaumont Theater building to Stegmeier's but they could be parallel in the sense that they were usually the starting point in the evening's festivities. From there the groups fanned out to the Ritz and the Plaza for dancing and to a myriad other places for drinking. It required considerable bird-dogging to unearth sufficient Scotch, rum or gin to satisfy their rabid drinking appetites, but they were usually obtainable in the right places. In an effort to make a little go a long way everyone soon learned the "short way home" by indiscriminately mixing whatever in the line of beer or liquor or both was available.[30]

Unconsciously this proved to be a good hardening process for the invasion; without it, the later bouts with Calvados and "jet juice" might have proved fatal. Never before had the men such a happy combination of circumstances to bolster their morale: plenty of women whose men were in the army, a pocketful of cartwheels, washers, and paper doilies (which the British used for money) and the pitch darkness of blackout. Women here were the same as anywhere else; it was just a question of accepting them under a different set of circumstances and customs. In a sense, the men went native. They came to learn some of the hidden charms of the English garden walls - at the cost of a few bruised knuckles - and to learn to ignore the British weather. That, they learned quickly, could be judged easily by the touching scenes of farewell in the shadows of the Midland Hotel with the six by six (2 ½ ton truck) waiting to whisk them away with a whine and a roar to Knutsford in eighteen minutes flat.[31]

There was nearly always something doing around Thorneyholme, even for those not out on pass. Beer was plentiful in many of the suites of the manor house. Packages from home and fish and chips from the stores in town provided a midnight snack. "Betty and her girl companions"[32] were usually within hailing distance so that even romance was not too far away. Keeping "the traffic" moving down the little lane that separated Thorneyholme from the adjacent property became a de facto part of the Special Orders for the Sergeant of the Guard and the OD.[33]

Then too there were sports. In games at Peover, Mobberly and Holmes Chapel, the team, which the 301st Signal Bn set up for sports, demonstrated its superiority not only to the ball clubs of various sections and units of Third Army Headquarters, but to the British public as well. This club, with eleven wins out of fifteen games played, ended its season with a score sheet showing some fine pitching, neat batting averages and good teamwork.

All in all, the stay at Knutsford was not a bad deal. Because of their congeniality, their enthusiasm and their willingness to join this new order of society, the men were popular. There is no doubt that the townspeople made great efforts to keep the men entertained, and the men met them half way. The GI's might have violated a few of the standing customs by leaving a wad of money on the bar, eating with the fork in their right hand, or by shying away from the garden wall in favor of a more comfortable attitude, but for the most part they complied with the rules and went along with the crowd. The Americans brought the pep and cheer typical of the American and for which the American is so envied and so often copied. They joined lustily in the barroom renditions of "Roll me over, lay me down, and do it again" and on the dance floor they soon learned the favorite English community dances: the Okey-Dokey, the Paul Jones, the Tango and others. They also left their mark on the people; the dancehalls rocked to the rhythm of jitterbugging English girls, "OK" was fast displacing "Aye" in the language of the Lancashire Lassies and the women, although they never would depart from the custom of drinking beer from a small glass, were learning how to use it as a chaser for something stronger.[34]

Patton encouraged all types of sports and recreation for his entire command.


[Colonel Richard J. Stillman]

Patton and Willie had become a familiar twosome in the English countryside. Although Patton was anxious to get to France and begin his military activities, he enjoyed many quiet evenings with cigars and scotch sodas with local friends. Willie was always included and slept on a rug in front of the fireplace.

Patton expected us to stay in good shape physically, and on the grounds to stay in shape next to Peover Hall my colleagues and I played baseball each afternoon weather permitting. Occasionally Willie would run off with the ball. Patton would watch from time to time and I was pleased as an outfielder, caught a well-hit ball headed for extra bases. He remarked "good catch, son."

The General would always take time to exercise. In addition to long walks with Willie, he exercised in his room each morning and played badminton with his aides. He did quite well and his young opposition did somehow manage to "let the boss win."[35]

[Patton]
**April 1, 1944 Saturday**

Talked to the 2d Infantry Division today, Major General W.M. Robertson, Brigadier General T.L. Martin (the artist), Brig. General G.P. Hays (Medal of Honor) in command of the artillery. Later we saw an attack by a battalion supported by the entire division artillery. The parade was as good as the other two, or nearly so, but the problem was poor in

concept though well executed in technique. The machine guns and mortars
were too far back, no marching fire was used, and infantry advancing by
rushes when there was no point to it. I was rather too severe in my
criticism to Robertson but told the men how good they were. It is a grand
division. Later I called on Lt. General Sir Allen Cunningham who commands
in Ireland. He is a brother to Sir Andrew who was not so impressive. He
took Abyssinia and was later relieved for reasons I do not understand,
but alleged to be because he showed lack of nerve, whereas in Abyssinia
he made attacks and conquered the country with practically nothing. In
fact, when the Italians surrendered to him at Addis Ababa, there were a
great many more of them than he had troops.

Dick Jenson was killed a year ago today.

Patton issued his letter of instruction and it was read by his staff. Among the things it said was,

> There is only one kind of discipline—perfect discipline.
>
> If you do not set up and enforce discipline, you are
> potential murderers. You  must set the example.
>
> There are more tired corps and divisions commanders than there are
> tired corps and divisions.
>
> Fatigue makes cowards of us all. Men in condition do not tire.
>
> High physical condition is vital to victory.
>
> Do not take counsel of your fears.[36]

In a footnote at the bottom of the instruction, Patton added, "Despite some similarities in speech, English and American are not the same. The English are foreigners to us, and we to them. General Montgomery told me that."[37]

April 16, 1944: The 81st Engineer Survey Liaison Detachment was assigned to Third Army Headquarters. This detachment of five officers and nine enlisted men were incorporated into the engineer section and charged with map distribution, supervision of map reproduction, and map supply and distribution.  Note: They performed these tasks through the planning stages, as well as in the field, during battle conditions as the army moved across France, Belgium, Luxembourg and through Germany into Czechoslovakia.[38]

Though still in a state of "limbo," the 6th Cavalry Regimental band performed that night.  Knowing of their predicament, and the relationship of the regiment to the band, after the performance, Patton began to quietly maneuver to have the group transferred and designated as the official 3rd Army band.[39]

[Patton]
**April 2, 1944 Sunday**

Hoped to fly back to England today but there was no visibility, so Hughes and I had a long talk with General Haislip, which I believe did a lot of good. I am quite impressed with him. Took a long walk.

G-2 Intelligence kept up with all theaters of operation. Col. Koch told Lt. Col Allen that he had come from SHAEF, London and had been told that the allies had suffered 100,000 causalities in Italy, of which 25,000 were at the Reggie beachhead. There was concern that the Germans had done quite a bit of maintenance in France on the fortification from Brittany to Brest.

There was speculation that the Germans may have gotten wind of Neptune … or perhaps they were just doing maintenance.[40]

[Patton]
**April 3, 1944 Monday**

Still weather not sound. Inspected ordnance and signal units, all excellent to superior. Took boat at Belfast at 2:00 and had a very quiet trip.

In the first week of April, an Army Exchange Officer was appointed and an American Red Cross Field Director joined Headquarters. Both were to operate under Special Services which had recently issued two programs of recreation and athletics designed for use either with or without standard equipment for Army troops.[41]

[Patton]
**April 4, 1944 Tuesday**

Landed at 0600 near Blackpool. Reached Peover at 0900 by car. Gaffey tells me that a War Department inspector is in London in connection with the killing of prisoners in Sicily. I tried two men, a Captain and a Sergeant for it and they pleaded at the trial that I had ordered them to do it. When the question of trying these two men for what was clearly barefaced murder came up, some of my friends advised me not to do it, as they said what has happened would happen, because that would be the natural line that the defense counsel would take. However, I did not believe then and do not believe now that I can condone murder for my own benefit.

When I addressed the 45th Division in Africa just before sailing for Sicily I got pretty bloody, trying to get an untried division to the sticking point. Among other things I said that if the enemy keeps shooting at you till you are right on top of him, you can't stop shooting

97

when he tries to surrender. If he wants to surrender he must do it in
time, or come to you with his hands up. If he snipes you from the rear,
you must kill him if you can. However, I made no statements by which the
wildest stretch of the imagination could be considered as directing the
killing of prisoners. Furthermore, it is interesting to remember that
this murdering took place on the 14th of July after the troops had been
ashore and in contact with the enemy, and had taken prisoners for three
days; therefore, had I ordered any killing, it would have started on the
11th and not on the 14th.

I just heard an amusing incident. Someone overheard a heated discussion
between Wedemeyer and Ike about me. Finally Wedemeyer said, "Hell, get
on to yourself, Ike; you didn't make him, he made you."


US Army General Albert C. Wedemeyer was a man of impeccable credentials. Wedemeyer was
highly respected by both British and American military planners and heads of state. He was the
foremost authority on German tactical operations and was the chief advisor to General Marshall
and the Joint Chiefs of Staff on war planning in Europe. He was the author of the "Victory
Program" that advocated the defeat of German armies in Europe as the prime objectives of the
U.S. In 1942, he'd studied Operation Torch, was there during its operation as an observer in North
Africa, and reported back regarding the operation to General Marshall. He knew Patton well.
They'd had many intense discussions regarding history, military tactics and planning.[42] General
Wedemeyer was now on his way to London by invitation of Lord Mountbatten and Prime Minister
Churchill, to attend a crucial planning session of the proposed cross channel attack.


[Robert S. Allen]

The first G-2 Briefing of staff in War Room at Peover hall was held at 1000
hours. Every one of the sections Chiefs were present. Patton was away
from camp. Show went off well.[43]


[Patton]
**April 5, 1944 Wednesday**

Codman, Odom and I left for London via Headquarters VIII Corps. I wanted
to talk to Middleton about the shootings and also about the two addresses
I gave the 45th Division, at both of which he was present as the then
Division Commander. I gave two addresses because the Division was camped
in two different spots, but the two talks were identical as nearly as one
can make them when speaking extemporaneously. His memory of what I said
was the same as my own and was also corroborated by Stiller and Codman,
who were present. We reached London at 1530 and called up Ollie Haines[44]
and asked him to come over with Lt. Colonel Williams, the Inspector
General who has been sent from Washington to make the investigation.
They asked me the regular questions about being willing to testify and

knowing my rights. Captain Compton of Company "A", 180th Infantry and Sergeant West, Company "C", 180th Infantry, were the two men who did the murdering on July 14 near Butera Airport. Captain Compton captured 43 Germans who had been sniping. Five of these were in civilian clothes, either in whole or in part. The Captain had these men shot without trial. Those in civilian clothes could have been shot legally - the rest not. Compton was later killed in Italy.  Sgt. West was conducting 36 prisoners to the rear, and when well out of the battle zone halted them on the side of the road and killed them.

In my opinion both men were crazy. At the trials, the defense counsels said that in my speech to the 45th Division on June 27th (I think it was), I had said that if the enemy resisted until we got to within 200 yards, he had forfeited his right to live. What I had said, as nearly as I can remember it, and corroborated by Middleton, Codman, Stiller, and later by Wedemeyer, was this: "In a close fight when you get within one or two hundred yards of the enemy and he shows signs of wishing to surrender, don't cease firing and go in to get him, but keep on shooting until he comes to you with his hands up." This is only simple common sense. Concerning snipers I said, "When you are sniped, especially from the rear, the snipers must be destroyed." Of course in neither case did I contemplate murder of men who had surrendered. The fact that Johnnie Waters is a prisoner would: aside from anything else, have made me the last one to do a thing for which they could retaliate on him. The testimony in the two cases as to what I said was different, which also indicates that the defense counsels were using quite unethical methods and manufacturing evidence out of whole cloth. Codman and I took Wedemeyer to dinner and had a very pleasant talk with him later.

While in London, Wedemeyer was contacted by General Handy of the U.S. Army Inspector General Department, concerning the matter.  Wedemeyer came to Patton's defense.  He wrote to General Handy regarding the matter.

While visiting with General Patton before the invasion of Sicily we arose in the morning of July 2nd and proceeded to a sector of the North African coastline to observe an amphibious landing by the 45th U.S. Division. We watched the men coming ashore and at the conclusion of the exercise each regimental combat team was assembled and critiqued. Patton addressed the men, exhorting them to advance rapidly after getting ashore.

He admonished them to be careful when the Germans or Italians raised their arms as if they wanted to surrender. He stated that sometimes the enemy would do this, throwing our men off guard. The enemy soldiers had on several occasions shot our unsuspecting men and had thrown grenades at them. Patton warned the members of the 45th division to watch out for the treachery and to kill

```
the s.o.b.'s unless they were certain of their real intention
to surrender.

I am sure that the captain and the sergeant who are now under
investigation for shooting the prisoners misunderstood Patton's
instructions as well as his intentions.[45]
```

After all the evidence was presented and motions made, Patton was ultimately cleared of any culpability.[46] The incidents, however, caused Eisenhower to once again caution Patton about keeping his mouth shut. Patton inquired whether his speech giving should be discontinued; Ike responded that this would not be necessary but advised him to be very cautious in future.

Provost Marshal Col. MacDonald informed Lt. Col. Allen that on April 5th, the first white/ black soldier confrontation occurred. At Norwich, near Chester, "white and Negro troops got into a brawling"[47] and for a while, local MPs had their hands full. They requested assistance and emergency platoons that the Provost Marshal had formed in anticipation of such an event were alerted; however, as things settled down, they were not dispatched.

[Patton]
**April 6, 1944 Thursday**

```
Hughes came in at 8 o'clock to see if I was in any trouble. I assured him
I was not. However, we decided to write Surles an accurate account of the
incident so that if any unscrupulous correspondent got wind of it, Surles
could immediately state the facts. I also told him that he could get the
additional sworn testimony from Lt. Colonel Williams, who was returning
to the U.S.  I went to see Bradley but he was busy. Saw Wedemeyer again
in the afternoon and went to the Theater with Hughes and Mrs. Prismall.
```

[Lt. Col. Robert Allen]

```
Patton keep diary. Also has complete file of all letters received
and sends.[48]
```

April 7, 1944, Good Friday: Patton attended a high level conference at General Montgomery's headquarters, located at St. Paul's School in Kensington, London. It was a day-long top secret meeting concerning the planning of Operation Overlord, the Planning of the Invasion of France and the landings at Normandy.

During this meeting, much of what General Patton's forces would do after they landed was discussed. Patton was to come ashore in support of Bradley's forces that had landed on D-Day. Patton's Third Army would breakout and swing westward to capture the Brittany Peninsula and its important ports such as Brest. When this was accomplished, Third Army would form a north to south front of about 140 miles facing east toward the Seine River and Paris, ahead of which they expected the Germans to make a firm stand blocking their way into Germany. The details of

Patton's invasion planning impressed Ike and his staff along with the airmen present.[49]

Montgomery stated he would not only take Caan on D-Day, but over the next 10 days, would secure a hub in which the Americans would pivot and would be south of Caan almost to Falaise.[50]

Operation Cobra, as it was subsequently designated, would later be formulated as part of the overall "breakout" plan. However, the breakout understood at this meeting depended entirely on Montgomery taking Caan and anchoring his forces to draw the enemy toward him and away from Bradley's so Patton could "breakout." Montgomery at this time, and many times thereafter, stated that he planned to support this strategy. He failed to come through, however, sold his failure to High command as a simple inability to achieve "this one." When failing to execute his own plans, Montgomery tended to blame others, and when successes occurred, regardless of whose, he would find a way to take the credit. Bradley pointed out that Montgomery was not Eisenhower's pick for command and thought rather that General Alexander was a far better field commander. However, the British people thought of Montgomery as the General who'd never lost a battle; and Churchill exerted considerable influence in Washington DC to see that Montgomery was the British Commander pick in Europe.[51]

[Patton]
**April 7, 1944 Friday**

Gaffey, Maddox, Muller and myself went to the briefing of the first U.S. Army and the Second British Army at St. Paul's School at 0855. General Montgomery gave a 2-hour talk, followed by Air Marshal Sir Thomas Leigh-Mallory and Admiral Sir Bernard Ramsey. The Navy was still quite gloomy and had lots of reasons why the thing would fail. But it was interesting to note that in the talks there was much better mutual understanding between the Air, Navy and ground troops than there had been at a similar meeting we had in Algiers before we took off for Sicily. I think that much of this good understanding has been due to General Eisenhower's efforts.

After lunch, Bradley, Gerow, and Collins gave the First Army plan and the plan of the VII and XIX Corps. The British then gave the plan of the Second British Army. As usual they were much more prolific than we are. They have not got the training in such conferences which we've received from the War College, and it always shows up.

The Prime Minister made the last talk and the best. He said, "Remember that this is an invasion, not a creation of a fortified beachhead.''

During Montgomery's lecture it was interesting to note that I was the only Army Commander of the four Army Commanders involved to be mentioned by name. The other three he mentioned by number. Had dinner with Ike, Mr. McCloy, McNarney, Bradley and Smith. McNarney jumped on Ike about the mishandling of replacements in Africa, which is correct, and they are doing a worse job here. I had quite a talk with them trying to justify an initial over strength of 15%. I base this on the fact that the normal

loss from disease and accidents runs around 8%, so that troops invariably
enter battle short. The first day's casualties cannot be replaced for a
few days or even a week. That is added to the first shortage so that at
the crucial point of a battle, usually the third or fourth day, there is
a serious shortage. If we started with the 15% over strength, we would
enter the battle the first day 7% over strength, and if we assume that
5% casualties per day will occur, we would still be 1% understrength at
the end of the third day.

It is further necessary to remember that the efficiency of a division is
not measured by its shortage in personnel. A shortage of 10% in personnel
reduces the effectiveness of a division about 20%, and as the losses
increase, the efficiency decreases in almost geometrical ratio. I can't
get anyone to realize this. That is because none of our topflight generals
have ever fought. As usual, Bradley said nothing. He does all the getting
along and does it to his own advantage. I expect I take chances because
at heart the army is not my living and beside I am a soldier --- a simple
soldier. Referring to the Inspector General incident Ike said, "You talk
too much." I said, "If you order me not to I will stop. Otherwise I will
continue to influence troops the only way I know, a way which so far has
produced results." He said, "Go ahead but watch yourself." All of them
but me are scared to death. I shall certainly attempt to say nothing
which can be quoted.

[Patton]
**April 8, 1944 Saturday**

Drove back to Peover by way of Henley and Turville Park where Papa and
Mama lived one summer in 1921. We had quite a time finding it. First
we got to Turville Grange where an old lady named Madame D. Hautpool
said she was sure they had never lived there, as she had lived there 30
years, and the dear queen, Alexandra, had visited her there during the
last dreadful war. Turville Park, where they did live, is now taken over
by the ministry of works and used as a storage place for things from
the British Museum. I was glad to have seen it as the family liked it
so much.

As activities in all sections increased, a tremendous amount of coordination with the upper echelons
of the Allied military required an almost constant presence of key Third Army staff in London.
Therefore, in early April, Third Army established a London office in Bryanston Square, adjacent
to First U.S. Army Group Headquarters, with the Deputy Chief of Staff, Tactical, in charge, to
maintain contact with Headquarters European Theater of Operations and Headquarters First
U.S. Army Group. Officers from G-1 through G-4, Medical, Quartermaster, and Signal Sections

were originally placed on duty in this office, and, as contacts became more necessary and frequent, other Sections sent representatives to London.[52]

G-2 Intelligence learned that the Germans were using tens of thousands of foreigners in Richwehr. Because the Nazis were desparate for manpower, most of their defense divisions consisted of Russians, PWs[53], Poles, Czechs, and others; some as much as 80%. Even the SS Waffen units, previously reserved for the Nazi-Party elite, had now become "diluted". As well, due to the shortage in manpower, their Infantry Divisions were also being reorganized into 3 Regiments -3 Battalions.[54]

[Patton]
**April 9, 1944 Easter Sunday**

```
Went to church and wrote a letter to Mrs. Sparks about the death of
her husband.
```

G-2 was informed that Third Army would be comprised of 3 Corps, XV, XX, VII; VIII would be transferred after the landings; 3 infantry divisions; 4 armored divisions; and 2 airborne. Intelligence estimates were made regarding the number of battle casualties. As the hospitalization of troops due to venereal diseases was concerning, particularly gonorrhea which was highly prevalent, and syphilis to a lesser degree, adequate supplies of prophylactics were made available. Efforts to control prostitution after the landings were discussed. As Intelligence had found that troops on "B" rations for over 30 days would experience weight loss and a decrease in efficiency, command paid close attention to the adequacy of rations. Adequate nutrition was planned; rations were to be reinforced with fresh bread, butter and fresh cooked vegetables.[55]

April 10, 1944 Monday: An Air Sub-section of G-3 was activated to fill the vital need for coordinating close combat Air support for ground troops and a G-2 Air Sub-section was organized for the purpose of securing information about the enemy from Air sources.

The Quartermaster Section began large scale planning to supply the forthcoming operation. During this period, the Inspector General Section made extensive alert inspections of and contact visits to many units, special attention being given to the indoctrination of troops. Schools in radio security were established by the Signal Section. To hasten communications, especially to higher headquarters, the Section set up an air courier system with officers as couriers, using planes of the Fourteenth Air Liaison Squadron which was assigned to Headquarters.[56] The concept, later adopted, allowed immediate dispersal of vital information gathered by the fight mission. Camera film would be immediately taken to signal corps photographic sections for development and then copies taken to Intelligence G2 sections where topographical units were assigned. The photographs would be studied, maps updated, printed and distributed both to headquarters and field units. This would later be quick enough to have less than a 24 hours turn around, so units in the field would have up to date information and maps.

G-2 Intelligence learned that SHAEF ordered all leaves cancelled and all were to be accounted for from 001 to 2400. The purpose for this was to round up AWOLS. There were thousands of them roving around without passes or furloughs.[57]

April 11, 1944 Tuesday: The final draft of the Joint Operations Plan, U.S. forces, for operation "OVERLORD" was received. Also at this time a "Mounting Plan" prepared by Headquarters European Theater of Operations was received which set forth the procedure involved for staging troops to the embarkation points. In short, this plan stated the method by which each unit in the United Kingdom would be moved from its present location to the concentration areas, there to receive the last necessary items of equipment, and then to the marshaling areas, wherein they awaited movement to the various ports of embarkation. The responsibility for the administrative control to insure the movement of each Third U.S. Army unit to the Continent rested with the A.C. of S. G-3. This entailed the compilation of all necessary movement tables, and the coordination of all changes in each unit's status from the time the unit was alerted for overseas movement until that unit reached the embarkation point. The data compiled enabled Headquarters European Theater of Operations to control and exercise the movement of all units in the United Kingdom to the designated embarkation points for the cross channel voyage.[58]

[Patton]
**April 12, 1944 Wednesday**

General F. U. Greer of the 79th Division called. He was the Colonel of the 18th Infantry in Tunisia and did very well. I had him made. We had him to lunch and had a very pleasant talk.

A circular was issued prescribing the personnel administrative plan and the organization and function of the administration centers. A casualty sub-section was added to the Adjutant General Section. Based on experience of past operations, a decision was made by the Adjutant General to centralize all administration in administration centers of divisions for all assigned and attached troops.[59]

[Patton]
**April 13, 1944 Thursday**

General R.C. Macon of the 83rd Division called. He commanded the 7th Infantry when we landed in Morocco and did well. I had him made. General Middleton came to see me and we had a talk on the use of separate tank battalions in support of infantry. I used many of his ideas in the memorandum I am writing on that subject. General Charles Hines, Chief of Anti-Air, Third Army came to lunch. After lunch I had General H. L. Earnest in to talk on the use of tank destroyers. He is to draw up a memorandum of them similar to the one I wrote on tanks. We also had a staff meeting to discuss a new directive for the employment of the Third Army. It is pretty general, and means that when we get to France we will fight. I have a feeling, probably unfounded, that either Monty or Bradley are not too anxious for me to have a command. If they knew what little respect I had for the fighting ability of either of them they would be even less anxious for me to show them up.

**Red Cross Clubmobile Program and Donut Girls**

On this day General Bradley took part in the American Red Cross Clubmobiles official dedication. Mr. Harvey D. Gibson, American Red Cross Commissioner in Great Britain made the presentation to Lt. General Bradley, who was there to represent the U.S. Army Ground forces in Europe. The new Clubmobiles were converted US army 2 ½ ton, 6 wheeled trucks capable of crossing rough terrain. The trucks were to be manned by female Red Cross "donut" girls who would take, free of charge, doughnuts, hot coffee, cigarettes and candy near the front lines as military situation permitted. In addition they would carry newspapers, a phonograph with an assortment of records, a radio receiving set and an amplifying unit with a range of a quarter mile. There was a "fleet of two or three vehicles that would be self-contained and will pull a trailer with a generator in the back of it. Other trailers would carry supplies. The girls will be trained in vehicle maintenance, driving on rough terrain and as well as training in all areas of their assignment."[60]

Unknown to General Patton at the time of this release, this program would be a part of his Third Army and even his headquarters in the near future. The Associated Press and wireless transmissions were sent to the United States. A story about this appeared in the New York Times and throughout most of the newspapers in circulation at the time.

This program was highly organized and employed women who received some pay, uniforms and were trained in the states and again in England. They had the assumed rank of Captain so if they were captured, they would be treated as officers according to the Geneva conventions. The Red Cross was worldwide so these lines of authority were respected, or at least, hoped to be. The clubmobile program was not new and had operated successfully in African and Pacific Theaters. This was a tough duty and was not for everyone. They would be in the field, in all kinds of weather conditions, sleep in tents and drive heavy trucks into the field to cater to the troops hot coffee and donuts. This was going to be very tough work in view of the fact they would make 1000 donuts a day and feed 500 troops out of each clubmobile in the hardest of environments. These women were not "camp followes" nor prostitutes. They were to maintain the highest standards and were highly supervised.

Clubmobile veteran Mary Redford said, "The standard for attractiveness in those days was not Rita Hayworth or Betty Grable, but the look was well scrubbed wholesome "girl next door." We were somewhere between dowdy and glamorous. We had to look friendly not seductive. In those days, before the sexual revolution, it was assumed that single young women took sexual morality seriously. And most of us did … if any soldier stepped out of line with his remarks he was usually chastised by his buddies, not by us. We the Red Cross girls, and USO girls, too, were respected. Even though we were surrounded by men, men who had been separated from their wives and sweethearts for months and years, we felt perfectly safe."

"Make no mistake," as Julia Ramsey put in her thesis, "these were not girls! In anything but name. Rather, these were intelligent, tough, and educated women who were often fiercely independent and in most cases fit the traditional female roles of the time much less closely than their on paper qualifications would indicate."[61]

The women who applied were screened heavily, had medical fitness exams, and several personal interviews. These women were to be paid professionals and given some overseas benefits. It was preferred they were unmarried and were as expendable as the American combat soldier, as they would be in harm's way. Once they were accepted into the program, they were sent to Washington DC and trained by the American Red Cross at American University. It was to be a six week course but later shorted to two weeks as the need was great and the time short. Once their training was completed they boarded a troop ship and traveled to England. There they were assigned to a Group and training continued. Once in England they learned how to use the equipment, drive the trucks and, of course, make donuts. The donut making was no easy task as it had to be done by the thousands, delivered and repeated each day. All the flour and supplies were huge, bulky and heavy. They had to do it all with little help. In England they were up at 5:30 a.m., dressed in their uniforms, and worked till 10 a.m. making donuts, then they delivered and served them and this lasted till about 2 p.m. and they traveled back to base. They then cleaned the trucks and got ready for dinner. This process was repeated daily. It was hard work in England and that would substantially change to harder work in the field in Europe.[62]

There were three women assigned to each clubmobile and 8 Clubmobiles to a Group and one Cinemobile run by two. After a hard day, they were often expected to attended events, in their dress uniforms in the evening, which were cut in the style of the uniforms of the period, were of a blue green color, complete with a service overseas cap, and purse. They had white gloves and were encourage to dress up and remind the young enlisted men why they were fighting. Their job was to entertain the enlisted men and not cater to the officers. This they did very well.

I've tried to include a description of the Red Cross Clubmobile program as it really existed as it has been given only lip service in other books on Patton, simply because Patton's niece was part of the program. The Red Cross women who did this job were every bit as important to the war effort as those who supported the troops on the home front. That there are very few books on the subject is a shame as they did a great job supporting the troops. In addition the women were subject to combat conditions and several were highly decorated. These would include bronze and silver stars and  in awards of purple hearts as a result of wounds. Some were in combat zones long enough to earn battle stars on the overseas ribbon. Some were killed in combat and some by car accidents. They were in the Army and had "Army Service Forces Certificate of Identity of Non-combatant" issued to them. They were subject to following and carrying out orders.

[Patton]
**April 14, 1944 Friday**

Played golf alone with a half-wit caddy and did worse than usual, also ran a little and walked about a mile. I am in good shape and wish the whistle would blow.

Colonel J.D. Page, who used to be executive to the artillery commander of the 9th Division, and who should have had a star, is here. Eddy said he was unhappy in the 9th under Ike's classmate, Rowel, who got the star, so I got him transferred to the 5th Armored Division. The artillery officer they had was no good.[63]

[Patton]
**April 15, 1944 Saturday**

Not a damn thing I can do. All the staff is working and we are doing all right. I inspected the engineers, artillery, G-3 and G-2 offices. This staff does not work with the same intensity as that of the Seventh Army. They have too much of an idea of shuffling papers. However, they are learning. I inspected the Army forward echelon messes and had Gay eat lunch at the Officer's mess; Stiller ate supper at the enlisted men's mess; and Captain Murnane, Gay's aide, ate supper at the rear echelon with the enlisted men. They all told me that the messes were in fair shape, but I think they can all be improved.

A white lieutenant from a colored ambulance company was arrested for entering a factory by climbing over a wire fence and carrying a concealed weapon. He was probably drunk. I called Colonel J.C. MacDonald, the Provost Marshal. The Lieutenant will be tried.[64]

April 16, 1944 Sunday: A training memorandum entitled "Use of Tanks in Support of Infantry," written by Army Commander General George S. Patton was distributed.

[Patton]

I had lunch with the Leicester-Warrens. They used to be De-Warrens, as I saw this on an inscription in their Chapel. I do not understand the methods by which people gain and lose names in England, but it seems very easy.

I also called on Colonel Goldschmidt, whose books on riding I used to read. I gathered from talking with him that he is a better writer than a rider.[65]

## A Birthday Party for Willie

Sometime in the middle of April General Patton decided to give Willie a birthday party. He reasoned that since Willie was coming with him overseas into combat, that Willie could be killed and, for that matter, so could he. Willie's true age was unknown but he was believed to be about 16 months old. Having no exact birth date Patton picked a day he could invite some of his closest staff members to dinner and used the occasion to celebrate Willie's birthday. So, one evening Patton arranged to have a birthday cake baked and invited Major General Gaffey (Chief of Staff), Lt. Col. Odom (Patton's personal physician), Brigadier General Gay (Deputy Chief of Staff), Captain Murnane (Assistant Secretary General Staff), and his two aides (Lt. Col. Charles Codman and Major Alexander Stiller). Also present was Aide to the Chief of Staff, Captain Taylor. The seating on Patton's right was Willie, Gaffy, Odom and Taylor. Patton was seated at the far end of the table. On Patton's left were Gay, Codman, Stiller and Murnane. Even on occasions such as this, proper seating and military service etiquette was followed. There are a least two photographs of this party taken by the signal corps stationed at Patton Headquarters. One of them has Willie to Patton's left as the guest of honor, sitting in a chair, having a piece of cake cut by General Patton as General Hobart Gay looked on.

The evening dinner, for the humans, consisted of a full semi-formal officer's mess complete with a cake with icing with birthday candles. To finish the flavor of the moment, the staff sang happy birthday.

Patton's private mess, when indoors, always followed military protocol and was complete with a white table cloth, china, silver service and the appropriate silverware, placed according to the formal service etiquette of the day. This practice was maintained throughout Patton's life. Willie, who was always at Patton's side, normally laid at Patton's feet during the meals he attended, which was often. Patton always tried to secure the best cooks and mess at his headquarters. Willie would often get juicy morsels slipped to him and upon getting it flicked to him, would catch it in his mouth without much movement.

(Stillman, Richard J./Riggs, Mary F. *General Patton's Best Friend: The Story of General George Smith Patton, Jr. and his Beloved Dog, Willie.* R.J Stillman Company, New Orleans 2001 Pages 27-30)

[Patton]
**April 17, 1944 Monday**

I had a staff meeting at 1100 to inform the staff, particularly the new part of it, that they are not following things through: that they issue orders but do not check to see that they are carried out. I said that I am not going to cut off any heads to produce results, but I am going to demand efficiency. Colonel Elliott Cutler, of the Medical Corps, was here for breakfast. He has a very good idea which he acquired from visiting the Russians, namely, to put the slightly wounded in a hospital by themselves, and the badly wounded and badly diseased in another hospital by themselves.

He says that doctors, particularly civilian doctors (and that is 99% of our Medical Corps), naturally spend most of their time on serious cases, whereas in war you should spend most of your time on the cases which can be got back to the front promptly. Furthermore, if the slightly wounded men associate with the badly wounded or diseased men, they learn a lot of symptoms which they then tell the doctors they themselves possess, and the doctors are big enough fools to leave them in the hospital when they should go back to the fighting. Cutler also pointed out that it has a great moral effect to get men back to their old unit, because in that case the soldiers see that getting wounded is not a very serious business.

Major General Floyd Scowden, Assistant Quartermaster of the U. S. Army (my old roommate) came to lunch and stayed for quite a talk on uniforms.[66]

April 18, 1944 Tuesday: During this time, Patton was reading *The Years of Endurance, 1793-1802*, by Arthur Bryant. The book was very popular among the English. It had been published in 1942. The book was about the principles that England held dear. Bryant was seeking to retrace the social history of his country backwards and was constantly reminded that the wealth, security and peace of the nineteenth century was founded on a great achievement of endurance and fortitude which took place in the lifetime of the grandfathers of the Victorians. In his book and the study of the

British people in struggle, Author Bryant shows how that faith was justified.[67]

Patton wrote home to Beatrice that he had read the book and found it a "swell book" and said it was a fine to buck up one's own self confidence and reinstate Providence but not in Destiny. (Destiny was Patton's code word for General Dwight David Eisenhower, who Patton used the first two initials of his name. D. D. and referred to him in early letters as Devine Destiny. Now it was just shortened to "Destiny." He went on to say, "The latter is not going to play much of a part in the invasion and it is too bad." Patton went on to write that he thought he was needed and that no one can plan their future and that those who try fail, but one can school your mind so that when opportunity knocks, he can use it fearlessly…"[68]

[Patton]
**April 18, 1944 Tuesday**

Mr. McCloy and Generals McNarney and Lee arrived in their special train at Knutsford at 7:45. We had breakfast on the train and then drove them to Peover. I showed them the map giving them the location of the Third Army and then took them for a briefing by the staff on the whole show. This was very well done and took 55 minutes. I mentioned to them, and so did Middleton, that in the setup, as now put out, there is a British Corps under the First U. S. Army, set to enter Paris. This is probably all right as they wish British, American and French to enter at the same time, but it is well to indicate this to the powers that be. I also said to them in private that I hoped the First U.S. Army Group would be functioning, so that American troops would not enter Paris under an Englishman. Mr. McCloy asked me what I thought of Monty. I said first that I preferred not to answer and then on being pressed I said I thought Monty was too cautious and would not take calculated risks. Both McCloy and McNarney urged me to say nothing that would get me criticized, as it was possible that if I get in trouble again, someone would bring up a resolution in the Senate demanding my recall. I told them that my methods had produced men who would fight and I would be untrue to myself if I failed to use them, regardless of what happens to me.  McNarney kept saying that the thing for me was to keep out of trouble so that I could lead the men. McCloy said that he would see that I command an Army in France in spite of hell.

General Waterhouse, an Englishman, came to lunch. He told me a good story about an alleged remark of General Moltke, the elder, which is as follows: "Officers have four attributes arranged in pairs---intelligence and stupidity, energy and laziness. An energetic and intelligent officer makes a good staff officer. An intelligent and lazy officer makes a fine commander. A stupid and lazy officer can be used, but God deliver me from an energetic fool."[69]

April 19, 1944 Wednesday: Col Koch approached Lt. Col. Robert Allen and asked him to become the Assistant Chief of Staff for G-2 Intelligence, Third Army. This would make him the XO of the section and that it would not interfere in his present assignment, which Robert Allen wished to continue. He explained that he would have a fuller picture of overall operations. Allen was asked to think it over.[70]

The 6th Cavalry Regimental Band arrived at Knutsford, Cheshire, England, and reported for duty as the band assigned to the Third United States Army. Though they would later be officially designed as the 61st Army Ground Forces Band, they would be known as Patton's Third Army Band.

## THE 6TH CAVALRY REGIMENTAL BAND
### (The 61st Army Ground Forces Band)
### OFFICIAL ROOSTER AS LISTED AT THE END OF THE WAR

CWO Gregorio A. Diaz*, band leader

Pfc Dixon T. Apel, Pfc Frederick W. Bickering, Pfc Leroy Brown, T-5 Clarence J. Chapman, Pfc William M. Drapela, Pfc Kenneth E. Gross, T-5 Earl E. Diehl Jr.,  T-5 Warren H. Dungan, T-5 Lousis J. Elster, T-Sg Richard W. Farrell, T-4 Benard L. Shendell,* T-4 Norman S. Hess, SSgt John A. Hooks*; Pfc Carence E. Holley*, T-4 Carl D. Howell*, T-Sgt Luther S. Jones*, T-4 Joseph J. Krol, Pfc William M. May, T-4 Hubart N. Mazerole*, T-5 Charles B. Mitchell, T-4 Delwin B. Murphy*, T-5 John G. Perkins, Pfc Roger H. Williams, T-5 Richard S. Winvick, T-5 Anthony D. Borrelli, Pfc Charles A. Edgerly, Pfc Robert Meisch, Sgt Ferris C. Frees.

Twenty-Eight men were originally assigned to the band.

* Designates original band members; these 8 soilders were in the band since 1941 and remained members throughout the war.

[Patton]
**April 20, 1944 Thursday**

Left at 0800 to give a talk to the 90th Division, commanded by Brigadier General J.W. MacKelvie, John A. Devine, Artillery, with Brigadier General S.P Williams the assistant Division Commander, at Bridgenorth. All the officers and senior non-coms were present. After I finished, General Middleton, the Corps Commander, gave a fine talk, using football as a vehicle of expression. When the troops were dismissed, we assembled all colonels and battalion commanders and had an informal talk. I was very favorably impressed with the appearance and discipline, and also the physical size of the men in the Division. After lunch we drove to the Headquarters of the XX Corps at Marlboro. I talked at some length to the Corps Staff. Walker tries hard but is fat and short---two qualities I always distrust.[72][73]

[Patton]
**April 21, 1944 Friday**

In the morning we inspected the Corps Artillery, who were having a Command Post Exercise. It was very bookish and showed lack of imagination. The problem was in the Downs and there were as far as the eye could see only three lines of trees which would be natural enemy artillery targets. However, they chose these lines of trees as points of concealment for their installations. Also the close defense machine guns were right in the position, and so would be unable to keep fire from reaching it. Before lunch we looked at a racing stable where some Astor horses were training. I thought that, from the confirmation standpoint, they were a poor lot. After lunch spoke to the officers and senior non-coms of the 28th Division, General Lloyd Brown, Brig. General Kenneth Buchanan and Brig. General B.H. Perry, Artillery Officer at Chislendon. Walker told me that they were pretty ratty but I thought them very good.  Talked to regimental and battalion commanders at some length, especially on use of assault fire. Walker and I then drove to Chippenham to see General "P" Wood 4th Armored Division and explained to him an illustrated exercise I want to put on to show the use of a tank platoon in close support of infantry. Wood was in a bad state as the result of having been ridden over by a peep, which would probably have killed any other man.[74]

[Patton]
**April 22, 1944 Saturday**

Left "P's" headquarters at 0600 and got to Castle Martin at the southwest end of Wales at 1100. Combat Command "B", under Colonel George Read of the 6th Armored Division was there, having firing and doing well. General R.W. Grow was also there. I inspected all types of firing. The bazooka was bad as they were firing at long ranges, 150 yards, and getting misses. The tactical dispositions were bad but the use of weapons good. It was also apparent that they took too long to get on targets of opportunity,and had failed to realize that, when light tanks attack medium tanks, they must do so by platoon or at least by section.[75]

The Army was allotted control over certain established training areas and artillery ranges. The G-3 Section placed artillery ranges under control of the Artillery Section, which coordinated and controlled their use on a monthly basis so that more than thirty Field Artillery, Tank and Tank Destroyer battalions used them during the month. AAA units were inspected to determine the status of their training and equipment, and all were sent to ranges for refresher and familiarization firing. The dual function of the Headquarters Commandant and Provost Marshal was altered late in the month and an Army Provost Marshal appointed, with a special staff section established under his command.[76]

[Allen]

G-2 Intelligence attended a two day conference ending on this day that involved the Air/ground put on by the 9th Air Force. General Quesada of the 9th Air force gave a colorful impression of the men. He stated that P-47 (Thunderbolts) which were rated as the best fighter bombers the allies have, will support the assaults. He explain they could operate in small bumpy fields expected in the assault areas. He was absolutely sure they could keep the German Air force from interfering in the assault (beach landings) He said he was hoping the German Air Force would come out in force so they could be annihilated.

He stated that allied radar was much better than the Germans as they can bomb though overcast and the Germans cannot. It was explained how the Airborne would go in early.[77]

[Patton]<br>**April 23, 1944 Sunday**

Left at 0800 and got to Peover at 1330. Drove along west coast of Wales. It was very pretty. The Burroughs family came to dinner and a very bad movie.[78]

Col. Koch's G-2 Intelligence section issued his first "estimate" as it was called, on this date. This was a compilation of known information and was as accurate as it could be known at the time. Throughout the war, Col. Koch kept a running tally of all German forces. As they were reduced, captured or eliminated, he updated his estimates. By process of elimination, he was able to have one of the most complete understandings of the forces facing the Third Army and those in all of the other areas of the Third Reich. No other G-2 intelligence sections employed this technique to the extent Patton's G-2 section did. This method also allowed the army commander to know the capabilities and effective forces the Germans were capable of launching. General Patton would use these to formulate his plans. Planning was going on daily as previously stated, Patton knew where he wanted to go if given the opportunity, and planned exactly how he would do it. He was miles and years ahead of those around him in similar command both above and below him.

Koch presented Estimate No.1 in the morning staff meeting in the war room.

On the same day the Section issued G-2 Estimate Number 1. Under enemy situation it reported that in the west (France, Belgium, and Holland) there were an estimated fifty-two German divisions, elements of German Army Group "B", commanded by General Feldmarschall Gerd Von Rundstedt, with Headquarters at St. German Ermain-En-Laye (R&O). The Army Group consisted of four Armies, the First German Army, with six divisions, occupied the area along the Bay of Biscay from NANTES (005), to the Spanish Border; the Nineteenth German Army with nine divisions along the Mediterranean from the Spanish to the Italian border; in Northern France and Belgium, the Fifteenth German Army with eighteen divisions; and Holland occupied by four divisions of the LXXXVIII German Corps. Three other divisions with no known assignment or attachment were also estimated in France.

113

The estimate outlined in detail the enemy situation as it then existed in the projected Lodgment Area, that part of France west of a line from CAEN (U06) to NANTES (005). Twelve divisions, under the Seventh German Army, were located in this sector, which included BRITTANY, the COTENTIN Peninsula, and extended east to CHARTRES (R30) and ORLEANS (F62).

Under "Enemy Dispositions," the estimate examined in detail ground, naval and air defenses. The over-all European situation, including the battle-fronts of Russia, Italy, Norway, Finland, Denmark, and the Balkans, was covered. One section contained assumptions and enemy capabilities, concluding with the following statements: "Except for the estimate of enemy capabilities to bring to and commit reinforcements in the target area, it is not feasible at this time to forecast the situation likely to confront Third U.S. Army when its first elements debark on the Cotentin Peninsula. The situation as it might affect Third U.S. Army is currently too obscure to prognosticate further at this time."[79]

Target Analysis No. 1, the first of a series of reports on Third U.S. Army's potential target area, was issued 23 April by the G-2 Section. It covered "Strategical Terrain Study", "Tactical Analysis of Terrain", and "Possible Airfield Sites Suitable for Landing Areas."

The band played its first appearance for the enlisted men of the Third Army Headquarters rear echelon.[80]

[Patton]
**April 24, 1944 Monday**

We gave the commanding Generals and staffs of the VIII and XV Corps a two-hour briefing on the assault plan. It was very well done. Decorated Haislip with the Oak Leaf Cluster on his DSM for work in the desert. Yet Muller and Gay, who ran a good war, can't get the DSM.[81]

[Patton]
**April 25, 1944 Tuesday**

General "Billy" (Ira C.) Wyche and two staff officers came to lunch and were briefed on plan. Gaffey, Gay, Maddox and I went over possible use of Third Army and I drew up a draft memorandum on it. We fear that Monty will steal our 28th Division to use against Havre and then we will have no amphibious division to get us ashore. It is too bad that no one in FUSAG has ever been to war --- they are not realists.

At 1800 Colonel Campanole, a British ensign, who is Campy's landlady's nephew, Stiller and myself went to Knutsford to see the opening of a British Welcome club. I had been asked to open it but declined as I did not want to be too prominent. In fact, I deliberately arrived 15 minutes late, but this did no good, as they were waiting for me. There were also some photographers in the yard, who took pictures but promised me not to publish them, as I told them I was not there officially.

There were about between 50 and 60 people at the meeting, mostly women.

Finally, the Chairman, Mrs. Constantine Smith, asked me to say a few words. When she introduced me, she said, "General Patton is not here officially and is speaking in a purely friendly way."[82]

Patton thought the staff briefing was excellent. He told his staff afterward, "I have won in battle and I'm going to win again. But I've won because I had good commanders and staff officers, and today's presentation is further evidence of that."[83]

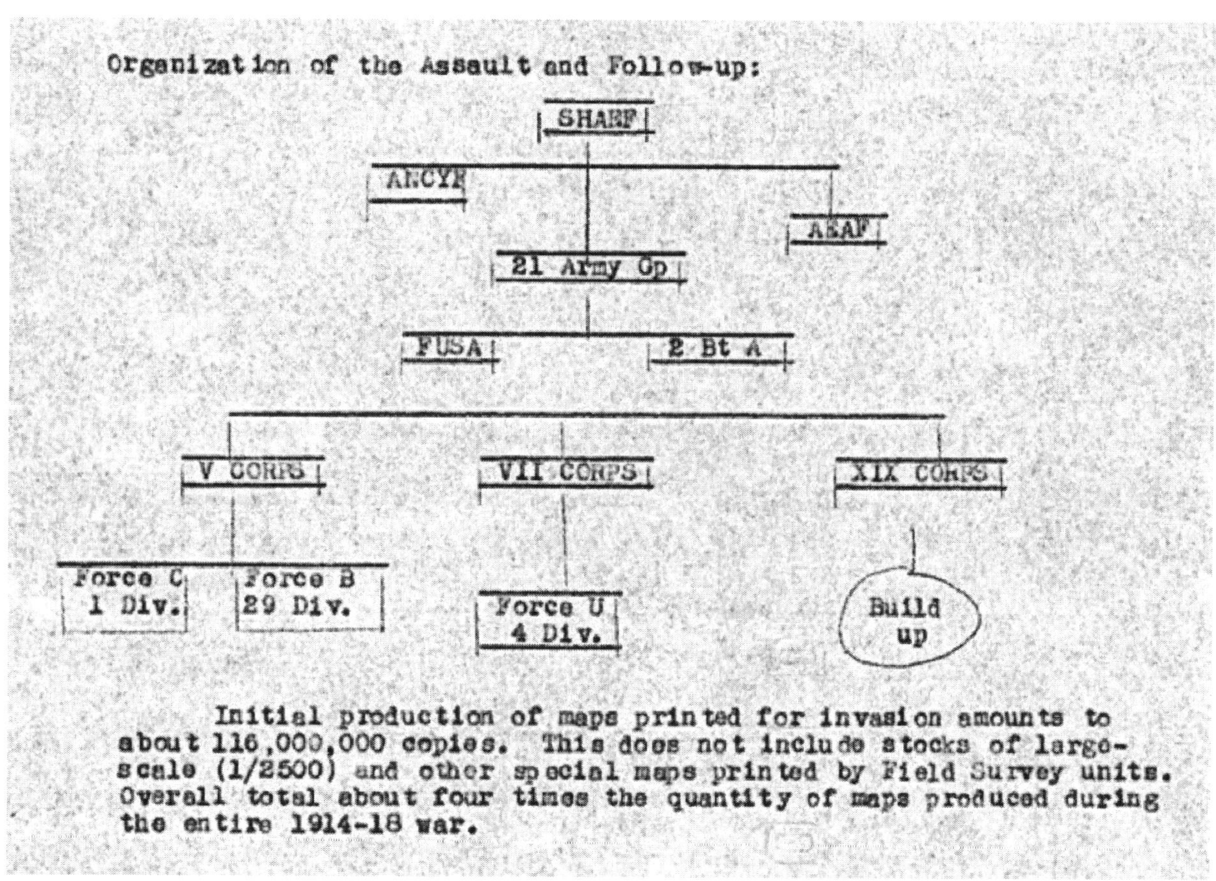


Taken from top secret organization chart of unauthorized G-2 Intelligence Journal kept by Robert Allen on information obtained on April 25, 1944.

## The Knutsford Incident

General Patton was invited by the British Ministry of Information to come to Knutsford on April 25 and make a few remarks to open a Welcome Club to Americans. Patton's presence in England had been kept a secret as part of a well-organized plan called Operation Fortitude. The plan was to convince the Germans that Patton was going to command the Army that would spearhead the invasion of Europe and that it was to be at Pas de Calais in France. Patton had not been seen in a combat role since Sicily. Patton really did not want to speak at this event; however, it was close and he felt it harmless. He planned to be there just for a little while and then excuse himself. He even planned to arrive late and hope it was over. At 6 p.m. his aide, Major Alexander Stiller, an old friend from years past, Colonel Nickolas Campanole, and Midshipman Bower, a nephew of his landlady drove to Knutsford in Patton's car. There is no evidence that Patton's English Bull Terrier, Willie, even came on the trip.

General Patton was told it was all off the record and no news people would be there. When he arrived there were three photographers there and Patton told them they could take pictures but that they could not officially be used or published. Patton went inside, was given a program and then went upstairs and was seated.

Patton's remarks:
```
Until today my experiences in welcoming has been to welcome the
Germans and Italians to the "Infernal Regions." In this I have
been quite successful.  I feel that such clubs as this are a very
real value, because I believe with Mr. Bernard Shaw, I think it
was he, that the British and Americans are two people separated
by a common language, and since it is the evident destiny of the
British and Americans, and, of course, the Russians, to rule the
world, the better we know each other, the better job we will do. A
Club like this is an ideal place for making such acquaintances and
for promoting mutual understanding. Also, as soon as our soldiers
meet and know the English ladies and write home and tell our women
how truly lovely you are, the sooner the American ladies will get
jealous and force this war to a quick termination, and I will get
a chance to go and kill Japanese.[84]
```

There seemed to be nothing to the speech nor any intent on Patton's part to cause any stir whatsoever. There were some other speakers and the event ended with no perceived incident by anyone.

In retrospect it appeared to Patton to be "a most innocuous statement of the policy of the three Great Powers as I understand it." After his talk, Mr. F. Johnson, Chairman of the Knutsford Urban District Council, proposed a vote of thanks to Miss Jeffery and to Patton. This was seconded by Colonel Thomas Blatherwick "in a rather lengthy speech."

Patton recalled later that "After this they played God Save the King and the Star Spangled Banner. They urged me to stay to supper, but I felt they would have a better time if I were not there, so I went home."[85]

<br>

**The Willie Incident:**
**Fact or Fiction?**

Patton's Bull Terrier has thought to be a cowardly dog ever since the movie was seen in 1970. In the movie a small Pekingese dog snapped and barked at Willie and he cowed down, and retreated. George C. Scott, playing Patton in the movie looked down and called him Willie, suggesting he was a wimp. The fact of the matter, the "Willie Incident" at Knutsford simply did not happen. The movie makers and script writer of the movie made it up. Willie never cowed down from any dog at any time. Had the incident really occurred, Willie would have probably mauled the dog, which was not there either. In fact, he had as his breed nature to be a fighter.

They are described thus:

> The English Bull Terrier breed was once a fierce warrior, but is far more gentle now. A Bull Terrier will defend its master but is not a "Guard Dog" and is not bred as one. They are courageous, fun-loving, active, clownish and show little fear. They are most loyal, polite, and can be trained to be highly obedient. They love deeply and are highly attached to their owner(s). If handled properly they will thrive on a firm and consistent leadership. With a lot of affection they make fine family pets. Bull Terriers are active and will be some with an active family. They do require a lot of companionship and supervision. Though the breed is a wonder dog they do not do well being left alone for a long period of time. They love people and are just as happy with grown ups or children. They are highly energetic and without the proper exercise they could overwhelm small children in their aggressive playing. They have also been known to be very protective, willful, possessive and sometimes jealous. They have been known to join in with family rough housing. They need a firm hand, training and a lot of exercise. They should have a lot of structure and can become destructive. They need to learn to socialize and the owner should be dominant in their handling of them. They will sometimes become very aggresive with other dogs and animals. They can be excellent watch dogs but are some difficulty in being trained and a proper trainer should be sought.

A Standard Bull Terrier:

Height: 20-24 inches (51-61 cm.) Weight: 45-80 pounds (20-36 kg.) They are a cross between a Bulldog and an Old English Terrier. There is some trace of the Spanish Pointer blood. These lines come together to what is now refered to as an English Bull Terrier breed. In the 1860's the white-coated variety, which was nicknamed the "White Cavalier." Many nobles of the period enjoyed the ownership and so they were "fashionable."

Patton's Willie was a "White Cavalier."
*Bull Terrier Kennel Club,* Book No 77

April 26, 1944 Wednesday:Generals of the XII and XX Corps were briefed on the operation "OVERLORD" at PEOVER HALL.

The Civil Affairs Mission for this section was presented on this date. The mission, responsibility, and object of Civil Affairs was outlined by the Army Commander thusly: "The sole mission of Civil Affairs Administration is to further military objectives. The exercise of Civil Affairs control is a command responsibility. The object of Civil Affairs is to assist in military operations." The order also said that the Army Commander would "provide policies for the Civil Affairs Section, including composition, size, relationship with other staff Sections, scope and general directives for operations."[86]

Simply put, their job was to see that civilian and army interaction was compliant with the rules and regulations of the Army and that, when occupying an area, they had good interaction with the civilian authorities and the population. It is ironic that Patton's interaction with the Ladies at Knutsford would have such a bad effect on Patton.


[Patton]


Just before lunch the public relations people from Ike's called up to know what I had said in my talk yesterday. They got Hap Gay on the line and told him to ask what I had said about British and Americans ruling the world. I told him that I said, "Since it was the evident destiny of England and the Americans, and of course the Russians, to rule the world, the better we knew each other, the better it would be.[87]


Unfortunately, the incident that was not one, became one. There were newspapermen there who published the speech in local newspapers. Then, it was picked up in the states. The statement about the Americans and British and Russians being destined to rule the world was what got all of the attention. Some reports had the Russians left out and others left it in. Regardless, the story took on a life of its own. Many of the elected politicians made assessments of it to the press, most all of them condemning Patton for suggesting anybody would rule the world. It revived the slapping incident to memory and it brought Patton to the forefront a man who could not control his tongue and, coupled with the slapping incident, brought his fitness to command into question.

General Marshall informed Eisenhower that the press in the states had lurid accounts of the incident in the newspapers. He also said he feared the remarks had caused a problem with regular army promotions to be submitted to Congress and Patton was one of them.

By the evening Patton knew he was in trouble. He called his friend Everett Hughes, sent him the program and a copy of his remarks, asking for his help so he was not misrepresented.[88]


[Patton]


General Gilbert "Doc" Cook of the XII Corps and Walker of the XX with staff came to lunch and we gave them the long briefing on the operation. Our staff did a really swell job and I was proud of them. Just before lunch the public relations people from Ike's called up to know what I

had said in my talk yesterday. They got Hap Gay on the line and told him
to ask me what I had said about British and Americans ruling the world.
I told him that I said "Since it was the evident destiny of England and
the Americans, and of course the Russians, to rule the world, the better
we knew each other the better it would be. Hap told me that some papers
said I mentioned the Russians and some did not.

Since it seems to have been a bad thing to do I will copy from the program
the names of the principal people present.

Honorable Mrs. Constantine Smith, Chairman of the Committee, opened the
show and introduced Miss Foster Jeffery, Order of the British Empire,
Regional Administrator of the Women's Voluntary Services.

Miss Jeffery made a speech, pronounced the club open, then asked me to
say something. I did. As far as I knew, no correspondents were present
and not more than 50 or 60 people, mostly women.

In any case I was really trying to be careful. Mr. F. Johnson, Chairman
of the Knutsford Urban District Council, made a speech thanking Miss
Jeffery and me. Then Colonel T. Blatherwick, D.S.O., C.B., made a speech.
Next Mr. A. Armstrong, the U. S. Consul from Manchester and finally Mr. G.
Mould of the Ministry of Information. I thanked everyone and went home.
When Mrs. Constantine Smith introduced me she said, 'General Patton is
not here officially', which was naturally an added reason for me to think
that no mention would be made of my presence or remarks in the press.
I was asked to stay to supper but felt that I did not wish that much
publicity and went home.[89]

All of the Third Army staff was told they could now sew back on their Third Army patches which
until now they had not been allowed to wear.

Intelligence reports were monitored by G-2 from all over the world. They reviewed reports
from the Pacific theater on this date referring to "Jap" defenses on Tarawa and their plan of
defense. They reviewed such things as sniper protective shield used by the Japs and anti-boat mines.
Since the planning for an amphibious landing was planned in Europe lessons learned in the Pacific
were important. They noted that the preliminary bombardment of the shoreline knocked out the
Jap communication system.[90]

[Patton]
**April 27, 1944 Thursday**

Colonel William Ganoe came to see me at 0900. He is the head of the
Historical Section for this theatre and is putting a team of nine officers
with each Army. The head man in our team was the professor of military
history at the University of Chicago, Maj. Cole. Colonel Ganoe told me,
an interesting thing. When Hooker assumed command of the Union army at

Chancellorsville, his plan was fine, and, to a point, well executed. After he got over the river, he received a letter from Mr. Lincoln in which Lincoln said he had given Hooker command under protest, and that he, himself, had no confidence in Hooker. Hooker promptly assumed the defensive position. So far as I am concerned every effort is made to show lack of confidence in my judgment and at the same time, in every case of stress, great confidence in my fighting. None of those at Ike's headquarters ever go to bat for juniors, and in any argument between the British and the Americans, invariably favor the British. Benedict Arnold is a piker compared with them and that includes Lee as well as Ike and Beedle.

Beedle called up at 1030 and said that he was giving me a verbal order from Ike that I am never to talk in public without first submitting what I am going to say to Ike and himself for censorship, thereby displaying great confidence in an Army Commander --- if I have not been relieved Beedle also said that due to my "unfortunate remarks" the permanent promotion of himself and me might never come off. How sad. In consonance with this order I am unable to talk with either the 79th, 80th, 83rd or 7th Armored Divisions, a restriction that will surely cost lives, yet if I break it I will get relieved and that would mean defeat and a still larger loss. "God show the right" and damn all reporters and gutless men.

The first group of Civil Affairs Section came to see me and we had a talk. Gaspar Bacon is one of them.[91]

April 28 1944 Friday: Patton was so shaken by the incident that when he was scheduled to appear for a ceremony, he sent General Gay in his stead and told him to park the car on a side street so it could not be seen. The incident had taken on a life of its own and Eisenhower was at the end of his tolerance for Patton.[92]

[Patton]

General de Brigade LeClerc, who commands the French 2nd Armored Division, which is now attached to the Third Army, came to call. We had a guard of honor for him, which pleased him. He is the man who marched to Tunisia all the way from Central Africa. He is a good type French soldier and, I believe, quite intelligent. He said one strange thing, however: that since his Division was the only French Division in the Third Army, it was very important that it should not be killed off too soon. He also pointed out that he had no replacements and asked me to use my good offices to secure them. He looks just like an American and I think speaks better English than he admits.[93]

The guard of honor was accompanied by a rousing number of songs played by the band.[94]

April 29, 1944 Saturday: On April 29th Eisenhower penned a strong letter of rebuke to Patton and told Patton that his habits of dramatizing himself and committing indiscretions for no other apparent reason but calling attention to himself had made him thoroughly weary of his failure to control his tongue and had begun to doubt his overall judgment, so essential to a high military position. He went on to say that his decision and the final outcome would depend on him hearing back from the War Department.[95]

[Patton]

A company of our Military Police battalion, and a band, and a group of nurses, took part in the Alderley Edge "Salute the Soldier Week." I had been asked to receive the salute there but felt that I had better keep out of the limelight, so General Gay took it. I looked on from a private automobile on a side street. Later, Colonel Goldschmidt and I went to look at some horses. They did not impress me very much. Apparently he and Colonel McFadden are mortal enemies.[96]

French General Le Clerc called upon Patton on this day. Patton was seen popping up the stairs just prior to his visit saying, "Got to get that French pronunciation record and brush up on my accent."[97]

April 30, 1944 Sunday: Eisenhower sent a short but serious message to General Marshall. It said that he had sent for Patton to allow him to present his case but unless something more came to light he would send him home.[98]

 The G-1 Section reported total strength of the Third Army as 219,800.[99]

[Patton]

Went to church. While I was there Beedle called up and told me to report to Ike, at Ike's office, at either 1100 or 1500 tomorrow. It can be anything from a reprimand to a reduction, or a new plan of campaign. These constant pickings are a little hard on the nerves, but great training. I feel that, if I get reduced and sent home, it might be quite important, as I would get into politics as an honest and straight spoken man and would either be a great success or a dismal failure. Gaffey was told by Hughes that, on the 28th, when Hughes went to see Ike, he was just writing a cable to General Marshall saying that he, Ike, had no further need of protecting me and would not resist my being recalled. When Hughes showed him my statements on the Knutsford speeches he said, 'Oh, hell" and tore the cable up. I do know from Mrs. Pressmall that Hughes is still worried about me --- so am I.[100]

[Patton]<br>
May 1, 1944 Monday

In spite of possible execution this morning I slept well and trust my destiny. God has never let me, or the country, down yet.

Reported to Ike at 1100. He was most cordial and asked me to sit down, so I felt a little reassured. He said, "George, you have gotten yourself into a very serious fix." I said, "Before you go any farther, I want to say that your job is more important than mine, so if in trying to save me you are hurting yourself, throw me out." He said, "I have now got all that the army can give me --- it's not a question of hurting me but of hurting yourself and depriving me of a fighting army commander." He went on to say that General Marshall had wired him that my repeated mistakes have shaken the confidence of the country and the War Department. General Marshall even harked back to the Kent Lambert incident in November 1942 certainly a forgiving s.o.b. Ike said he had recommended that, if I were to be relieved and sent home, I be not reduced to a Colonel, as the relief would be sufficient punishment, and that he felt that situations might well arise where it would be necessary to put me in command of an army. I told Ike that I was perfectly willing to fall out on a permanent promotion so as not to hold the others back. Ike said General Marshall had told him that my crime had destroyed all chance of my permanent promotion, as the opposition said that even if I was the best tactician and strategist in the army, my demonstrated lack of judgment made me unfit to command. He said that he had wired General Marshall on Sunday washing his hands of me. (He did not use these words but that is what he meant).

I told him that if I was reduced to a Colonel I demanded the right to command one of the assault regiments; that this is not a favor but a right. He said no, because he felt he would surely need me to command army. I said, I am not threatening, but I want to tell you that this attack is badly planned and on too narrow a front and may well result in an Anzio, especially if I am not there. He replied, "Don't I know it, but what can I do?" That is a hell of a remark for a supreme commander. The fact is that the plan which he has approved was drawn by a grounp of British in 1943. Monty changed it only by getting 5 instead of 3 divisions into the assault but the front is too short. There should be three separate attacks on at least a 90 mile front. I have said this for nearly a year. Ike said he had written me a "savage" letter but wanted me to know that his hand is being forced in the United States. He talked to the Prime Minister about me and Churchill told him that he could see nothing to it. That "Patton had simply told the truth." Ike then went on to excuse General Marshall on the grounds that it was an election year etc. It is sad and shocking to think that victory and the lives of thousands of men are pawns to the "fear of They", and the writings of a group of unprincipled reporters, and weak kneed congressmen, but so it is. When I came out I don't think anyone could tell that I had just been killed. I have lost lots of competitions in the sporting way, but I never did better. I feel like death, but I am not out yet. If they will let me fight, I will; but if not, I will resign so as to be able to talk and then I will tell the truth and possibly do my country more good. All the way home, 5 hours, I recited poetry to myself.

> "If you can make a heap of all your winnings
> And risk them on one game of pitch and toss
> And lose, and start at your beginning
> And never breathe a word about your loss"

"If"

"I dared extreme occasion and never one betrayed."

My final thought on the matter is that I am destined to achieve some great thing --- what I don't know, but this last incident was so trivial in its nature, but so terrible in its effect, that it is not the result of an accident but the work of God.

His Will be done.

General Leroy Lutes of the U. S. Service of Supply was here when I got back after supper and we gave him a briefing and entertained him. I hope to get some equipment as a result.[101]

---

**If**
**by Rudyard Kipling**

If you can keep your head when all about you
Are losing theirs and blaming it on you;
If you can trust yourself when all men doubt you,
But make allowance for their doubting too:
If you can wait and not be tired by waiting,
Or, being lied about, don't deal in lies,
Or being hated don't give way to hating,
And yet don't look too good, nor talk too wise;

If you can dream---and not make dreams your master;
If you can think---and not make thoughts your aim,
If you can meet with Triumph and Disaster
And treat those two impostors just the same:

If you can bear to hear the truth you've spoken
Twisted by knaves to make a trap for fools,
Or watch the things you gave your life to, broken,
And stoop and build'em up with worn-out tools;

If you can make one heap of all your winnings
And risk it on one turn of pitch-and-toss,
And lose, and start again at your beginnings,
And never breathe a word about your loss:
If you can force your heart and nerve and sinew
To serve your turn long after they are gone,
And so hold on when there is nothing in you
Except the Will which says to them: "Hold on!"

If you can talk with crowds and keep your virtue,
Or walk with Kings---nor lose the common touch,
If neither foes nor loving friends can hurt you,
If all men count with you, but none too much:
If you can fill the unforgiving minute
With sixty seconds' worth of distance run,
Yours is the Earth and everything that's in it,
And---which is more---you'll be a Man, my son!

Academy of American Poets, Retrieved from
http://www.poets.org/viewmedia.php/prmMID/15241

[Patton]
**May 2, 1944 Tuesday**

On May 2nd Marshall cabled back saying the decision was Ike's to make. He did say that in his view he should not do anything to weaken his hand for Overlord, and if he thought relieving Patton would weaken his hand he should continue him in command. He also said that he did not want him to be burdened in reducing him in rank and he could send him home if he saw fit. Consider only Overlord and its success.

The only commander Ike thought to replace Patton with was General Truscott who was in a battle and doing well in Italy. If it was not for that fact, Ike may have relieved Patton. Marshall was clever in his letter and took Ike off the hook in two ways. He suggested that Ike did not have to relieve him if he weakened his hand for Overlord by doing so. And that he needed to reduce Patton in rank. That, coupled with the fact that there was no better combat general, and certainly no one close available, Ike decided to retain Patton.[102]

[Patton]
**May 3, 1944 Wednesday**

Went to the Station Hospital 164 to have my teeth cleaned. It is a very good hospital - - the best I have seen in any theater. At the request of Lt. Colonel Clune, I had an informal inspection, and wrote a letter afterward to General Kenner stating that it was an excellent hospital and that Clune should be promoted.

When I got back Gay handed me an Eisenhower dispatch telegram which said in effect: "Since the War Department has placed the decision of relieving you on me, I have decided to keep you. My letter on this subject will be put in the official file (cover page). Go ahead and train your army."

I felt much better and wrote Ike, thanking him. He called up in person and was very nice. Sometimes I am very fond of him and this is one of the times. When I read the wire, I called to Gay, "The war is over," which I always say when I mean that trouble is over. Captain Murnane heard me and thought I meant that the war was over for me. So when Hugh Gaffey, Gay, Codman, Stiller and I all took a drink to celebrate, he thought we were very callous.

General Raymond McClain, who used to be artillery officer of the 45th Division, called. He was at Salerno and Anzio. He said that at Salerno, Clark got badly scared, although the counter-attack was nothing to what we had at Gela, and he was there too. As the result of this scare the battle-cry of the Anzio landing was "No more Salernos" with the result that they were timid. He also said that for the first day and most of the second, the high ground could have been had for the walk. Later, the Germans built up fast. I had heard that this build-up was made by using the motorized reconnaissance units from all the available units, and later bringing in the infantry. McClain agreed this was possible because in no other way could they have gotten identification from so many other divisions in such a short time. He personally had identifications from the Herman Goering, the 3rd Armored, the 1st Panzer, the 71st, 65th., 114th, 26th and 715th Infantry Divisions, and one SS division.

McClain is a National Guard officer of great courage and efficiency. I asked for him as a reserve division commander but General Bradley, who also knows his ability, got him first.

Brigadier General Jack Thompson came to dinner. He commands the advanced section of the 7th Armored Division. Gaffey, Gay, Thompson and I went to the Bells of Peover Inn to celebrate. 7th Armored has been delayed two weeks. At the Bells of Peover they wanted L25 for a bottle of champagne so we did not drink it.[103]

[1] Allen 17-20.

[2] Patton, Diary entry March 24, 1944.

[3] R. J. Stillman, Riggs 22-23.

[4] Allen 17-20.

[5] Allen, Robert S. Collection; RSA Journal 1,2,3,4, 1944-1945; National Infantry Museum & Soldier Center, 1775 Legacy Way; Columbus, GA 31903 Unpublished typed (transcript transferred from Patton Museum, Fort Knox Kentucky), March 24, 1944

[6] The author met and spoke with Mr. George Patton Waters regarding the origin of the ring when they first met on September 1, 2010 at the 6th Cavalry Museum Fort Oglethorpe Georgia. During this encounter, Patton Waters allowed the author to examine the ring and even offered to loan it to him for the duration of his portrayal of Patton on that day. Though extremely honored ... and more than a bit temped, the author declined for fear of losing such a precious family heirloom.

[7] Allen 17-20.

[8] Rosevich

[9] T/O refers to the Table of Organization, as directed by the Army Field Manual. Thus, the troops arrived as one large group but were thereafter quickly divided by their assignments and units where they remained, for the most part, from that point forward.

[10] Wallace 15-19; Third Army

[11] C. C. Smith, *My War Years*, 1940-46:Service on Gen. Patton's Third Army Staff 34.

[12] An alpine light was a flame placed in front of a mirror to provide light. The fuel source of the flame varied from candles, gas and wood.

[13] 301st Signal Corp. Battalion 75.

[14] Koch 71.

[15] Allen, Robert S. Collection; RSA Journal entry March 25, 1944.

[16] Women's Royal Naval Service.

[17] In the movie "Patton", this quote was erroneously attributed to General Montgomery. Additionally, the whole of the Patton/Montgomery encounter in the town square of Messenia, Sicily where these words were supposedly uttered is a complete fabrication, no doubt added for an enhanced dramatic effect.

[18] Allen, Journal entries March 26-27, 1944.

[19] Allen, Journal entry March 27, 1944.

[20] Koch 72.

[21] Third Army, We Followed Patton, 652nd Engineer Topographical Battalion excerpts 40, unnumber pages; C. C. Smith 34-37.

[22] The 652 Engineer Topographic Battalion was one of the topographical battalions that produced maps in England and in the field under battle conditions. Third Army, We Followed Patton, 652nd Engineer Topographical Battalion excerpts from unnumber page.

[23] Koch 75.

[24] *Ibid.*

[25] Third Army, Planning in the United Kingdom 11; James H. O'Neil was born on January 14, 1892, and after receiving his Bachelor of Arts degree (1911) and Master of Arts degree (1913) from Loyola University (Chicago), he entered St. Paul's Seminary in St. Paul, Minnesota, and was ordained on May 20, 1915. Father O'Neil was then assigned to the Diocese of Helena, Montana and appointed to the faculty of Carroll College in Helena in the fall of 1915. While at Carroll, he was Professor of Physics, Registrar, Dean of Men, and Vice President (1921–26). In 1926, Father O'Neil entered the Chaplain Service of the US Army. He saw duty throughout the United States (1929–1934; 1936–1942) and the Philippine Islands (1927–1929; 1934–1936), and served on the staffs of General Jacob Devers (1942–44) and General George Patton (1944–45) in the European Theater of Operations. On this date Chaplain O'Neil finished and presented his plan and initiated his plans calling for complete religious coverage of all units.

[26] Allen, Journal entry, March 29 1944.

[27] *Ibid.*

[28] Allen, Journal entry, March 30, 1944.

[29] Allen, Journal entry, March 31, 1944.

30 301st Signal Corp. Battalion 75-76.

31 *Ibid.*

32 This refers to the slang term for prostitutes that originated from the 1941 exploitation movie "Escort Girl" where Ruth Ashley, played by Betty Compson, and Gregory Stone, played by Wheeler Oakman, were the joint owners of the Hollywood Escort Bureau … which was not on the up-and-up.

33 301st Signal Corp. Battalion 75-76.

34 *Ibid.*

35 R. J. Stillman, Riggs 38.

36 Allen, Journal entry, April 1, 1944.

37 *Ibid.*

38 Third Army, We Followed Patton .

39 Diaz family collection;

40 Allen, Journal entry, April 2 1944.

41 Third Army, Planning in the United Kingdom 11.

42 Wedemeyer 220-227; Blumenson, *The Patton Papers* Vol.2 431-432.

43 Allen, Journal entry, April 4, 1944.

44 Col. O.L. Haines.

45 Wedemeyer 226.

46 Col. Odom informs us that both of the accused were later convicted, punished and returned to their units. Odom, however, does not clarify regarding the specifics of the charges in which they were found guilty. Both men were killed in the fighting before the end of the war.  C. B. Odom 37.

47 Allen, Journal entry, April 5, 1944.

48 Allen, Journal entry, April 6, 1944.

49 O. N. Bradley Pg 233-235

50 *Ibid.*

51 *Ibid.*

52 Third Army, Staff Reports Section Reports Command Part 1, G-3 Part 4.

53 Now referred to as POWs; Prisoners of War.

54 Allen, Journal entry, April 8 1944.

55 Allen, Journal entry, April 9th 1944.

56 Third Army, Planning in the United Kingdom 12.

57 Allen, Journal entry, April 10 1944.

58 Third Army, Planning in the United Kingdom 11.

59 Third Army, Planning in the United Kingdom Pg 11.

60 Press release, 13 April 1944, Number 1912 Headquarters, European Theater of Operations, United States Army. Author's personal collection, 31 May 1944.

61 J. A. Ramsey 55-56.

62 J. A. Ramsey 64-67.

63 Patton, Diary entry April 14, 1944.

64 Patton, Diary entry April 15, 1944.

65 Patton, Diary entry April 16, 1944.

66 Patton, Diary entry April 17, 1944.

67 Bryant overview of book

68 Blumenson. *The Patton Papers*. Vol.2, 437.

69 Patton, Diary entry April 18, 1944.

70 Allen, Journal entry, April 19, 1944 entry.

71 Diaz Family Collection.  Gregorio A. Diaz, CWO; Bandleader, 61st Amy Ground Forces Band, Third U.S. Army.

72 BAP He proved to be the shining exception to the rule.

73 Patton, Diary entry April 20, 1944.

74 Patton, Diary entry April 21, 1944.

75 Patton, Diary entry April 22, 1944.

76 Third Army, After Action Reports Vol.1, 12.

[77] Allen, Journal entries, April 21-22, 1944.

[78] Patton, Diary entry April 23, 1944.

[79] Third Army, After Action Reports Vol.1, 12.

[80] Diaz family collection.

[81] Patton, Diary entry April 24, 1944.

[82] Patton, Diary entry April 25, 1944.

[83] Allen, Journal entries, April 25, 1944.

[84] Blumenson. *The Patton Papers*. Vol.2, 450-451; D'Este, Eisenhower, *A Soldier's Life* 591-594.

[85] *Ibid.*

[86] Third Army, After Action Reports Vol.1, 12.

[87] Patton, Diary entry April 26, 1944.

[88] Blumenson, *The Patton Papers* Vol.2 450-451; D'Este, Eisenhower, *A Soldier's Life* 591-594.

[89] Patton, Diary entry April 26, 1944.

[90] Allen, Journal entry, April 26, 1944.

[91] Patton, Diary entry April 27, 1944.

[92] Blumenson, *The Patton Papers* Vol.2 450-451; D'Este, Eisenhower, *A Soldier's Life* 591-594.

[93] Patton, Diary entry April 28, 1944.

[94] Diaz family collection.

[95] Blumenson, *The Patton Papers* Vol.2 450-451; D'Este, Eisenhower, *A Soldier's Life* 591-594.

[96] Patton, Diary entry April 29, 1944.

[97] Allen, Journal entry, April 28, 1944.

[98] Blumenson, *The Patton Papers* Vol.2 450-451; D'Este, Eisenhower, *A Soldier's Life* 591-594.

[99] Third Army, After Action Reports, Vol. 2.

[100] Patton, Diary entry April 30, 1944.

[101] Patton, Diary entry May 1, 1944.

[102] Blumenson, *The Patton Papers* Vol.2 450-451; D'Este, Eisenhower, *A Soldier's Life* 591-594.

[103] Patton, Diary entry May 3, 1944.

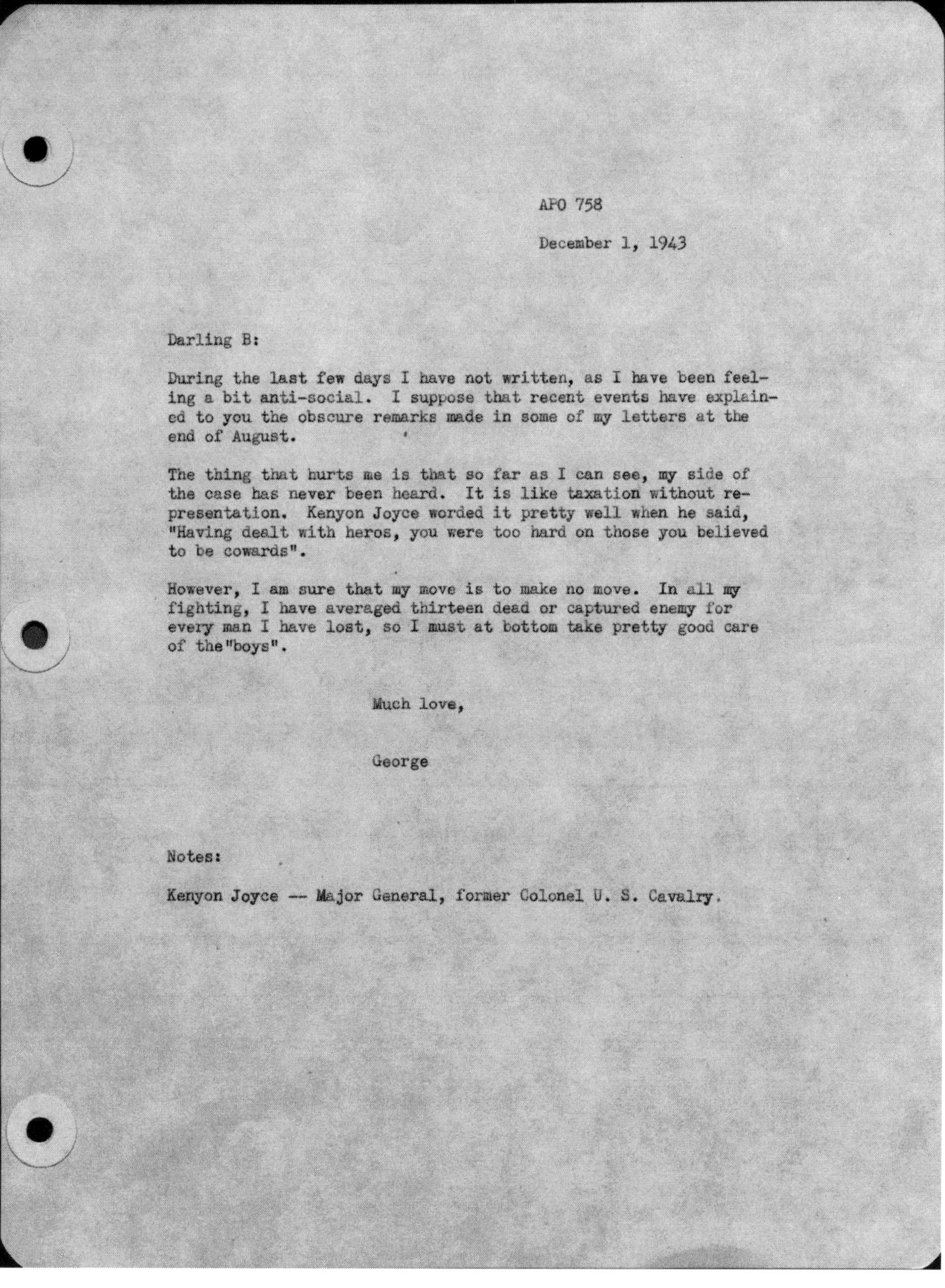



Letter to Beatrice about Kenyon Joyce, December 1, 1943. Patton wrote home that he has not been given a chance to give his side of the story and he is in very low spirits.
(Image courtesy *The Patton Papers*, Library of Congress.)

Patton speaks to the 2nd Infantry Division giving his famous speech in April of 1944, Northern Ireland. (Image courtesy *The Patton Papers*, Library of Congress.)

Patton leaves from the speech and returns to Peover, England, after giving his famous speech in Northern Ireland. (Image courtesy *The Patton Papers*, Library of Congress.)

Kay Summersby in her 1941 British uniform. She was in the drivers pool when she was assigned to General Eisenhower. They soon became friends, and later much more than friends.
(Eisenhower Presidential Library Archives)

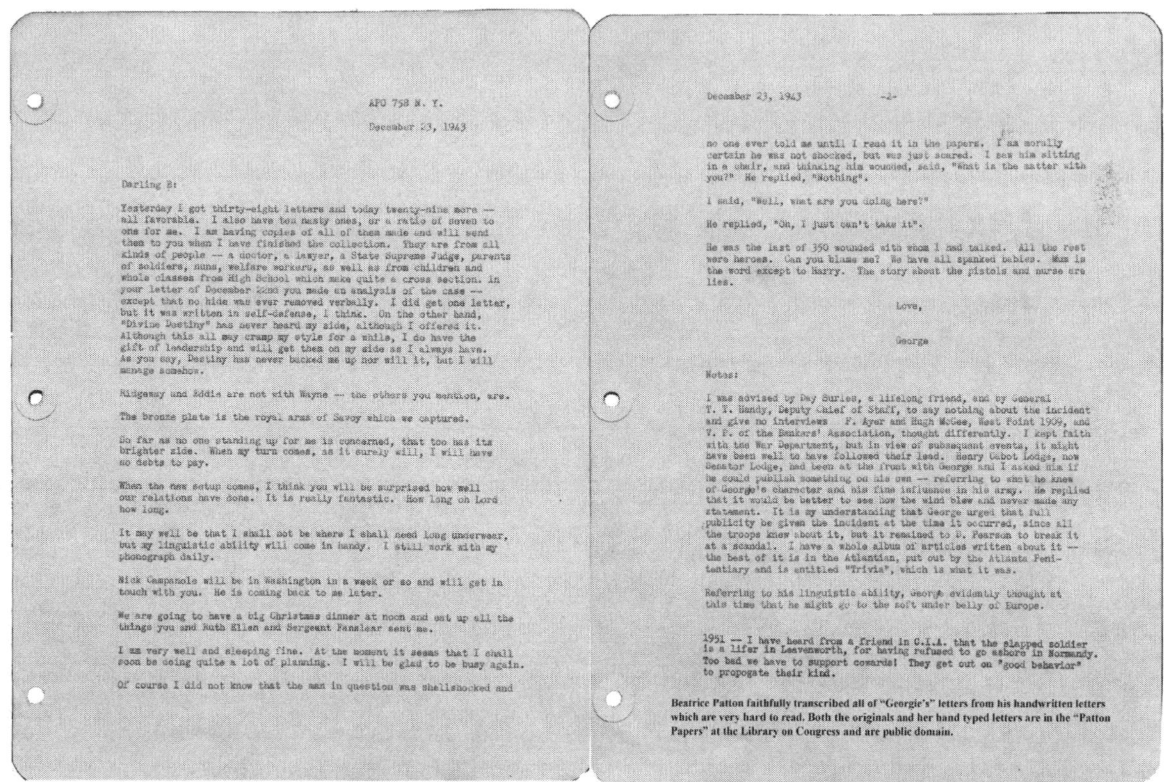

APO 758 N. Y.

December 23, 1943

Darling B:

Yesterday I got thirty-eight letters and today twenty-nine more — all favorable. I also have ten nasty ones, or a ratio of seven to one for me. I am having copies of all of them made and will send them to you when I have finished the collection. They are from all kinds of people — a doctor, a lawyer, a State Supreme Judge, parents of soldiers, nuns, welfare workers, as well as from children and whole classes from High School which make quite a cross section. In your letter of December 22nd you made an analysis of the case — except that no hide was ever removed verbally. I did get one letter, but it was written in self-defense, I think. On the other hand, "Divine Destiny" has never heard my side, although I offered it. Although this all may cramp my style for a while, I do have the gift of leadership and will get them on my side as I always have. As you say, Destiny has never backed me up nor will it, but I will manage somehow.

Ridgeway and Eddie are not with Wayne — the others you mention, are.

The bronze plate is the royal arms of Savoy which we captured.

So far as no one standing up for me is concerned, that too has its brighter side. When my turn comes, as it surely will, I will have no debts to pay.

When the new setup comes, I think you will be surprised how well our relations have done. It is really fantastic. How long oh Lord how long.

It may well be that I shall not be where I shall need long underwear, but my linguistic ability will come in handy. I still work with my phonograph daily.

Nick Campanole will be in Washington in a week or so and will get in touch with you. He is coming back to me later.

We are going to have a big Christmas dinner at noon and eat up all the things you and Ruth Ellen and Sergeant Fanslear sent me.

I am very well and sleeping fine. At the moment it seems that I shall soon be doing quite a lot of planning. I will be glad to be busy again.

Of course I did not know that the man in question was shellshocked and

---

December 23, 1943        -2-

no one ever told me until I read it in the papers. I am morally certain he was not shocked, but was just scared. I saw him sitting in a chair, and thinking him wounded, said, "What is the matter with you?" He replied, "Nothing".

I said, "Well, what are you doing here?"

He replied, "Oh, I just can't take it".

He was the last of 350 wounded with whom I had talked. All the rest were heroes. Can you blame me? We have all spanked babies. Mum is the word except to Harry. The story about the pistols and nurse are lies.

Love,

George

Notes:

I was advised by Day Suries, a lifelong friend, and by General T. T. Handy, Deputy Chief of Staff, to say nothing about the incident and give no interviews  F. Ayer and Hugh McGee, West Point 1909, and V. P. of the Bankers' Association, thought differently. I kept faith with the War Department, but in view of subsequent events, it might have been well to have followed their lead. Henry Cabot Lodge, now Senator Lodge, had been at the front with George and I asked him if he could publish something on his own — referring to what he knew of George's character and his fine influence in his army. He replied that it would be better to see how the wind blew and never made any statement. It is my understanding that George urged that full publicity be given the incident at the time it occurred, since all the troops knew about it, but it remained to D. Pearson to break it at a scandal. I have a whole album of articles written about it — the best of it is in the Atlantian, put out by the Atlanta Penitentiary and is entitled "Trivia", which is what it was.

Referring to his linguistic ability, George evidently thought at this time that he might go to the soft under belly of Europe.

1951 — I have heard from a friend in C.I.A. that the slapped soldier is a lifer in Leavenworth, for having refused to go ashore in Normandy. Too bad we have to support cowards! They get out on "good behavior" to propogate their kind.

**Beatrice Patton faithfully transcribed all of "Georgie's" letters from his handwritten letters which are very hard to read. Both the originals and her hand typed letters are in the "Patton Papers" at the Library on Congress and are public domain.**

Letter to Beatrice from Patton regarding slapping, December 23, 1943. Patton was still fretting over the slapping incident and not sure of his future and wrote home to Beatrice. Some years later, Beatrice took his letter to him and typed it so it could be read. The notes in the margin are hers.
(Image courtesy *The Patton Papers*, Library of Congress.)

Ike, just after his meeting with President Roosevelt, 1943. Eisenhower was with President Roosevelt after he was just told that he would be the Supreme Allied commander. Kay sat in the car with the president and they shared lunch. Roosevelt wrote home to his daughter that he was sure that Ike and Kay were lovers.
(Image courtesy *The Patton Papers*, Library of Congress.)

Patton gave his famous speech to tens of thousands of soldiers. It was full of strong language and the soldiers loved it. Here, General Patton is still in Northern Ireland at Greencastle, Country Down, March 30, 1944.
(Image courtesy *The Patton Papers*, Library of Congress.)

General Patton speaks in Knutsford and was told no reporters would be there. His speech got him in far more trouble that the slapping incident, but not because it was noteworthy. Eisenhower was away and General Beedle Smith handled the press inquiries in a way to make a bigger deal than it was. It almost lost Patton his command and career. (Image courtesy *The Patton Papers*, Library of Congress.)

Patton, seen here in a L5 plane, was a pilot in his own right.
He flew or was flown all over England and later in Europe.
(Image courtesy *The Patton Papers*, Library of Congress.)

Patton is believed to have taken this picture of his headquarters in Peover, England, as he flew over it in March or April of 1944.

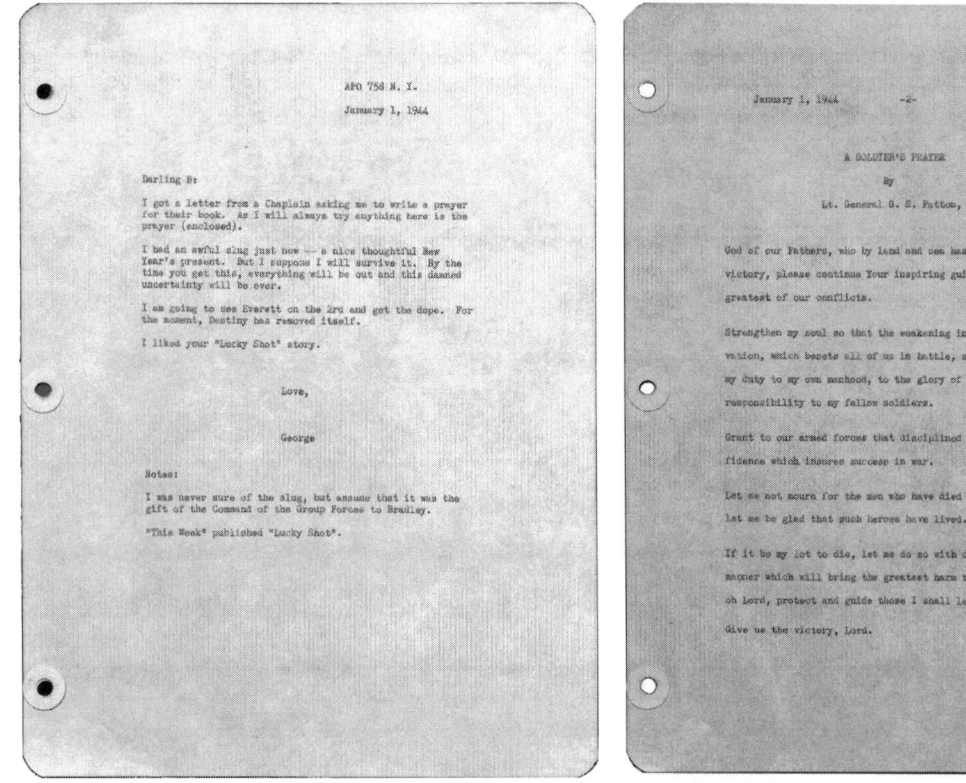

AFO 758 N. Y.

January 1, 1944

Darling B:

I got a letter from a Chaplain asking me to write a prayer for their book. As I will always try anything here is the prayer (enclosed).

I had an awful slug just now — a nice thoughtful New Year's present. But I suppose I will survive it. By the time you get this, everything will be out and this damned uncertainty will be over.

I am going to see Everett on the 2rd and get the dope. For the moment, Destiny has removed itself.

I liked your "Lucky Shot" story.

Love,

George

Notes:

I was never sure of the slug, but assume that it was the gift of the Command of the Group Forces to Bradley.

"This Week" published "Lucky Shot".

January 1, 1944     -2-

A SOLDIER'S PRAYER

By

Lt. General G. S. Patton, Jr.

God of our Fathers, who by land and sea has ever led us on to victory, please continue Your inspiring guidance in this the greatest of our conflicts.

Strengthen my soul so that the weakening instinct of self-preservation, which besets all of us in battle, shall not blind me, to my duty to my own manhood, to the glory of my calling, and to my responsibility to my fellow soldiers.

Grant to our armed forces that disciplined valor and mutual confidence which insures success in war.

Let me not mourn for the men who have died fighting, but rather let me be glad that such heroes have lived.

If it be my lot to die, let me do so with courage and honor in a manner which will bring the greatest harm to the enemy, and please, oh Lord, protect and guide those I shall leave behind.

Give us the victory, Lord.

Patton wrote home to Beatrice on January 1, 1944, that he was asked to write a prayer. It lifted his spirits and he sent a copy home. Years later, Beatrice typed the hand written letter from his original. The notes are from Beatrice.

Reporter Drew Pearson as he appeared in 1944. He was not liked in many circles and Patton hated him. He knew more than he let on in public. Assistant G-2 Robert Allen had worked with him before the war, so Patton was able to get a better insight to him from Allen.

**The Blessings of the Colors for Battle June 14, 1944 Peover Hall**

General Patton ordered a general assembly of the 3rd Army Headquarters and assembled was an honor guard manned by the 503rd MP battalion and participating to their left was the now official 61st Army Ground Forces Band. The Honor guard marched forward and dip the Third Army Colors. At that moment the Army chaplain came forward and official Bless the flag of the Third United States Army and read some scriptures and prayed.

The Chaplain of the Third Army, Col. James Hugh O'Neil offered a prayer for the blessing of the colors.

On June the 14, 1944 General Patton had his command assembled and Chaplain James O'Neil blessed the colors for battle. The Third Army colors were dipped down and brought up. Chaplain O'Neil stepped forward and performed the blessing. This marked the beginning of the campaign and the Third Army Headquarters would soon be off to France and engaged in battle.

The Patton Vans were CCKW GMC made maintenance vans that were converted to cabin sleepers for General Patton, General Gaffey, and General Gay. They were delivered to Patton headquarters in Peover, England. Of the three, only General Patton's exists today and is on display inside the Patton Museum, Fort Knox, Kentucky.

The secret Scambler Phone and CV1052 frequency changer. Patton had two phones in his sleeping quarters van. One was a T 6 phone that was not a secure line and the other was a scrambler phone. The scrambler phone had to have a frequency changer mainframe. It consisted of a wooden or metal chest containing the tube-based circuitry to modulate the signal and scramble or descrambled the signal into normal speech patterns. By 1944 they had introduced a unit what would run on 110 volts, which would work with most Army generators. Patton's van and work trailer had such generators. Patton was not fond of the phone as it often did not do what it was intended to. Patton's use of colorful language was often heard throughout the camp when he was frustrated with the phone. The phone had a light green handset and a black bake lite base. One button needed to be pushed to scramble the voice when talking. (Image courtesy of Andy Grant)

PATTON'S PRE-INVASION SPEECH MADE AT PEOVER HALL, DURING MAY 1944,
AT KNUTSFORD, ENGLAND

The Corps Chaplain gave the invocation, the men standing with bowed heads, asking divine guidance for the great Third Army that they might help speed victory to enslaved Europe. Maj. Gen. Cook then introduced Lt. Gen. Simpson, whose army was still in America preparing for their part in the war.

"We are here", said Gen. Simpson, "To listen to the words of a great man. A man who will lead you into whatever you might face with heroism, ability and foresight. A man who has proven himself amid shot and shell. My greatest hope is that some day soon I will have my own great army fighting with him, side by side."

General Patton arose and strode swiftly to the microphone. The men snapped to their feet and stood silently. Patton surveyed them grimly. "Be seated" the words were not a request but a command. The generals voice rose high and clear. "Men, this stuff we hear about America wanting to stay out of this war, not wanting to fight is a lot of BULLSHIT. Americans love to fight traditionally. All real Americans love the sting of battle. When you were kids you all admired the champion marble player, the fastest runner, the big league ball players and the toughest boxers. The Americans love a winner and will not tolerate a loser. Americans play to win, all of the time. I wouldn't give a hoot in hell for a man who lost and laughed. That's why Americans never lost, and never will lose a war, for the very thought of losing is hateful to all Americans.

He paused and looked over the silent crowd, "You are not all going to die. Only two percent of you here, in a major battle, would die. Death must not be feared. Every man is frightened at first in battle. If he says he isn't, he's a GODDAM liar. Some men are cowards, yes, but they will fight just the same, or get the hell shamed out of them watching men who do fight who are just as scared. The real hero is the man who fights even though he is scared. Some get over their fright in a few minutes under fire, some take hours, some it takes days. The real man never lets the fear of death overpower his honor, his sense of duty to his country, and his innate manhood. All through your career of army life you men have bitched about what you call this CHICKEN-SHIT drilling. That is all for one reason, INSTANT OBEDIENCE OF ORDERS, AND TO CREATE CONSTANT ALERTNESS.

I don't give a damn for any man who is not always on his toes. You men are veterans or you wouldn't be here. YOU ARE READY. A man to continue breathing must be alert at all times. If not, some German Son-Of-A-Bitch will sneak up behind him and beat him to death with a sock full of shit." AND THAT IS NO HORSE-ASS WAY TO DIE.

The men roared. Patton's grim expression did not change. "There are 400 neatly marked graves somewhere in Sicily, "he roared," All because ONE MAN went to sleep on his job." He paused and the men grew silent." But they were German graves", he said softly, "Because we caught the BASTARDS asleep before they did."

PATTON'S PRE-INVASION SPEECH, Cont, page 2

The General clenched his microphone tightly, his jaw out-thrust, "An army is a team, lives, eats, sleeps and fights as a team. This individual heroic stuff is a lot of crap. The bilious BASTARDS who write that kind of stuff for the Saturday Evening Post don't know any more about real battles than they do about _______.

The men slapped their legs and rolled in glee, this was the old boy as they had imagined him to be, and in rare form too, he had it.

We have the finest food, the finest equipment, the best spirit and the best men in the world. Patton bellowed. He lowered his head and shook it pesively. Suddenly he snapped his head up, facing the men belligerently. "Why by God", he thundered, "I actually pity those SON-OF-A-BITCHES we are going up against, by God, I do." The men howled and slapped delightedly. There will be many barrack tales about the Old Man's choice phrases. This would become part and parcel of Third Army History.

My men do not surrender," Patton continued, "I don't want to hear of a soldier under my command being captured unless he is hit. Even if you are, you can still fight. And that's not just BULLSHIT either. The kind of man I want is like a lieutenant in Libya, who, with a Luger against his chest, jerked off his helmet, swept the gun aside with his other hand, and busted hell out of the Boche with his helmet. Then he jumped on the gun and went out and killed another German. By this time, the man had a bullet through his chest. THAT'S A MAN FOR YOU.

He halted and the crowd waited. "All the real heroes are not story book combat fighters, either, " he went on. "Every man in the army plays a vital part. Every little job is essential to the whole scheme. What if every truck driver decided he didn't like the whine of those shells and turned yellow and jumped head-long into a ditch. He could say to himself, "they won't miss one in thousands". What if every man said that? Every man does his job. Every man serves as a whole. Every man, every department, every unit is important in the vast scheme of things. The Ordnance men are needed to supply the guns, the Quartermaster to bring up the food and clothing for us, because where we are going, there isn't a hell of a lot to steal. Every last man in the mess hall, even the one who heats the water to keep us from getting Diarrhea, has a job to do. Even the Chaplain is important, for if we get killed and he were not there to bury us, we'd all go to hell. Each man must not only think of himself, but think of his buddy fighting beside him. We don't want yellow cowards in this army. They should be killed off like flies. If not they will go back to the states after the war and breed more like them. The brave men will breed more brave men. One of the bravest men I saw in the African campaign was one of the fellows who was on top of a telegraph pole in the midst of a furious fire while we were plowing toward Tunis. I stopped and asked him what in hell was he doing up there at that time. He answered, "Fixing this wire sir." "Isn't it a little unhealthy right now? I asked. "Yes sir, but this GODDAM wire has got to be fixed. "There was a real soldier. There was a man who devoted his all to his duty. No matter how great the odds, no matter how seemingly insignificant his duty may have seemed at that time. You should have seen those trucks on the way to Gabes, the

PATTON'S PRE-INVASION SPEECH, Cont, page 3

drivers were magnificent. All the day they drove along those SON-OF-A-BITCHING roads, never stopping, never diverting from their course with shells bursting all around them. We got through on good old American guts. Many of the men drove for over 40 consecutive hours.

The general paused, staring challengingly out over the silent sea of faces. You could hear a pin drop anywhere on the vast hillside. The only sound was the breeze stirring the leaves and the animated chirping of the birds in the branches on the generals left.

"Don't forget, " Patton roared, "You don't know that I am here at all, no word of that fact is to be mentioned in any letter. The world is not supposed to know what they do with me. I'm not supposed to be commanding this army, I'm not supposed to be in England. LET THE FIRST BASTARDS TO FIND OUT BE THE GERMANS. Some day, I want them to raise up their hind legs and howl, JESUS CHRIST, It's the GODDAM THIRD ARMY AND THAT SON-OF-A-BITCH PATTON AGAIN.

The men roared and cheered delightfully. This statement had real significance behind it, much more than met the eye, and the men instinctively sensed the fact and the telling fact they themselves would play in World History because of it, they were being told as much now. Deep sincerity and seriousness lay behind the generals colorful words, and well they knew it; but they loved the way he put it as only he could.

"We want to get the hell over there, "Patton yelled." We want to get over there and clean the GODDAM thing up. And then we'll have to take a little jaunt against the purple pissing Japanese and clean out their nest before the Marines get all of the BASTARDS.

The crowd laughed and Patton continued quietly. "Sure we all want to go home, we want to get this thing over with, but you can't win a war laying down. The quickest way to get it over is to go get the BASTARDS. The quicker they are whipped, the quicker we go home. THE SHORTEST WAY HOME IS THROUGH BERLIN. When a soldier is lying in a shell hole, if he just stays there all day, the Bocher will get him eventually, and probably get him first."

The hell with taking it; give it to them first. There is no such thing as fox-hole war anymore. Foxholes slow up an offensive. Keep moving. We'll win this war but we'll win it by fighting and showing our guts. "He paused, and eagle like eyes swept over the crowd and hillside.

"There is one thing you men will be able to say when you go home. You may all thank God for it. Thank God that at least 50 years from now, when you go home and are sitting around the fireside with your grandson on you knee and he asks you what you did in the great World War II, you won't have to say that you say that you shoveled shit in Louisiana."

This speech was made in May 1944, near Patton's headquarters at Peover Hall in England. It is a little more of his colorful speech than most. He had a written speech before him and only followed it in general. That is why there are so many variations of the same speech. Lt. Col. Codman, Aide-de-camp to General Patton, kept a copy of the original speech in his briefcase. If asked what Patton said, he would produce the official version, which did not always match verbatim to what he had just said. His speech varied depending on how he felt at the moment.

This is one of several of Patton's famous speeches in the author's collection. The soldiers would write down in short hand then go back and have it typed out. These hand typed speeches were kept by the soldiers who had them all their lives. After their death they wound up in various auctions and sold as collectables.

Patton's bull terrier, Willie.

# CHAPTER 3

## GO AHEAD AND TRAIN YOUR ARMY

On May 4th, Patton was told he could retain his command but SHAEF sent a public relations officer to Patton, who told Patton that he should make no more public statements. Patton, knowing Ike, asked, "What did he really say?"

"He said you were not to open your God damn mouth publicly until he said you could." Patton burst into laughter.[1]

This incident, more than any other, chastised Patton to his soul. He was now afraid to speak out for the first time in his life. He was loyal and appreciated the chance to command that he kept his mouth shut and only wrote his fears in his diary and in letters to his wife. The tragedy of this was he saw the things that needed to be said and had he spoken up, he could have prevented a lot of things from interfering with the fighting of the war.[2]

[Patton]
**May 4, 1944 Thursday**

I felt all tense, so took pills with a bromide, with no effect so far. Gaffey and Maddox went to London to get our final plan approved.[3]

[Patton]
**May 5, 1944 Friday**

Wrote a paper on the use of armored divisions. Major General Moore, Chief Engineer of NATOUSA, came to call. It is a very cold rainy day but I have completely gotten back in the swing of things, thank God.[4]

Willie had the free run of the headquarters and often came into the War room, which was off limits and secret. Allen made note that Willie had once been owned by an officer in the RAF who was shot down over Europe.[5]

[Patton]
**May 6, 1944 Saturday**

A War Department Army Historical Section was attached on 6 May to the G-3 Section for the purpose of writing the history of the Third U.S. Army and its supporting troops for the War Department Record.[6]

In Knutsford there was a parade that was called the salute to the soldier and the Third Army band marched in the parade.[7]

[Patton]

Colonel F.M.S. Miller, Third Army Air officer, has arranged a number of flights of airplanes of all sorts over our troops so they can get some idea of how they will look. They fly in a specified order so the troops can pick them out as they have the list. For example a flight consisting of a P 38, two different kinds of Spitfire, a Mosquito, and a P-51 -- always in that order -- will arrive at a given camp at a given hour and circle four times, diving once.

I went out in a *Mosquito in one of these demonstrations and was up for nearly two hours. I had never flown at 300 m.p.h. before and the effects of gravity and centrifugal force are quite interesting. When you pull out of a steep dive, which has been at a rate of better than 300 miles per hour, you are actually pushed down uncomfortably on the seat and have difficulty in moving your legs or arms. When banking at the same speed, you have the same effect of centrifugal force. Further, at that speed, even with my flying experience, it is very difficult to recognize ground forms. However, I could see from the plane that the men were very much interested and were getting valuable instruction out of the exercise.[8]

### The Wooden Wonder and The Flying Circus

The de Havilland Mosquito was a British made and operated fast, twin-engined aircraft with shoulder-mounted wings. The most produced variant, designated the FB Mk VI (Fighter-bomber Mark 6) was powered by two Merlin Mk 23 or Mk 25 engines driving three-bladed de Havilland hydromatic propellers. The typical fixed armament for an FB Mk VI was four Browning .303 machine guns and four 20 mm Hispano cannon while the offensive load consisted of up to 2,000 pounds (910 kg) of bombs, or eight RP-3 unguided rockets. The Mosquito was one of the few operational, front-line aircraft of the World War II era to be constructed almost entirely of wood and, as such, was nicknamed "The Wooden Wonder." It had a two-man crew.

The Flying Circus, as it was called, was part of the Royal Canadian Air Force and had been combined with US airmen and planes for a serious purpose. It was put together to display all of the different planes in the allied arsenal of flying craft from bombers to small reconnaissance aircraft. They were to fly over pre-scheduled areas of England so the ground troops could learn to recognize their silhouettes and know the difference between allied aircraft and axis aircraft. This had proven to be a real problem and in several of the minds of all the generals that this should not ever happen again. The 430th squadron was part of that unit. (Sweetman, Bill, *The Great Great Book of WWII Airplanes*, pages 317-367[9])

There was a young C/O pilot named Richard Rohmer who flew a P51 Mustang in that squadron. He was participating in training missions over England. He received orders that his squadron was to fly in to Ramsberry and that the next day they would be inspected by General Patton. They flew in the night before to Ramsberry, a Royal Air Force airfield near Liverpool. They were told that at 0800 hrs. on the morning of May 8th, General Patton was going to inspect the squadron. They were ready and lined up at the appointed time. Their P51 fighters were in a straight line, wingtip to wingtip.

[Patton]
**May 7, 1944 Sunday**

Gay and I went calling in the afternoon.[10]

There was some fear of the use of poison gas by the Germans. There were secret reports given to G-2 that the Germans were devoting considerable time to anti-gas training. In Bordeaux and Toulon areas, German service personnel were wearing respirators on an extensive scale. There were frequent gas alerts in Rennes. Intelligence also had reports that a large German firm, Frederick Strael & Co. of Konstanz got a big order to start production of gas-proof suits.[11]

[Rohmer]
**May 8, 1944 Monday**

At 8 a.m. in the morning, a jeep with its top down appeared on the roadway between the buildings in front of us swung south and pulled around to the southernmost aircraft and stopped. There he was, General Patton himself. Standing rigidly I turned my head slightly to see him climb out of his vehicle, returning the salute of our squadron commander. Without further ado Patton began to walk down the line of aircraft, passing in front of each pilot. He did not stop to talk to any of my colleagues. But he did stop when he got to me. There he was right in front of me! I was stiff, ramrod attention, at my tallest. My flat officer's cap was barely on my head, polka dot scarf neatly in place. The General was elegantly dressed. He had a wedge cap on over his white hair. The left breast of his khaki battledress jacket was covered with a multitude of ribbons. Light tan riding breaches were above highly polished riding boots and silver spurs. On each hip was a revolver, the famed ivory handled guns. He towered over me, all six foot two of him.

General Patton looked down on me, examining the boyish face. He then look up at the looming noise of the huge Mustang. Then back down at me. "Boy," he demanded, "how old are you?"

"I am twenty sir."  His eyes went up to the aircraft again, then back down to me. His right arm lifted as he pointed up to the airplane, but his eyes were still fixed on mine and he asked in his high pitched voice, "Do you fly that goddam airplane?"

"Yes Sir." With that he dropped his arm.

"Son of a bitch," he said incredulously. With a shake of his head he turned and walked off.[12]

[Authors note: The young pilot never forgot that day. He flew through the entire rest of the war, and was highly decorated for his service. He rose to the rank of Major General and went on to write many books, one of which was just quoted. His book, *Patton's Gap*, on pages 42 and 43 where these quotes appear, examines a question and gives the answer of who would later be held responsible for a major blunder of the war, namely the Falaise Gap.]

[Patton]

Left in the morning to talk to the officers of XII Corps and then to see "P" Wood about the tank and infantry attack on April 15. I wrote a paper on the tactical use of the separate tank battalion in an attack with infantry showing when infantry leads and when tanks lead and how they are to support each other. We first went to see the sand table demonstration which was along the lines I had prescribed. We will go and see a rehearsal in the morning. I made the corrections, shortening the attack order.[13]

Six weeks after the Third Army's arrival in the United Kingdom the complete intelligence report for operation Overlord was published. The topical section began to expand on the mapping to include more of the continent and surrounding areas. Detail studies were undertaken to determine best routs, tonnage allowed on roads and bridges, and great interest given to known fortified positions.[14]

Headquarters command of the Third Army called for a detailed chart from all sections regarding packing up and moving in preparation for pulling out toward the front. Word was received that they would be moving to Eristoke, near Bristol.[15]

[Patton]
**May 9, 1944 Tuesday**

Left Wood's house at 0800 and got to the Downs in time. All arrangements were made. In the first rehearsal, the infantry advanced by rushes when defiladed, and failed to use their weapons. I called the officers together and explained errors to them. Had lunch. In the second rehearsal I accompanied General Holmes Dager in a half-track with a radio.

The support and reserves were so far back as to be wholly useless. The tanks did better but the officers and non-coms of infantry just went along as members of the chorus and gave no orders. It was very sad.

When the tanks jumped off on the second objective the infantry were slow following. The occupation of the position was poor and the employment of anti-tank guns awful. I again assembled the officers and gave them hell. I hope they improve. The majority of the general officers of the Third Army came to dinner including the Frenchman, LeClerc.

        J.S. Wood, Major General, 4th Armored Division
        I.D. White Maj. Gen. 79th Inf. Division
        W.H. Walker Maj. Gen. XX Corps
        G.S. Patton Lt. Gen Third Army
        W.C. McMahon 8th Div.
        Lloyd Brown 28th Div.
        De B LeClerc 2nd French Armored Div.
        R.C. Grow Maj. Gen. 6th Armored Div.
        L.R. C. Irwin Maj. Gen. 5th Div.
        L.P. Oliver Maj. Gen. 5th Armored Div.
        Eugene Ragnier, Brig. General 5th Armored Div.
        H.R. Gay, Chief of Staff, Third Army
        J.B. Thompson 7th Armored Div.
        R.C. Macon 83rd Div.
        Col Allen G-3 XV Corps
        J.A. Holly, Col. Armored Force
        H.L. Ernest, Tank Destroyer
        J.E. Slack Brig. Gen. Artillery Officer XX Corps

After dinner we had a very good conversation and I read them the draft
of the paper I am writing on armored divisions and asked for comments
I got very few as none of them know anything about armored divisions.
Furthermore very few officers ever project what they do in training into
battle, which is a very sad commentary on our system. During the evening
I received an invitation, which is tantamount to an order, from General
Eisenhower, to be present at an official luncheon in London on the 12th.[16]

[Patton]
**May 10, 1944 Wednesday**

We had all the regimental and battalion commanders of infantry, and a
separate tank battalion commanders, of the Army assembled. The demonstration
was a great success except that this time the reserve company was too
close. I was delighted and feel I have at last illustrated the use of
marching fire and of tanks and infantry. It strikes me as a sad reflection
in our state of preparedness for war that I had to personally conduct and
drive the rehearsals, but so it is. On the other hand it was depressing
to realize that had I not personally practically commanded the battalion
on the second rehearsal the thing would not have come off. Our officers
do not realize the necessity of utilizing all the means at hand, all
weapons, to accomplish victory.

As the result of an invitation from Ike to a lunch on Friday, the
12th, I came to London.[17]

[Allen]

Lt. Col. Hal Forde reported to G-2 Intelligence to be placed in charge
of Map and photo intelligence, once he gets a handle on it. It was noted
that he was the only one in headquarters that had a handle bar moustache.
Col. Koch said to Lt. Col. Allen that Forde was an expert in this field.[18]

[Patton]
**May 11, 1944 Thursday**

General Hughes and I drove to Cheltenham to see Colonel Walter Leyma
about replacements. I think that at last I succeeded in making them
understand that a unit is never 100% effective, because, due to sickness
and accidents, there are always some 2 to 8% of the men not available.
Therefore, when you go into battle, you are that much short.

To correct this we should always have 15% over strength in basic privates
and lieutenants. With this over strength we could enter battle at 100%
and still have enough over to account for casualties in one or two days

of fighting. This would breach the gap which always exists between the requisition for replacements and the arrival of the replacements.

In order to make this over strength fully effective, the men should be with the units for at least a month before they go in. This will give them a feeling of personal interest in the unit.

Every war that I know about has had a crisis on replacements. Many wars have been lost because of a lack of them. Had the British expedition to the Low Countries under the Duke of York in 1793 received the 10,000 replacements it asked for instead of the 2,200, which it actually got, it is highly probable that the Revolutionary French armies would have been stopped, and that instead of the British going through eighteen years of consistent defeat, England would have been victorious and then the Napoleon Era would never have existed. It is a scandal that we have so few replacements and so many SOS troops.[19]

Patton wanted the very best he could find for his personal staff. Colonel Charles Odom was one such man. He had graduated from Tulane University, spent eight years in surgical training at Charity Hospital in New Orleans. He entered military service in June 1943 as a Lt. Colonel. He was later assigned to General Patton's staff in North Africa and served with him throughout the war. His official title was surgical consultant of the Third Army. He made all the recommendations for surgical procedure and saw they were carried out in the commands of Third Army. In England he was part of the surgical team looking into the medical planning for operation Overlord and subsequently would be invaluable to the medical needs of Patton's Third Army. He was Patton's good friend and was referred to as Patton's personal physician, even though his duties were through the Third Army command. Colonel Charles Odom submitted his plan for Operation OVERLORD, dated 11 May 1944. It was pointed out that early, skilled surgical care of battle casualties is the principal function of medical installations supporting a field army. This care was based on the following principles:

1. First aid and primary care include only dressing of wounds, control of hemorrhage, splinting of fractures, and treatment of shock. These measures are carried out at battalion aid stations and at collecting and clearing stations.
2. Definitive surgery is not to be undertaken in installations forward of field hospital platoons.
3. A most important consideration in the early care of the wounded is the proper sorting of casualties. This sorting (triage) permits lightly wounded to be returned quickly to duty, while seriously wounded casualties are evacuated to field or evacuation hospitals, the echelon at which they are treated depending upon their transportability.

In this medical plan, casualties were divided into two groups, as follows:

(1) A transportable group, consisting of those who could withstand movement to the rear without deterioration; and
(2) a non-transportable group, consisting of casualties who would do poorly when moved

and whose wounds (or the status resulting from whose wounds) required immediate treatment.

There were a number of categories in the non-transportable group, as follows:

1. Casualties, usually those with multiple wounds, who remained in shock in spite of intensive resuscitative therapy.
2. Casualties with abdominal wounds, particularly those with possible concealed hemorrhage. In evaluating these patients, it was emphasized that another fact had to be taken into consideration, that all previous experience had shown that patients who had undergone laparotomy could not be safely moved for at least 7 or 10 days. In other words, the triage of this group required the evaluation of both the postoperative circumstances and the casualty's present status.
3. Casualties with large sucking chest wounds or massive intrathoracic hemorrhage.
4. Casualties with transthoracic or thoraco-abdominal wounds. It was pointed out that these wounds are difficult to diagnose and are likely to be missed because the path of the missile is frequently unexpected. In wounds of the buttocks, for instance, the missile may come to rest in the thorax, while in wounds of the shoulder, it might lodge within the peritoneal cavity. If X-ray facilities were available, it was recommended that they be used to settle the matter.
5. Casualties with wounds about the face and neck causing mechanical interference with respiration. Patients in this category would usually require tracheotomy before evacuation.

Shock was the most important cause of death in casualties who did not die immediately of their wounds. If it was not treated promptly and vigorously, it was likely to become irreversible. Its prolongation, even if the patient did not die immediately, often led to a subsequent fatality from anuria. Among the casualties who died in anuria, prolonged, profound shock seemed to be the single constant factor; transfusion reactions did not seem of great importance in this connection. Alkalinization and other methods were found to be of no value in either the prevention or the treatment of this complication. The important consideration was to bring the casualty promptly out of shock.

Adequate shock therapy, based on the use of plasma and stored whole blood, was probably the most important single method of lowering the mortality and morbidity from combat wounds. Operation was performed as soon as possible after resuscitation and was regarded as part of the resuscitative routine. Teams were set up in all forward hospitals for the treatment of shock and the administration of blood. The chiefs of laboratory services were responsible for the supervision of the hospital blood program.

Plasma was available to all medical units as far forward as battalion aid stations. It was used in liberal quantities in the prevention of shock and in resuscitation until a field hospital could be reached. It was of value, however, only as a temporary expedient. No casualty could be properly prepared for surgery without the use of whole blood. Plasma and whole blood were originally used in the proportion of 2 pints of plasma to 1 pint of blood, but, as the campaign progressed, more and more blood was used.

Before D-day, the policy was formulated that the Third U.S. Army would have attached to it a blood bank detachment for the receipt, storage, and delivery of whole blood. The blood was to be delivered daily to all hospitals on a so-called "milk run." Plans were also made, and hospitals were equipped, to obtain whole blood from hospital personnel.

These plans were based on the provision of blood by the theater blood bank in the United Kingdom Base. During initial operations, 190 pints were delivered daily for the use of the whole Third U.S. Army. This supply was entirely inadequate, even with supplementary provision of whole blood secured by bleeding hospital personnel. Late in August, supplies from the Zone of Interior became available, and from 500 to 700 pints of blood were received daily. This was an entirely adequate provision. There was only one occasion thereafter on which whole blood was badly needed and was not available in sufficient quantities. Colonel Odom was dispatched by the army surgeon to theater headquarters, then in Paris, and a conference with Maj. Gen. Paul R. Hawley, Chief Surgeon, ETOUSA, and General Cutler, his consultant in surgery, insured an adequate supply for all immediate needs and future necessities.

When morphine was indicated, a dosage of one-quarter of a grain (15 mg.) was usually adequate, although occasionally one-half grain (30 mg.) was required for the control of pain. Larger doses were never repeated. The time and amount of the injection were always recorded.

Chemotherapy. In the Third U.S. Army medical plan for Operation OVERLORD, soldiers wounded in action were directed to take, by mouth, 4 grams of sulfadiazine in tablet form from their first aid package as soon as possible unless the wounds involved the abdomen. At least half a canteen of water was to be drunk within the next 5 or 10 minutes. The medical officer who first dressed the wound was instructed to frost it lightly with sulfanilamide powder. The powder was available in 5-gm. packets, and, under no circumstances, regardless of the size and number of his wounds, were more than two packets (10 gm.) to be used for a single casualty. Sulfadiazine by mouth when definitive surgery had been accomplished. The maintenance dose was 1 gm. orally every 4 to 6 hours or 2 gm. parenterally every 8 to 12 hours. After debridement, or after definitive surgery, all wounds were again lightly dusted with sulfanilamide powder, and sulfonamide therapy was also continued by the oral or parenteral route.

Medical officers were instructed to be constantly on the alert for a possible reaction to the sulfonamide drugs. If a reaction occurred, the medication was to be discontinued.

By the time the May 1944 medical plan was issued, the experience in the Mediterranean theater had shown that the sulfonamide preparations in a wound act as foreign bodies. The local use of sulfonamides was therefore discontinued entirely within a few months after the invasion of the Continent. They were found to be of no therapeutic value, and wound healing was actually delayed when crystals were used. Local reactions were not uncommon, and after the wounded man had resumed his activities the wound sometimes broke down.[20]

Note: The surgical consultant to the Surgeon, Third U.S. Army, had the same duties as surgical consultants in other field armies. He advised the Surgeon on a variety of matters, such as (1) evaluation and assignment of personnel, (2) organization and functioning of surgical sections of hospitals in the forward area, (3) the quality of medical service rendered, with suggestions for its improvement, (4) changes in concepts and techniques of surgical management of combat injuries, (5) indoctrination of new medical personnel, (6) the results being obtained in the care of battle casualties, and (7) future planning. Col. (later Brig. Gen.) Thomas D. Hurley, MC, Surgeon, Third U.S. Army, and Col. John Boyd Coates, Jr., MC, Executive Officer, had the task of supporting the advancing Army by leapfrogging medical units which were leapfrogged across each other. Since the surgical consultant moved with the command post of the army, it was often possible for him to recommend advantageous hospital locations to the Operations and Training Subsection. Also being thoroughly familiar with the abilities and capacities of the various medical units, he was often able to recommend the use of one unit instead of another as better suited to the immediate job to be done.

[Patton]
**May 12, 1944 Friday**

General Eisenhower had a lunch at the Officers Club at Widewing to commemorate the African campaign. As many as possible of the British and American participants in that Campaign were present, including Tedder, Conyngham, Doolittle, Admiral Cunningham, Spaatz, Hughes, Gaffey, Huebner, Eddy, Smith and myself --- 32 in all. Ike made an excellent speech. He said, as nearly as I can remember, "We are gathered here to commemorate our success in Africa. On looking around, however, and making a mental calculation, it just occurs to me that if each one of the general officers, air marshals, and admirals here had used a machine gun for half an hour, some 350,000 rounds could have been fired against the enemy, so perhaps we would have gained a greater victory had we used you more directly. But seriously, it is hardly a time to stress past victories too strongly, so I ask that we all stand and drink a silent toast to our fellow soldiers who will never leave Africa." I made suggestion to Air Marshal Conyngham that I hoped neither he nor I would shortly be the object of a similar toast.

After lunch General Gaffey and I went to see Beedle Smith about the constant demands being made on the Third Army by the SOS for men, and the failure of the SOS to get us equipment. We got no satisfaction at all out of him except being told to go and see General Bull, G-3 of SHAEF.

After leaving Smith, Ike asked me to come in for a chat. We had a very pleasant few minutes together lecture and all.

Hughes and I went for a walk and visited a saddle shop on Oxford Street, also the Curtis Gun shop. Here we met the Purdy Brothers who ran an office more like a club than anything else. *We saw Beedle's shot gun, which they are giving him, and he, in exchange has presented the son of the one of them with an electric train, value $20.00, and two U. S. Army carbines which he had no right to present. The shot gun is probably priced at $2,000.00. It is the cheapest swindle either of us had ever seen.[22]

Hughes also wrote in his diary that there was a toy train set traded in for the guns. This issue was pursued by Hughes and General Saylor informed Hughes General Smith had reported them lost and had paid for them. Hughes wrote that Beedle got mad when he mentioned it and blamed Patton for it. Hughes stated he wrote a memo on the subject.[22]

[Patton]
**May 13, 1944 Saturday**

Read and loafed. In the afternoon, Codman and I went to Marian Hall's for tea and met a Colonel Johnson, who is interested in prisoners of war. We had Marian Hall and James Hazen Hyde's daughter-in-law to dinner. Later we called on the Lunts and Sandy Patch. The Lunts are entertaining but colorless-sort of human phonograph records.[23]

[Patton]
**May 14, 1944 Sunday**

Colonel and Mrs. Robert Henriques took Codman and me to lunch at the Cavalry Club Church at St. Paul's. Later we went out and had dinner with Doolittle.[24]

There was a ceremony for the 301st Operation Signal Battalion. Colonel Elton Hammond presented the battalion colors to the unit in a colorful ceremony. Colonel Hammond was the Third Army's Signal Corps Chief of Staff headquarters. As such he was in command of all signal communications coming in and out of the Third Army to all other commands up the chain of command and down to the smallest unit. This would include overseas traffic, stateside and throughout the entire European Theater going and coming from Third Army Headquarters. The 301st was responsible setting up and making it all function from Third Army Headquarters.[25] The Third Army Band attended and played for the presentation of the colors for this event.[26]

May 15, 1944 Monday: Patton attended a formal dress rehearsal for Operation Overlord in London. The day was cold and frigid. The meeting was held in a lecture room of St. Paul's School. There was a row in front for the VIP's but many of the top generals in attendance wore their great coats and huddled amongst each other to stay warm. There was a large model of the invasion area and maps posted all along the walls. This was one of, if not the largest gathering of top leadership of the war in England. The attendees were King George VI, Field Marshal Jan Smuts of South Africa, Churchill, Eisenhower, Tedder, Montgomery, Brooke, and the other British chiefs of staff, Adm. Sir Bertram Ramsay (the naval commander in chief), Marshal Sir Trafford Leigh-Mallory (the air commander in chief), Bradley, Lt. Gen. Miles Dempsey (the British Second Army commander), Lt. Gen. Courtney H. Hodges, Lt. Gen. H. D. G. Crerar (the Canadian First Army commander); the British, Canadian, and U.S. corps and division commanders; and a host of other senior officers from SHAEF and Whitehall.

Patton was late. General Montgomery ordered the doors shut promptly at 0900 hrs and had posted two MPs at the outside to insure no one entered the room.

As the conference started to commence there was a large hammering on the doors. This continued until Montgomery, visibly angry, ordered the doors opened and in walked General Patton. General Montgomery re-opened the proceedings.[27]

[Patton]
**May 15, 1944 Sunday**

All the senior commanders and their chiefs of staff assembled at St. Paul's School for the final briefing for the attack. The King, the Prime Minister, and Field Marshal Smuts were also present. General Eisenhower started with a short talk emphasizing the fact that any existing disagreements between the Air, the Navy, and the Ground must be ironed out today. Then Admiral Ramsey of the Navy told how difficult it was going to be to get troops ashore. Air Marshal Leigh-Mallory followed, telling what the Air Force had done. Then the Chief of the British Bomber Command spoke and made what I considered a very ill-timed argument in favor of bombardment instead of attack. Bradley and Spaatz made short and good speeches. The King said a few words, but it was rather painful to watch the efforts he made not to stammer. At lunch I sat opposite Mr. Churchill who asked me whether I remembered him, and when I said I did, he immediately ordered me a glass of whiskey.

After lunch there were more talks; Admiral Kirk made a weak, stilted one, and the British opposite number made a fine fighting talk. Smuts talked a lot, but repeated himself and was not impressive. Finally the Prime Minister made a really great fighting speech, worth all that preceded it. He took a crack at overstressing Civil Government and said that his views would hurt the feelings of his dear friend, General De Gaulle. Also that we were worrying too much about governing France before capturing it. It was a very fine fighting speech and I intend to write him a letter about it. Returned to Peover.[28]

After lunch there were more talks. These included Admiral Kirk, senior American naval commander, and General De Gaulle The top commanders closed with Smuts, then Winston Churchill and General Eisenhower closed with a short talk and even stated that disagreements between the air, navy and ground forces must be ironed out today. He finished his speech by remarking, "In half an hour Hitler will have missed his one and only chance of destroying with a single well-aimed bomb the entire high command of the Allied forces."

Patton was only a spectator at this event and did not get up to speak. However, he did make his presence known in typical Patton fashion. When one of the Canadian Generals got up to speak, Patton found the speech so boring that he said in a whisper, but loud enough to be heard around him that in Patton's typical profane language that "if the &%$^& don't set down he was going to $%##" No one seemed to recall the exact curse words but it got the desired effect and Montgomery's Chief of Staff got up and whispered in the ear of the Canadian General, and he did sit down. Admiral Hall, U. S. Navy and General Henry D.G. Crerar, commander of Canadian forces, were sitting next to Patton and recalled it years later that it was timed perfectly and so funny they had to snicker (laugh) at the remarks, which caused a little bit of a shuffle around them.[29]

[Patton]
**May 16, 1944 Tuesday**

Made a talk to the officers and senior non-coms in the 79th Division and also to the Staff of the VIII Corps. Middleton made a good talk, as usual. I also addressed the Technical School of the Third Army.[30]

[Patton]
**May 17, 1944 Wednesday**

Made a talk to the officers and senior non-coms, also addressed Third Army School of Administration. As in all my talks, I stressed fighting and killing. In addition to the $870.00 odd I already owe Sgt. Meeks, I owe him as of today an additional $347.75.[31]

[Patton]
**May 18, 1944 Thursday**

Smith called me on the phone to say that someone had told Ike that the discipline and esprit of the 5th Armored Division was bad, owing to their being on housekeeping duties in the marshaling area. Damn these people who listen to rumors, and double damn those who spread them. In this case I think it was Kenner who talked too much. Middleton and Maddox are going south to talk with the Navy about the Belle Isle operation and will look into it. Today I marked on my map the places I think I will have to fight. I did it before Sicily, and was correct. The only worry I have about this show is how I am going to get the Army across and assembled on the other side. For the fighting I have no worry.[32]

A Tank Destroyer staff section was established on 18 May. Authority to issue one tank dozer blade for medium tanks M1 in each Armored Division prior to leaving the United Kingdom was requested of Services of Supply, European Theater of Operations.[33]

The 6th US Cavalry Group was assigned to 3rd Army under "Plan Unicorn." The plan's name is interesting in that the 6th Cavalry Regiment had its origins as far back as May of 1861 and was a continuous horse cavalry regiment from then until February of 1942. They had adopted the "Rampant Unicorn" on the unit's crest distinctive insignia (aka DCI) and their patch was a Rampant Unicorn raised on its hind legs. They were reorganized as a mechanized cavalry regiment as the Joints Chiefs of Staff had decided to do away with horse mounted cavalry. From March through September 1943 they trained as a mechanized cavalry regiment. In October, they were given orders to ship to Scotland and continue training. Many of these men were career veterans of the mounted horse cavalry and skilled in quick cavalry tactics. They were then trained as reconnaissance to employ infiltration tactics, fire and maneuver. Patton had a use for them as his eyes and ears. Because of their training, they could operate quickly and get information back and forth. They were highly capable of fighting their way out of a fix to get messages flowing. The

151

problem came with army communication nets that were not reliable and slow. Messages were in code, took time to transmit and decode and were subject to atmospheric interference, interception and field radios were a.m. frequencies using tube combinations with replaceable crystals used to change frequencies. Fast mobile warfare could not wait on messages being slow to arrive or slow to dispatch. In North Africa this was overcome by specialized units called SIAM. This stood for "Staff Information And Monitoring" Service. The idea was to use real communication messages in real time and to physically hand carry messages by using men in the field. Since mechanized cavalry was trained to move quickly they were ideal for this type of assignment. Patton personally named this group Army Information Service (A.I.S.), for Third Army. Though they were official designated as that, they had the nickname "Patton's Household Cavalry," which they thoroughly loved.  The force earlier had been designated as the 6th Cavalry Group, 6th Cavalry Reconnaissance. The 28th US Cavalry Reconnaissance squadrons reinforced and consisted of approximately 1624 officers and men and were commanded by Colonel Edward M. Fickett, who was a career army officer and had been a mounted officer in the horse cavalry. This unit was trained in communications but was still a small but formidable fighting force capable of quick and decisive action. They were to also be responsible for augmenting Headquarters' command post security.

Since the 6th Cavalry Group had left the states as a mechanized cavalry regiment, it kept its designated band assigned to it. They were top notch musicians and it was obvious to the commanding generals that entertainment, ceremonies and other official functions would indeed require a band. In an unprecedented move, the band was kept intact during re-organization, but army regulations would no longer allow it to be attached to a smaller organic unit. Patton, having heard the band during an inspection trip, quickly moved to have it reassigned as the Third Army 61st Army Ground Forces Band.[34]

[Patton]
**May 19, 1944 Friday**

For over a month we have been trying to get a new command post nearer the embarkation area. We had it all set when Smith called up and told my Chief of Staff we would not move. I believe that this decision was based on a total lack of understanding of where the Third Army is, and also a lack of imagination which cannot picture that the best laid plans may not work, in which case it will be necessary for me to be on the round. People who lack both inspiration and experience are a menace in war.

If this show does not go as planned, and I think it won't, they will need me at once, and here I run too far away.[35]

Conferences were held for the A.C. of S. G-4s for all corps and divisions. They were oriented on procurement policies and procedures for Continental operations and given a resume of the supply picture as foreseen at that time.[36]

[Patton]
**May 20, 1944 Saturday**

Middleton and Maddox got back and told me that the 5th Armored Division is all right.[37]


By May 20, all Medical units which had been in the United Kingdom for three weeks or longer were ninety percent equipped. The forty-five general surgeons and ninety surgical technicians requested for Landing Ship Tank duties by Headquarters European Theater of Operations, reported for briefing. A Chief Nurse was assigned.

In the evening, Lady Leese held a party at her estate for the 3rd Army Staff. General Patton was in attendance. Three other general were also in attendance. It was done in a formal manner where the guests were announced by the butler in livery and then went down to the receiving line. The party started at 8 p.m. and lasted till midnight. There was a long table at one end of the ball room with sandwiches, cakes, cider (very popular in England), beer, coffee, and later soup.[38]

May 21, 1944 Sunday: G-2 Intelligence reviewed the news from Italy as their job was to learn from all theaters to be able and prepared to use the information learned in France and beyond. It was learned that there were 26 Allied divisions in use and there was a new offensive to crack Hitler's line in Rome. There is some speculation that the Italy offense was hoped to be wrapped up so the division there could be transferred to this theater for the attack on Europe and Southern France. The Operation, Operation Anvil, was the operation Patton was working on when he was brought to France. The idea was that Anvil would be coordinated with the invasion of Northern France and cause Hitler to split his forces. They also expected the Russians to resume their offensive.[39]


[Patton]
**May 22, 1944 Monday**

General Stephen Henry and Dr. Boles, an adviser to the Secretary of War, and Mr. Rowe of the American Fruit Company, who is to be an advisor to General Eisenhower, came by and we had quite a talk. I think it may have done some good as they all work for the Secretary of War. Also the rest of the Civil Affairs section came to report in. I memorized the map for quite a while and can almost draw it from memory now.

Major General C. P. Beckett and Major General Caesar, his Chief of Staff for the Western Defense Command, AA Section called. He had the AA at Malta and told me that he nearly lost 8% of his men and 7 months of the blitz. He also told me that, at the end of that time, he had expended half his ammunition and still had 1400 rounds per gun. I just heard the full story of Beedle Smith at Messina.

After Keyes, Gay and I took off to enter the town, Smith and Lemnitzer arrived and decided to follow me "if it was quite safe." Murname took them when they got to the top of the pass. Smith asked if we were under fire and was told it could happen. Just then one of our batteries of 155 guns let go, firing at Italy. Smith thought it was enemy shells arriving and jumped from the car into the ditch in one leap and he refused to leave it even when Lemnitzer and Murnane told him it was quit safe. When I got back he was still pale gray and shaky.[40]

The Build-Up Control Organization Section of Headquarters, known as BUCO, left for PORTSMOUTH, where it operated under BUCO West, supervising the priorities and loading of units moving to the Continent.

A conference at Third Army Headquarters was held at which representatives of the G-4 Section, First U.S. Army Group, Ninth U.S. Air Force, Advance Section Communications Zone, and European Theater of Operations U.S. Army were present, determined "That not more than fifteen divisions could be fully supported by ST. MALO (S71) and COTENTIN Peninsula area." Entrance of further divisions would have to await capture and development of QUIBERON BAY (M99) area in order for such troops to be maintained. The Finance Section obtained 3,760,000 Francs in "Invasion Money" for the use of contracting and purchasing offices."[41]

There was an interesting story about Patton while he was in Casablanca told by Lt. Col. Barnard "Bunny" Carter who was now in the G-2 Auxiliary section. He told Robert Allen, one day, (Patton) was walking down the Main street of Casablanca, passed a Sergeant who didn't salute. Stopped him and asked why not. "I don't salute generals. They don't need it," was the reply. Patton bellowed, "Lock the son of a bitch up!" in a voice that could be heard a block away.[42]

May 23, 1944 Tuesday: There was a school in London for G-2 Intelligence officers which Lt. Col. Robert Allen attended. He observed that London was very dirty, drab and overrun by the U.S. military. He learned that Lt. General Omar Bradley would be head of the First United States Army Group. He was told that V-1 bombing had hit near Army headquarters there and that included near Whitehall. Plans were to have four US Armies in England and part of the European campaign that were not yet part of it. The total manpower would exceed 1,250,000 troops. They were also going to form the 2nd French Armored Division that would be sent to France as well. Allen attended the senior officer mess and said the food was "reasonable excellent."[43]

[Patton]
**May 24, 1944 Wednesday**

At the invitation of Colonel Everett Bush, Third Army Quartermaster, I gave a talk to all corps and division quartermasters. In this I stressed that it was their duty to see that the troops were supplied and in doing it I expected and demanded that, when the need arose, they would perform the impossible.

General Oliver flew up to see me about the reports by Smith that the 5th Armored is low in morale and discipline. I am convinced that he is doing a good job. Before the Division house warming this housekeeping and I kicked to the limit of my ability to keep duty--Oliver spoke to every man telling him whether it was pleasant or not, it was a vital duty and

154

they must perform it. Since then, he has spent his whole time inspecting the various units and from everything I hear, the Division is doing an excellent job.

The only two places I can think of that the reports came from were from R. O. Barton who command the 4th Division, and who moved into an area recently vacated by one of his own battalions. It was dirty, and as the 5th Armored Division got there at the same time as Barton did, there was no time to clean it prior to his arrival. He may have kicked, or General Kenner may have talked too much, without knowledge. He often does. This is his own fault. One of the allegations made against the 5th Armored Division was that there were a great many men AWOL.

In April, 40 men went AWOL, of whom 39 came back. In every case this was due to the difficulty of movement in England. At the present time there is only one AWOL in the Division. The Civil Affair Section had a housewarming which we attended.[44]

The XX Corps and attached units were alerted for overseas movement.[45]

Lt. Col. Allen finished up his schools. Among the subjects learned were the Rakin Plan which, in the event Germany collapsed, provided a plan of action. Another was the Subsex plan. This was a combined British and American operation developed by the British SIS (Secret Intelligence Service) and USA OSS/SI. This plan was in collaboration with the French underground for the purpose of obtaining information by the use of undercover agents in enemy occupied territory.[46]

[Patton]
**May 25, 1944 Thursday**

Just read in the daily mail that the Senate Military Affairs Committee has tabled my promotion. I hope they let the others through. If I get no more out of this war but a permanent Major Generalcy I will "not" be a failure. General Hawley, Chief Surgeon SOS, came in and we had a good talk. I think he is O.K. He is coming to dinner and will spend the night.[47]

[Patton]
**May 26, 1944 Friday**

General Paul Baade of the 35th Division reported in to me. We also had the chief nurses of the First Army Group and the WVS for lunch. They are both majors.

I am leaving in the morning to see the air control system and the briefing of a bomber raid. I took a flight in an L-5 today.[48]

While the Publicity and Psychological Warfare Section was being organized, a Public Relations Officer was named on 26 May to take charge of arrangements for Public Relations and a Press Camp for war correspondents who were to be assigned to the Army during combat operations.[49]


[Patton]<br>**May 27, 1944 Saturday**

Flew to Northolt Airfield and motored to Uxbridge, which is the Tactical Air Force Command Post. I saw Conyngham and was shown how the system works. There was quite a lot of eyewash -- the control room is 60 feet underground. We then flew to a place in East Anglia to visit the 354th Fighter Group of P-51's and saw them get in from a mission.

Brigadier General O. P. Weyland, who commands the XIX Tactical Air Support, which works for the Third Army, asked me to talk to both officers and men and to stress teamwork.

We next drove to the Wing Headquarters (two Groups) commanded by Colonel B. M. Hovey and looked at a lot of installations. They seem to have everything they possess in vans. We then drove to the 303d Fighter Group, P-47's. This outfit had failed in an attack on a bridge at ROUEN this morning, so were going to take off again. I saw the orders issued by the use of a map and an enlarged photo of the target area thrown on a screen. I consider this method of issuing orders extremely good. It was also interesting to see that the Colonel, just promoted from Lt. Colonel, was to lead the attack in person in the first plane. Most of these men had flown in about 18 missions. Their faces were tense, but not too much so. The 52 planes took off by pairs in some 7 minutes, a great piece of administrative discipline.

The soldiers all seemed to have cameras and all taking pictures of me. I feel sure that, as a result of today, we've added greatly to the entente between the ground and air forces. At lunch a perfectly strange Lt. Colonel came up and asked me to autograph a copy of "Soldier's Burial," which I wrote in the last war and which he said his daughter had secured from Little Bea. I read it over to see if it was o.k. and did as he asked. We flew back to Peover.[50]


General Patton attended the weekly briefing of his G-2 intelligence, which was secret and was very complicated. Patton talked and stated he believed the Germans would counter-attack from the southeast—ground troops always go where other ground troops go. He said nothing about the TUSA plans. He said he had written Eisenhower for permission to move the HQ south of England. He stated General Bull, Eisenhower's G-3 had turned it down so Patton went over his head.[51]

## XIX Tactical Air Command

Brigadier General O.P. "Oppie" Weyland was to be Patton's air support and was assigned to General Patton's Third Army as such. His chain of command was up the chain of command in the Army Air Corps, through the 9th Air Force, but, his XIX Tactical Air Command was to be in support of General Patton's Third Army. Though Patton was a Lt. General and Weyland was a Brigadier, they would soon develop a relationship of mutual respect and admiration. Weyland had been doing exactly what Patton had been doing, building his command. He had arrived in England in January and had since then begun building and training his command. Initially he had started out in February with only 30 officers and 77 enlisted men. Weyland had graduated from what is now Texas A&M ROTC program and worked his way up the chain of command. His command was  initially composed of the *P-51 fighter bombers. At this time, when Patton visited his command, he had 11,965 officers and enlisted men. They now had operational flying units and in addition to the P-51 Mustangs they also had the *P-47 Thunderbolt.[52]

### Mustang and Thunderbolt Fighter-Bombers

The North American Aviation P-51 Mustang was an American long-range, single-seat fighter and fighter-bomber. From late 1943, P-51Bs (supplemented by P-51Ds from mid-1944) were used by the USAAF's Eighth Air Force to escort bombers in raids over Germany.

### Data for P-51D and P-51K

<u>General Characteristics:</u>

Crew: 1
Length: 32 ft. 3 in (9.83 m)
Wingspan: 37 ft. 0 in (11.28 m)
Height: 13 ft. 4½ in (4.08 m:tail wheel on ground, vertical propeller blade.)
Wing area: 235 sq. ft. (21.83 m²)
Empty weight: 7,635 lb. (3,465 kg)
Loaded weight: 9,200 lb. (4,175 kg)
Max. takeoff weight: 12,100 lb. (5,490 kg)
Powerplant: 1 × Packard V-1650-7 liquid-cooled supercharged V-12, 1,490 hp (1,111 kW) at 3,000 rpm;[88] 1,720 hp (1,282 kW) at WEP
Zero-lift drag coefficient: 0.0163
Drag area: 3.80 sqft (0.35 m²)
Aspect ratio: 5.83

<u>Performance:</u>

Maximum speed: 437 mph (703 km/h) at 25,000 ft. (7,600 m)
Cruise speed: 362 mph (580 km/h)
Stall speed: 100 mph (160 km/h)
Range: 1,650 mi (2,755 km) with external tanks
Service ceiling: 41,900 ft. (12,800 m)
Rate of climb: 3,200 ft./min (16.3 m/s)
Wing loading: 39 lb./sqft (192 kg/m$^2$)
Power/mass: 0.18 hp/lb. (300 W/kg)
Lift-to-drag ratio: 14.6
Recommended Mach limit: 0.8

<u>Armament:</u>

Six M2 Browning 50 cal machine guns, three per wing with 1,880 total rounds (400 rounds for each on the inner pair, and 270 rounds for each of the outer two pairs) 2× hardpoints for up to 2,000 lb. (907 kg) of bombs 6 or 10× T64 5.0 in (127 mm) H.V.A.R rockets (P-51D-25, P-51K-10 on) (Grinsell, Robert, P-51 Mustangs, *The Great Great Book of WWII Airplanes*, pages 54-100)

### P-47 Thunderbolt

The Republic P-47 Thunderbolt was the largest, heaviest, and most expensive fighter aircraft in history to be powered by a single piston engine. It was heavily armed with eight .50-caliber machine guns, four per wing. When fully loaded, the P-47 weighed up to eight tons, and in the fighter-bomber ground-attack role could carry five-inch rockets or a significant bomb load of 2,500 pounds; over half the weight the B-17 bomber could carry on long-range missions. The P-47, based on the powerful Pratt & Whitney R-2800 Double Wasp radial engine, was to be very effective as a short-to-medium range escort fighter in high-altitude air-to-air combat and, when unleashed as a fighter-bomber, proved especially adept at ground attack in both the World War II European and Pacific Theaters. Armament of eight 0.50 in (12.7 mm) machine guns. These statistics will vary depending on model and modification throughout the war. (Matricardi, Paolo, Angelucci, Enzo, *Complete Book of World War II Combat Aircraft* 1933-1945 , Militarcy Press New York page 273.)[53]

[Patton]
**May 28, 1944 Sunday**

When I returned last night I found General Kenner, now Chief Medical

Inspector for General Eisenhower, here. We had a long talk. Tonight
General Gaffey is taking Kenner and me to dinner at the Bells of Peover.

Just as we were leaving, Colonel Bagby of the Air Corps, on the staff
of Leigh-Mallory, came by. He is a civilian whom we knew in Africa. He
seemed to be very much interested in selling us the idea of putting on
the "Swordhilt" operation and getting me to express an opinion, but as
he had no credentials, Gaffey and Gay wouldn't commit themselves, and I
didn't any more than speak to him.[54]

The Third U.S. Army was assigned supply priority to No. 5, which equaled eighty percent of all organization equipment. The A.C. of S. G-4 issued a memorandum to A.C. of S. G-4s of corps and divisions saying supply discipline is an essential part of training and a continuing function of command; that the standard of supply discipline is an indication of the general efficiency of an organization and its commander.[55]

May 29, 1944 Monday: There were quite a few troops in corps and division now assembled near Peover. Patton had them assemble in a place he could talk with them and gave his famous speech:

> Men, this stuff we hear about Americans wanting to stay out of this war, not wanting to fight, is a lot of bullshit; Americans love to fight traditionally. All real Americans love the sting and clash of battle, "When you were kids, you all admired the champion marble player, the fastest runner, the big league football players, the toughest boxer. Americans despise cowards. Americans play to win, all the time. I wouldn't give a hoot in hell for the man who lost and laughed. That's why Americans never lost, nor ever will lose a war, for the very thought of losing is hateful to Americans.
>
> You are not all going to die, only two (2) percent of you here, in a major battle, would die. Death must not be feared. Every man is frightened at first in battle. If he says he isn't he is a God damned liar. Some men are cowards, yes, but they fight just the same or get the hell shamed out of them, watching men who do right who are just as scared. Some get over their fright in a few minutes under fire, some take hours. For some it takes days. The real hero is the man who fights even though he is scared. But the real man never lets his fear of death overpower his honor, his sense of duty to his country, and his innate manhood. All through your army career you have bitched about what you call, "This chicken shit drilling." That is all for a purpose. Drilling and discipline must be maintained in an army, if only for one reason: Instant obedience to orders tends to create constant alertness. I don't give a damn for a man who is not always on his toes.
>
> You men are all veterans or you wouldn't be here. You are ready. A man, to continue breathing, must be alert at all times. If not, sometimes a German son-of-a-bitch will sneak up behind him and beat him to death with a sock full of shit. There are four hundred neatly marked graves somewhere in Sicily, All because one man went to sleep on his job. But they are German graves for we caught the bastards asleep before they did.

An army is a team; lives, sleeps, fights as a team. This individual heroic stuff is a lot of crap. The bilious bastards who wrote that kind of stuff for the Saturday Evening Post don't know anything more about real battles than they do about fucking. We have the finest food, the finest equipment, best spirit, and the best men in the world. Why, by God, I actually pity those sons of bitches we are going up against. By God, I do.

My men don't surrender, I don't want to hear of any soldier under my command of being captured unless he is hit. Even if you are hit, you can still fight. That is just not bullshit either. The kind of man I like was a Lieutenant in Libya, who with a Luger against his chest, jerked off his helmet, swept the gun aside with the other hand, and busted hell out of the Boche with his helmet. Then he jumped on the gun and went out and killed another German. By this time the man had a bullet through his lung. That's a man for you.

All real heroes are not story book combat fighters either. Every man in the army plays a vital role. Every little job is essential to the whole scheme. What if every truck driver suddenly decided he did not like the whine of those shells and turned yellow and jumped headlong into the ditch? He could say to himself, "They won't miss me, just one guy in a thousand." What if every man said that? Every man does his job. Where in the hell would we be now. No, thank God, Americans don't say that; every man does his job. Every man serves the whole. Every department, every unit, is very important to the vast scheme of things. The Ordnance men are needed to supply the guns, the Quartermaster to bring up the food and clothes to us for where we're going there isn't a hell of a lot to steal. Every last man in the mess hall, even the one who heats the water to keep us from getting the GI shits, has a job to do. Even the chaplain is important, for if we get killed and if he is not there to bury us, we'd all go to hell.

Each man must not only think of himself but of his buddy fighting beside him. We don't want yellow cowards in this Army. They should all be killed off like flies. If not, they will go back home after the war and breed more cowards. The brave men will breed brave men. Kill off the goddamn cowards and we'll have a nation of brave men.

One of the bravest men I ever saw in the African campaign was on top of a telegraph pole in the midst of furious fire while we were plowing toward Tunis. I stopped and asked what the hell he was doing up there at that time. He answered, "Fixing the wire, sir." "Isn't it a little unhealthy right now?" I asked. "Yes sir, but this goddamn wire's got to be fixed." There was a real soldier. There was a man who devoted all he had to his duty, no matter how great the odds, no matter how seemingly insignificant his duty might appear at the time.

You should have seen those trucks on the road to Gabes. The drivers were magnificent. All day and all night they rolled over those son-of-a-bitching roads - never stopping, never faltering from their course, with shells bursting around them all the time. We got through on good old American guts. Many of those men drove over 40 consecutive hours. Those weren't combat men. But they were soldiers with a job to do. They did it - and in a whale of a way. They were part of a team. Without them the fight would have been lost. All the links in the chain pulled together and that chain became unbreakable.

Don't forget, you don't know I'm here. No word of the fact is to be mentioned in any letters. The world is not supposed to know what the hell became of me. I'm not supposed to be commanding this Army. I'm not even supposed to be in England. Let the first bastards to find out be the goddamn Germans. Someday I want them to raise up on their hind legs and howl, "Ach, it's the goddamn Third Army and that son-of-a-bitch Patton again."

We want to get the hell over there. We want to get over there and clear the goddamn thing up. You can't win a war lying down. The quicker we clean up this goddamn mess, the quicker we can take a jaunt against the Japs and clean their nest out too, before the Marines get all the goddamn credit.

Sure, we all want to be home. We want this thing over with. The quickest way to get it over is to get the bastards. The quicker they are whipped, the quicker we go home. The shortest way home is through Berlin. When a man is lying in a shell hole, if he just stays there all day, a German will get him eventually and the hell with that idea. The hell with taking it. My men don't dig foxholes. I don't want them to. Foxholes only slow up an offensive. Keep moving. And don't give the enemy time to dig one. We'll win this war but we'll win it only by fighting and by showing the Germans we've got more guts than they do.

There is one great thing you men will all be able to say when you go home. You may thank God for it, thank God that at least 30 years from now - when you're sitting around the fireside with your grandson on your knees, and he asks you what you did in the great war - you won't have to cough and say, "I shoveled shit in Louisiana."

Alright now, you sons of bitches, you know how I feel.  I will be proud to lead you wonderful guys into battle anytime, anywhere. That's all.[56]

[Patton]
**May 29, 1944 Monday**

Kenner left this morning. Spoke to all Corps and Army troops in this vicinity, and at the end of the speech, had all field officers present themselves and gave them a special talk. I emphasized that it was the military duty of the Medical Corps to get men back to the front and that serious sick and wounded should be separated from the lightly wounded ones, not only to keep up manpower but to reassure the others.

At dinner we had General Walker, XX Corps, and his Chief of Staff, Colonel Parson Menoher, General Cook of the XII Corps with his Chief of Staff Colonel R.J. Canine; General Haislip of the XV Corps with his Chief of Staff, General Middleton of the VIII Corps with his Chief of Staff, Colonel

Cyrus H. Searcy; General Weyland and myself, all of whom are Southerners. Present also were General Gaffey and General Gay. The other members of the mess ate outside.

After dinner we had quite an informal talk. The only point I tried to stress was that, in case of doubt, follow the old Confederate maxim of "Marching to the sound of guns." I believe the dinner was very satisfactory.[57]

[Patton]
**May 30, 1944 Tuesday**

Lt. General W. H. Simpson, now commanding the Ninth U. S. Army, and his Chief of Staff, General J.E. Moore, arrived at 1430 and we had a guard of honor. After supper we gave them the short briefing, and as Colonel Maddox was absent, I took the G-3 part on myself. I did this with malice forethought because I know that General Simpson trusts too much to his staff and does not know what is going on, so I thought it was a good idea for him to see that I did. It had the desired result. He was quite impressed by the fact that I could also be my own G-3 ---of course I always am.[58]

[Gay]

Lt. General Simpson and three of his staff were guests of General Patton and spent the night.  Hobart Gay, Assistant Chief of Staff wrote that General Simpson would be an Army Commander and more than likely command the Ninth Army. At 2030 hours they were briefed on Operation Overlord.[59]

[Patton]
**May 31, 1944 Wednesday**

Simpson and I left at 0800 for Headquarters XII Corps. Codman came with us. General Moore followed in second car. I spoke to all Corps and Army troops in the area stressing the need of getting men back to the front. At 1445 Codman and I drove to Headquarters First Army at Bristol. Bradley and Hodges were there and we had a very useful evening.

I forgot to mention that this morning Lee phoned stating that he would arrive in Peover, and then be at Headquarters VIII Corps. I sent him a note saying that I could not meet him, as I was busy. What he is doing is putting on a tactical show when he actually does not know the level of supplies in his own SOS. It is very unfortunate that he both commands the SOS and acts a Deputy Theater Commander. He is good for neither.[60]

The strength of the Third U S Army on 31 May had grown to 253,500, as the G-1 Section reported to the commanding General.[61]

General Patton and General Simpson left the 3rd Army Headquarters at 0800 and drove to the headquarters of XII Corps, where General Patton delivered a fiery speech to the assembled officers and non-commissioned officers of the corps and army troops stationed in the area. Col. Codman was given a copy of the speech for safekeeping.[62]

General Lee, who was the commanding General of ETOUSA and accompanied by his G-1, G-3 and G-4, and Col. Jacobs, who commands the Western Base section, paid an official visit to Third Army Headquarters. They flew in from London and were met by General Gay and motorcycle escorted from the airport. After meeting with heads of the different staff sections, he was escorted by General Gay to the HQ of VIII Corps. From VIII Corps he was escorted to the 79th Division. All of which was overseen by General Gay.[63]

Patton drove to General Bradley's headquarters in Bristol and Chet Hansen, Bradley's aide-de-camp, gave Patton a military escort complete with M.P.s. Chet Hansen did not care much for Patton and remarked that most of Bradley's headquarters were not fans of his and all of it stemmed back to Sicily and the slapping incident.[64]

June 1, 1944 Thursday: Patton met with General Bradley in the first part of the morning and went over his final plans. General Montgomery had invited the four Army commanders to spend the night and both Patton and Bradley left and drove to Bristol in a black Packard automobile and then flew to Portsmouth to visit Monty. As General Montgomery lived nearby in Southwick, Montgomery, Bradley and Patton had tea and then went to Monty's office without aides or staff. There they went over the plans. Patton wrote that Montgomery was especially interested in Third Army plans. After supper General Dempsey and Crerar arrived. The meeting of the commanders took place that evening. In all the meeting was looked upon as pleasant and General Montgomery and Patton "got along," and had a good evening together. At the close, the generals gambled a little and a little money changed hands in a friendly card game. Afterward Patton returned to Bristol and stayed at the Holms Hotel. He was with Bradley and his staff. After he arrived they took in a movie, "The Bridge at San Luis Rey."[65]

While General Patton attended this meeting his Third Army was still shaping up. On this date the "Publicity and Psychological Warfare Section" became officially known as the G-6 Section. From the publicity standpoint, an organization to service war correspondents in the field was contemplated. This included a field hotel, transportation, conducting officers, a censorship group to censor correspondents' copy at Army level, and communications facilities by which censored copy could be transmitted on to main communications centers in England and the United States.

The Psychological Warfare Branch of the G-6 Section was organized to monitor enemy and other radio broadcasts, to originate leaflets and other publications to persuade the enemy that his cause was lost, and to lift the morale of the French citizenry in occupied areas by such means as news broadcasts by mobile units. Radio-monitored intelligence was considered of particular significance in determining the enemy situation. Personnel of this branch consisted of American and British civilians and British officers in addition to U.S. Army personnel."[66]

[Patton]

The beginning of a fateful month. Bradley went over all his final plans with me this morning. He is much more cheerful than he was, and if everything moves as planned, there will be nothing left for me to do. Naturally I hope something turns up.

Bradley and I left at 1530 and flew to Portsmouth to see General Montgomery, who lives at Southwick. General Montgomery, Bradley and I had tea and then we went to his office, and without the aid of any staff officers, went over the plans. Montgomery was especially interested in the operations of the Third Army and it was very fortunate that, two nights ago, I had rehearsed the whole thing for General Simpson, so I was very fluent. He said twice to Bradley, "Patton should take over for the Brittany, and possibly for the Rennes Operation."

After supper we had in General M.C. Dempsey, commanding the Second British Army, and General H.P. G. Crerar, commanding the Canadian Army. I was quite interested in General Montgomery's indirect approach.

The official meeting of the four Army Commanders and De Guingand, Chief of Staff for General Montgomery, took place at this time.

General Dempsey had the Corps in Sicily which failed to take Catania. He is not very impressive looking, and I take him to be a yes-man. The Canadian is better, but not impressive. De Guingand is very clever but is extremely nervous and continuously twists his long, black oily hair into little pigtails about the size of a match. General Montgomery was very anxious to get the exact location of all Command Posts on D Day, and also the succession of command down to, and including the third generation. The estimate here is that the Germans will have four divisions and 700 tanks at least 200 of which are small Renaults, against us on D Day, and up to 1800 tanks on D plus 1 if all goes as planned. However, it never does go as planned. In fact no operation I have undertaken would have succeeded had the G-2 estimate of any enemy potentiality been 50% correct. We will have some 600 tanks ashore by dark on D Day.

During our first conversation with General Montgomery he called someone in London on the telephone -- I think it was General Ismay — and told him to dissuade the Prime Minister from visiting him on Sunday. Referring to this conversation he said, "If Winnie comes, he'll not only be a great bore but also may well attract undue attention here. Why in hell doesn't he go and smoke his cigar at Dover Castle and be seen with the Lord Mayor? It would fix the Germans attention to Calais."

At dinner, General Montgomery produced a betting book and asked me whether or not England would be at war again in ten years after the close of the present war. He bet she would not, therefore, to be a sport, I had to bet she would. Also his Quartermaster offered to bet me $40.00

that an American horse would not win the next Grand National. In order
to stick up for my country I had to risk the $40.00. The only chance is
that, since England has bred no horses during the war, American horses
may have a chance.

When the port was passed, General Montgomery toasted the four Army
Commanders. Nobody did anything about it, so I said, "As the oldest Army
Commander present, I would like to propose a toast to the health of
General Montgomery and express our satisfaction in serving under him."
The lightning did not strike me. After dinner we gambled in a simple way.
At first I won too much but finally succeeded in finishing a slight loser.
I have a better impression of Monty than I had.[67]

[Patton]
**June 2, 1944 Friday**

At breakfast told Monty goodbye. He said, "I had a good time and now
we understand each other. We left by air for Bristol at 0830 and flew
over the lines of an ancient British camp and also a Roman camp on the
adjacent hills. Perhaps some old battle. Codman and I then drove to
Marlborough, the Headquarters of the XX Corps and then to Moreton-on-
Marsh to address Corps and Army troops. We then drove to Sennybridge in
Wales where we have 30 battalions of artillery doing firing. We spent the
night at a British camp with Lt. Colonel H. H. Gardiner, who is a very
charming gentleman. Hodges will be on the "Achenar" from tonight on.
Bradley will be on the "Augusta" Saturday night. Montgomery's command
post will be at Grande Campe on, and after, D plus 2.[68]

General Patton proceeded to where the XX Corps was billeted and gave another of his fiery
speeches to the men assembled to hear him. This was both an intended speech to inspire the men
and a ploy designed to show General Patton attending to business and throw off spies as to the real
invasion day and place, which was now imminent.[69]

Lt Col. Robert Allen broke down the plans in place to date:

Air offensive against Nazi Europe began January 1, 1944. Fortitude Cover plan to hide
invasion plans of Brittany included bombing Brittany positions, communications, storage
points, and beach defenses in Dieppe and Pas de Calais. Swordhilt Plan to capture Brest
and landing at Morlaix, or St. Brieuc area and seizing port from land side. Weeks ago we
were told to suspend planning on this operation.

Crossbow British designation for pilotless aircraft installations of Germans on invasion
coast. This is a real secret weapon we've been bombing and not rocket-gun position. Ski-
slide sites for these aircraft established by TIS now numbering 83 divided equally aligned
on London, Worthing and Plymouth. Most sites in Pas de Calais and Cherbourg.

According to Ninth Air Force plan, 3,200 vessels take part in invasion and will be protected by 800 aircraft.

The Navy will have:

3 US Battleships
Nevada-14 inch guns
Texas 14 inch guns
Arkansas 12 inch guns

US Cruisers
Tuscaloosa 8 inch guns
Augusta 8 inch guns
Quincy 8 inch guns
HMS Monitor –Ebris 2-15 inch guns
Cruisers
Glasgow 6 inch guns
Enterprise 6 inch guns
Hawkins 7.5 inch guns
Black Prince 5.25 guns
Bellona 5.25 guns

22 U.S. destroyers
135 LC crafts various type - gun, tank, smoke[70]

June 3, 1944 Saturday: General Bradley drove to Plymouth to head toward the invasion area and board the heavy cruiser USS Augusta.[71]

[Patton]
**June 3, 1944 Saturday**

Starting at 0800 we inspected battery positions. They were well dug in and camouflaged, but the guns were too close together. At 1030 I spoke to all the officers and the senior non-commissioned officers of Corps and Army Artillery. Also to Major General Halsted, British Commander of the Bristol area. At the close of all talks, I always have the field officers stay over for more personal and informal conversation. After lunch we saw firing by the Corps Artillery under General Ott, using forward observers, airplanes, and sound ranging. It was not too good because they took too long to switch from one target to the other. I will send General Gaffey down to pep them up.

Flew back to Peover to dinner. Nothing had happened except we have to provide 2,000 men for prisoner of war escort. Apparently Lee and company were caught wholly flat-footed.[72]

General Patton proceeded to Sunnybridge Range where he gave the same speech he had given to other units based on the substance of the speech he had put in Col. Codman's possession.  General Patton returned to headquarters at 1830 hrs.[73]

Patton attended church services in the chapel at Peover with General Gay and Gaffey.[74]

[Patton]<br>June 4, 1944 Sunday

```
All of us went to church. I am awfully restless and wish I were leading
the assault. When I visited the XII Corps on the 31st I saw a British
2-inch mortar with a range from zero to 500 yards. This should be a
valuable weapon in conjunction with our 60-mm because that instrument
will not shoot short enough, and so we have a zone from zero to about
500 yards in which we can get no vertical fire.
```
[75]

{Patton}<br>June 5, 1944 Monday

```
Today might be D-Day. I listened to the radio at 0600, but no news. In
fact there has been no news all day. I called Hughes and asked him to get
off a radio of congratulations to Alexander, Keyes, and Clark on their
success in Italy. At 0900 we received a report signed Eisenhower to the
effect: Enemy intelligence, no change. Bombarding forces still at sea.
Ships and craft in assault force at anchor, waiting. Convoy proceeding
according to plan. U. S. LST, No. 2498, sunk off Portland Bill 1600. 4th
of June no casualties.

I think that this means that the attack has been postponed until tomorrow.
Bradley hoped that this would be the case because the tide situation on
the 6th is better than that of this morning, and gives more time for
daylight naval bombardment. I still believe in night attacks.
```
[76]

Third Army was receiving "Sitrep" through intelligence channels (Sitrep was short for situational reports and were as up-to-date information that was known at the time). The invasion of France was underway and stuck at sea with bad weather. It was too late to turn back and Sitrep number 0501289 was read. It stated, "Bombarding forces still at sea, ship and craft of assault forces are at anchorage ready to proceed. Convoys proceeding according to plan.  U.S. LCT 2498 capsized and sunk afternoon of 4 June. Believed no casualties."

General Gay put into the Third Army log, which he referred to as a diary, some prophetic words, "It may be of interest to the historians reading this to note in the light of history just what the Sitrep means" He was saying the invasion was on and this was the first indication of it they had received.[77]

Patton traveled to Camp Bewdley, near Stourport, England and gave his famous speech. This speech had a dual purpose. It was highly visible as all his speeches were. It was given both to inspire the troops to show Patton in public in order to continue Operation Fortitude. While Patton was giving this speech, Operation Overlord was underway for the Normandy Invasion and Patton knew it.

This speech, unlike most of his speeches, was being recorded. There was capability to record on vinyl disks, in real time and that recording could be played back immediately. Those making the recording were from the United States Office of War Information, referred to as the O.W.I. Its job was to collect timely war information and help consolidate information for dissemination throughout the government agencies and abroad. After the recording of the speech, the disks were rushed off to the states and presented to the O.W.I. in the hopes it could be released to help with the war effort—a timely, fiery speech from none other than General Patton himself. Upon arrival, the senior men of the O.W.I. sat down with pencils in hand ready to write down the speech. Patton had been particularly fiery and profane; so much so, the speech was never released during the war. Like most things that were hushed up and made secret, it would eventually leak out. This speech was considered so profane by censorship laws at the time, it could not be printed. It did get a brief airing—but highly abbreviated—in a small publication called "Politics" in August 1945. The speech was later pieced together by a number of historians and it appears below as he is believed to have said it at the time, unedited.

Patton would be addressing a sea of soldiers and after the pomp and circumstances of introductions and a guard of honor, complete with a band, Patton came to the platform. The soldiers were called to attention and Patton came to the microphone:

Be seated. Men, this stuff that some sources sling around about America wanting out of this war, not wanting to fight, is a crock of bullshit. Americans love to fight, traditionally. All real Americans love the sting and clash of battle. You are here today for three reasons.

First, because you are here to defend your homes and your loved ones. Second, you are here for your own self-respect, because you would not want to be anywhere else. Third, you are here because you are real men and all real men like to fight.

When you, here, every one of you, were kids, you all admired the champion marble player, the fastest runner, the toughest boxer, the big league ball players, and the All-American football players. Americans love a winner. Americans will not tolerate a loser. Americans despise cowards. Americans play to win all of the time. I wouldn't give a hoot in hell for a man who lost and laughed. That's why Americans have never lost nor will ever lose a war; for the very idea of losing is hateful to an American.

You are not all going to die; only two percent of you right here today would die in a major battle. Death must not be feared. Death, in time, comes to all men. Yes, every man is scared in his first battle. If he says he's not, he's a liar. Some men are cowards but they fight the same as the brave men or they get the hell slammed out of them watching men fight who are just as scared as they are. The real hero is the man who fights even though he is scared. Some men get over their fright in a minute under fire. For some, it takes an hour. For some, it takes days. But a real man will never let his fear of death overpower his honor, his sense of duty to his country, and his innate manhood.

Battle is the most magnificent competition in which a human being can indulge. It brings out all that is best and it removes all that is base. Americans pride themselves on being He Men and they ARE He Men. Remember that the enemy is just as frightened as you are, and probably more so. They are not supermen."

All through your Army careers, you men have bitched about what you call "chicken shit drilling." That, like everything else in this Army, has a definite purpose. That purpose is alertness. Alertness must be bred into every soldier. I don't give a fuck for a man who's not always on his toes. You men are veterans or you wouldn't be here. You are ready for what's to come. A man must be alert at all times if he expects to stay alive. If you're not alert, sometime, a German son-of-an-asshole-bitch is going to sneak up behind you and beat you to death with a sock full of shit!

There are four hundred neatly marked graves somewhere in Sicily, All because one man went to sleep on the job. But they are German graves, because we caught the bastard asleep before they did.

An army is a team. It lives, sleeps, eats, and fights as a team. This individual heroic stuff is pure horse shit. The bilious bastards who write that kind of stuff for the Saturday Evening Post don't know any more about real fighting under fire than they know about fucking!

We have the finest food, the finest equipment, the best spirit, and the best men in the world. Why, by God, I actually pity those poor sons-of-bitches we're going up against. By God, I do.

My men don't surrender.  I don't want to hear of any soldier under my command being captured unless he has been hit. Even if you are hit, you can still fight back. That's not just bull shit either. The kind of man that I want in my command is just like the lieutenant in Libya, who, with a Luger against his chest, jerked off his helmet, swept the gun aside with one hand, and busted the hell out of the Kraut with his helmet. Then he jumped on the gun and went out and killed another German before they knew what the hell was coming off. And, all of that time, this man had a bullet through a lung. There was a real man!

All of the real heroes are not storybook combat fighters, either.  Every single man in this Army plays a vital role. Don't ever let up.  Don't ever think that your job is unimportant. Every man has a job to do and he must do it. Every man is a vital link in the great chain.

What if every truck driver suddenly decided that he didn't like the whine of those shells overhead, turned yellow, and jumped headlong into a ditch? The cowardly bastard could say, "Hell, they won't miss me, just one man in thousands," But, what if every man thought that way? Where in the hell would we be now? What would our country, our loved ones, our homes, even the world, be like?

No, goddamit, Americans don't think like that. Every man does his job. Every man serves the whole. Every department, every unit, is important in the vast scheme of this war. The ordnance men are needed to supply the guns and machinery of war to keep us rolling.

The Quartermaster is needed to bring up food and clothes because where we are going there isn't a hell of a lot to steal. Every last man on K.P. has a job to do, even the one who heats our water to keep us from getting the 'G.I. Shits'.

Each man must not think only of himself, but also of his buddy fighting beside him. We don't want yellow cowards in this Army. They should be killed off like flies. If not, they will go home after this war and breed more cowards. We got to save the fucking for the fighting men. The brave men will breed more brave men. Kill off the goddamned cowards and we will have a nation of brave men. One of the bravest men that I ever saw was a fellow on top of a telegraph pole in the midst of a furious fire fight in Tunisia. I stopped and asked what the hell he was doing up there at a time like that. He answered, "Fixing the wire, Sir". I asked, "Isn't that a little unhealthy right about now?" He answered, "Yes Sir, but the goddamned wire has to be fixed." I asked, "Don't those planes strafing the road bother you?" And he answered, "No, Sir, but you sure as hell do!" Now, there was a real man. A real soldier. There was a man who devoted all he had to his duty, no matter how seemingly insignificant his duty might appear at the time, no matter how great the odds.

And you should have seen those trucks on the road to Tunisia. Those drivers were magnificent. All day and all night they rolled over those son-of-a-bitching roads, never stopping, never faltering from their course, with shells bursting all around them all of the time. We got through on good old American guts. Many of those men drove for over forty consecutive hours. These men weren't combat men, but they were soldiers with a job to do. They did it, and in one hell of a way they did it. They were part of a team. Without team effort, without them, the fight would have been lost. All of the links in the chain pulled together and the chain became unbreakable.

Don't forget you men don't know that I'm here. No mention of that fact is to be made in any letters. The world is not supposed to know what the hell happened to me. I'm not supposed to be commanding this Army. I'm not even supposed to be here in England. Let the first bastards to find out be the Goddamned Germans. Someday I want to see them raise up on their piss-soaked hind legs and howl, "Jesus Christ, it's the Goddamned Third Army again and that son-of-a-fucking-bitch Patton."

We want to get the hell over there,  The quicker we clean up this goddamned mess, the quicker we can take a little jaunt against the purple pissing Japs and clean out their nest, too. Before the goddamned Marines get all of the credit.

Sure, we want to go home. We want this war over with. The quickest way to get it over with is to go get the bastards who started it. The quicker they are whipped, the quicker we can go home. The shortest way home is through Berlin and Tokyo. And when we get to Berlin I am personally going to shoot that paper hanging son-of-a-bitch Hitler. Just like I'd shoot a snake!

When a man is lying in a shell hole, if he just stays there all day, a German will get to him eventually. The hell with that idea. The hell with taking it. My men don't dig foxholes. I don't want them to. Foxholes only slow up an offensive. Keep moving. And don't give the enemy time to dig one either. We'll win this war, but we'll win it only by fighting and by showing the Germans that we've got more guts than they have or ever will have. We're not going to just shoot the sons-of-bitches, we're going to rip out their living Goddamned guts and use them to grease the treads of our tanks. We're going to murder those lousy Hun cocksuckers by the bushel-fucking-basket.

War is a bloody, killing business. You've got to spill their blood, or they will spill yours. Rip them up the belly. Shoot them in the guts. When shells are hitting all around you and you wipe the dirt off your face and realize that instead of dirt it's the blood and guts of what once was your best friend beside you, you'll know what to do!

I don't want to get any messages saying, "I am holding my position." We are not holding a Goddamned thing. Let the Germans do that. We are advancing constantly and we are not interested in holding onto anything, except the enemy's balls. We are going to twist his balls and kick the living shit out of him all of the time. Our basic plan of operation is to advance and to keep on advancing regardless of whether we have to go over, under, or through the enemy. We are going to go through him like crap through a goose; like shit through a tin horn!

From time to time there will be some complaints that we are pushing our people too hard. I don't give a good Goddamn about such complaints. I believe in the old and sound rule that an ounce of sweat will save a gallon of blood. The harder WE push, the more Germans we will kill. The more Germans we kill, the fewer of our men will be killed. Pushing means fewer casualties. I want you all to remember that.

There is one great thing that you men will all be able to say after this war is over and you are home once again. You may be thankful that twenty years from now when you are sitting by the fireplace with your grandson on your knee and he asks you what you did in the great World War II, you WON'T have to cough, shift him to the other knee and say, "Well, your granddaddy shoveled shit in Louisiana."

No, Sir, you can look him straight in the eye and say, "Son, your granddaddy rode with the Great Third Army and a son-of-a-goddamned-bitch named Georgie Patton!"[78]


Politics magazine had an editorial regarding the speech which summed it up when it said, "… this speech would be considered by later historians as typical of the style of this war as Caesar's and Washington's and Trotsky's set speeches to their troops were in their wars. At once flat and theatrical, brutal and hysterical, coarse and affected, violent and empty-in these fatal antinomies the nature of World War II reveals itself: the maximum of physical devastation accompanied by the minimum of human meaning."

[Authors note: This speech began like all of his others and again there is no evidence that it started with the words "No Bastard ever won a war".... This beginning is believed to have come from what they call "literary license" and there is no historical, factual base that he said it in his famous speech. There is always the chance that the original vinyl disk of Patton giving this speech may someday be found. This, at least, does confirm that a recording of Patton making the speech did exist at one time. ]

The staff meeting was held at 1100 in the war room. Several matters of importance were handled by various sections on 5 June, the following being examples. The A.C. of S. G-3 ordered officers from that section on duty in the War Room twenty-four hours a day to maintain situation maps. The final draft of the operation "CHASTITY" was completed, presenting the operational manner in which BELLE ISLE (M77) and the QUIBERON BAY area would be secured. XII Corps and attached units were alerted for overseas movement. Finance obtained 352,256,000 francs for use of disbursing officers. The A.C. of S. G-4 was informed it was probable that Third U.S. Army units would be equipped with major essential T/E or T/BA items of equipment, but not far in advance of operations. VIII Corps was equipped with its essential T/E equipment and arrangements were made to carry additional ammunition for 155 howitzers and eight-inch howitzer battalions.

Intelligence Estimate of Enemy strength was compiled by G-2 Colonel Oscar Koch who was certainly one of the finest intelligence officers in the European Theater. He was a brilliant, quiet man. He kept a running estimate of German and Axis forces strength totals: Where they were, how many had been killed and wounded and those that had been captured. He was in touch with every level of intelligence officers from SHAEF and British intelligence and then worked up his own estimates. He was conservative in his estimates and they were highly accurate. Patton had complete confidence in him and would often act on Koch's estimates without even the question of their accuracy. His reports were extremely detailed. As a result, Patton knew exactly where the enemy was, could be, may be going and the "who, what, where and why," as best as it could be known at the time. Colonel Koch was aided by "Ultra" information but there was far more to the intelligence of predicting, based on that raw information of radio intercepts. On this date, the day before the D-Day invasion, Colonel Koch published his enemy strength estimates to the General. The G-2 Section Estimate No. 4 was issued the same day, reporting a total of sixty and one-half enemy divisions in the west (France, Belgium and Holland). This was an increase of eight and one-half divisions since Estimate No. 1, dated 23 April. The report dealt in detail with the CHERBOURG (012) area. The COTENTIN Peninsula was estimated to include six and a half enemy divisions. The enemy had forty-five infantry and two tank battalions on or in the immediate vicinity of the CHERBOURG Peninsula. ROMMEL, with headquarters at LA ROCHE GUION (R57), was reported to be in command of Army Group B, which included the Seventh and Fifteenth German Armies and the LXXXVIII German Corps, It was also indicated that parachute divisions were being concentrated in France. The enemy had shown an increasing trend to thicken his coastal defenses and it appeared that he was building up double, and in some places triple, lines of defense. In the first line were limited employment type infantry divisions; in the second, field type infantry divisions; and in the third, Panzer divisions. History now shows the incredible accuracy of Colonel Koch's intelligence reports.[79]

## G-2
### Third U.S. Army Functional Overview

Third Army consisted of five functional branches: Administration, Combat Intelligence, Air, Security, and Auxiliary Agencies. Although the G-2 itself was relatively small, with only 19 officers and 25 enlisted men, with intelligence attached to the G-2. Koch and Colonel Robert S. Allen, his assistant G-2, coordinated and supervised the intelligence staff. The Administration Branch handled the G-2's personnel and logistic matters. It received and distributed reports from higher headquarters and disseminated G-2 products. The Combat Intelligence Branch, collected, processed, and produced intelligence for the Third Army. The branch maintained G-2 situation maps and charts, conducted briefings, and exchanged tactical information with subordinate and higher headquarters. It also prepared intelligence estimates, periodic reports, and other studies. An order of battle team from MI (Military Intelligence), specially trained on the German Army, augmented the branch.

### G-2 Air

Commanded by Colonel Harold M. Forde, produced and disseminated intelligence from visual and photographic aerial reconnaissance. Has a small planning group at army headquarters, the rest of the branch was with the XIX Tactical Air Command (TAC), the Third Army's air component. At the XIX Tactical Air Command post, the air reconnaissance coordinating officer consolidated corps and army air reconnaissance requests. At the airfields, ground liaison officers briefed and debriefed pilots and disseminated the results. At the photo squadron's airfield MI teams manned the photo center, interpreting photographs and preparing reports. The Security Branch is where Combat Intelligence related with combat operations. This branch's task was to deny information about the Third Army to the enemy. It published CI directives, arranged security training, and issued passwords and replies. Counterintelligence Corps attachments helped the branch maintain security. The Auxiliary Agencies Branch supervised and coordinated the use of intelligence attachments to the G-2. It received and disseminated these teams' reports. In addition, the Third Army Signal section coordinates Signal Intelligence with the Army corps and divisional levels.

Maj. Melvin Heflers was the G-2 ULTRA Intelligence officer and disseminated Ultra Intelligence from the British Special Liaison Unit.[80]

[Patton]
**June 6, 1944 Tuesday**

The war is on. At 0700 the BBC announced that the German radio reported Allied landing boats from west of Le Havre to the Cherbourg Peninsula. It is a nice bright day for a battle. I hope I get in before it is all over. All the reports that we have state that things are going well. Our troops--that is, British paratroops--are in Caen and British tanks are reported nearing that town. Fighting also reported on the Cherbourg-St. Lo Road, at (103-882) which must be the U. S. Airborne Troops.

I have horrible feelings that the fighting will be over before I get in but I know this is not so, as destiny means me to be in.

There is a report that all 23 bridges of the Seine west of Paris are out as the result of our bombardment. Of course, these bridges can be promptly replaced by rafts, or pontoons, if the Germans want to do so. I feel sure that all the so-called information we get over the radio is imaginary, as, from my previous experiences in landings, I know that were I on the beach I would not know a damn thing at the time of the operation, so how can the commentators know anything?

The Prime Minister and the King both made fine speeches on the landing. We failed to pick up Mr. Roosevelt's speech. I started to pack up my clothes a little bit, always hoping, I suppose, that someone will get killed and I will have to go.

General Charles Hines, Chief of the Third Army Anti-air Artillery, spent the night.[81]


When Patton was informed that the landing had occurred and the Normandy Invasion had begun, it prompted him to bring his Command Post to operational status. Directly after Colonel Koch had delivered his report, Patton entered the war room. He was exuberant and beaming. He said the following:

> Congratulations Gentlemen, the war is finally on. We aren't in it yet, but we will be very soon. When we do get in it, Third Army either will make glorious history or we won't be around to alibi why we didn't. …The secrecy on the invasion was well kept, but it is essential to continue airtight security regarding us. The Germans still do not know that Third Army is in England and it is vital this be kept from them until they find out when we kick them in the teeth.[82]


At 1100 hours a decoration ceremony was held, at which the Soldiers Medal was awarded by General Patton to Pfc. Frank Yurchak, Pvt. Charles W. Bowers, and Pvt. Carmine A. Broccio. Guard of Honor, consisting of one company of the 503rd MP Battalion and Band from the 6th Cavalry, were present.[83]


June 7, 1944 Wednesday: A staff meeting was held at 1100 hrs. They were briefed through a "Sitreps" that heaviest fighting was on "OMAHA" beach by American troops of the 1st and 29th

Divisions. Present at the staff meeting were the heads of all the staff sections. The staff studied the roads on the Cotentin and Brest Peninsulas. Several staff officers left after the meeting headed by Colonel Bratton to reconnoiter the area of VII Corps with the view of moving the HQ to that area. (In preparation of Third Army debarkation.[84])

[Patton]

Radio still full of platitudes. We hear that Omaha Beach[85] in front of VII Corps is giving trouble. It is a bad beach with a wide lagoon behind it. Until it is taken Cherbourg can't be attacked. Any delay there will be very bad for the whole operation, but we will not get a good picture of what is going on until tomorrow or the next day.

I have just found that the trouble is at Utah[86] and not Omaha beach. If they stick there it will leave a gap between us and the British.

Went for a drive in an M-29 snow buggy --- a sort of full track that can swim. I drove it. It might be useful in flooded areas. Began to pack seriously, sorting out different things. Time certainly drags on, it is only 1500 and seems 2000.[87]

[Patton]
**June 8, 1944 Thursday**

We have a staff meeting daily at 1100 and the G-2 and G-3 description of the situation as we get it, but the facts are very meager and from 18 to 24 hours old. Apparently things are not going too well and one gets the impression that people are satisfied to be holding on, rather than advancing. There will probably be some sort of a major operation in the morning.[88]

[Gay]

Staff meeting was held at 1100, at which the tactical situation incident to Operation Overlord was presented by G-2 and G-3. Reports indicated that some 45,000 troops have been unloaded over the beach at "OMAHA" as of 2200, 7 June. Patton Headquarters, TUSA, was being asked by the medical authorities to have the XX Corps moved so adequate hospital space could be shifted to where they now were, due to heavy casualties. Orders were received that the markings of corps, vehicles and shoulder patches could be marked exactly as Army regulations and that CP signs were now approved for divisions, corps and armies with the shoulder sleeve insignia. (This is significant as Third Army existence had been a closely guarded secret.) Orders were issued to Third Army to sew on their 3rd Army patches.[89]

June 9, 1944 Friday: There was a staff meeting held at 1100. The tactical situation on the continent was discussed. General Holmes and Colonel Ryan, Civil Affairs Officers of SHAEF and FUSAG, paid an official visit to HQ to inspect the Civil Affairs section.[90]


[Patton]
**June 9, 1944 Friday**

Time drags terribly. Things are clearly going badly on V Corps front at Omaha beach. I think the British are over stressing their successes.

Went over the papers in the case of Lt. Colonel Whitside Miller. I fear he will have to be reduced to his permanent rank and sent home. I sent the Third Army Inspector General down to have a final look. I came to this decision very reluctantly after I had the question carefully examined by the Third Army Inspector and had also talked to Colonel Smith, Miller's Tank Group Commander. Had Colonel Smith used due diligence, Miller would not have made as big a fool of himself as he has.

General Holmes and Colonel Ryan of the Civil Government came up to give us the dope on civil government. It is pretty hazy but will have to work. DeGaulle is making a mess of things.

Had Colonel Smith, Tank Group Commander, in to give him hell on not finding out about the Miller business sooner.[91]


June 10 1944 Saturday: A staff meeting was held at 1100 and the tactical situation was discussed as it applied to Operation Overlord. It was decided that all operational orders should be kept up to date as to be ready to embark when ordered.[92]


[Patton]
**June 10, 1944, Saturday**

D plus 4.

There is still no information on either the 700 or 8:00 radio. I think that today, or possibly yesterday, was a very critical time. Have been wearing my shoulder holster ever since D-Day so as to get myself into the spirit of the part. I suppose I am one of the few emotional soldiers who have to build up a role, but I have always hoped to be a hero, and now may be the time to attain my ambition. Talked to the Public Relations Officers of the Corps and Divisions and told them how important their function is. I want credit to go to the soldiers and junior officers. To this end they are to see that the correspondents get news of the actual front.

Got an order from ETO dated 6 June, AG 381.099 Subject: "Organization and Command of U. S. Forces", showing the stages of the operation and specifying that the 21st Army Group takes the northern group of armies and FUSAG gets the southern group, that is First and Third American Armies, when General Eisenhower takes personal command on the Continent. This is a very important paper.[93]

Patton told Beatrice through a letter to her brother Frederick Ayer, that on June 10 and he had apparently inspected his new mobile headquarters. There were three mobile headquarter vans made from 2 ½ ton ordnance trucks. He took some pictures of the three vans. These vans were to be significant and prove to be highly useful. Patton had envisioned a fluid, highly mobile warfare on the continent of Europe. An army field commander has way too much to deal with and still have to worry about billeting and the re-set up of valuable documents, charts and maps. A mobile headquarters was not uncommon but one that was used like a "travel trailer" was innovative. "I have a truck to sleep in. It is quite swell - like the cabin of a cruiser only you can stand up. There is a bed with an air mattress, a wash stand, clothes closet, desk map board, heater and a 110 volt electrical circuit with a built in radio; also sort of canvas porch effect. The horrors of war are fast departing and fear of booby traps has gone. It can also black out and has a huge map board so one can work at night. It is made out of an obsolete truck body but runs well or at least well enough.[94][95]

[Authors note: The shop portion of the van was a ST6 and was originally a small arms maintenance workshop and manufactured by Perley A. Thomas Car works High Point, North Carolina, which is known today as Thomas Buses. Sometime in March of 1944 the conversions began near Patton's Headquarters in Peover, England. In 1965, one of the original builders visited Fort Knox where the van came to be put on display after the war. An article that appeared in the "Turret" newspaper stated that Technician 5th Grade Joseph Owczarczak, "was then a "shop clerk" in charge of maintenance and repair shop of the 911th Ordnance Heavy Automotive Company. Twenty men from the company and ten French civilians actually built the vans. Mr. Joseph E. Owczarczak stated he was included because of his position in the company and his knowledge of the French language and people. He passed instructions on to the French civilians."[96] Inside the Turret Fort Knox Kentucky Friday May 7, 1965.]

LTC Paul Harkins wrote in a footnote to War As I knew It that "Once in a while it was necessary to use radio telephone, which was handled over a regular telephone system installed in the truck. One of the two telephones—incidentally, it had a green receiver—was a direct line to General Bradley and General Eisenhower. This particular telephone had a device supposed to scramble the words as they passed over the wire and come out spoken at the other end. Most of the General's oaths [profanity] were used at this device. It seemed he could never get it in phase and complained that it scrambled his words before he uttered them."[97]

**The Scrambler Telephone System**

"In 1939, the British war office requested the GPO (General Post Office in England) research and development department to design equipment that will provide 'telephonic communication that is proof against casual or intentional eavesdropping.' The system that they developed was based on a tube based Frequency Changer mainframe that 'scrambled' the speech signal using a process based on ring modulation with a 2.5kc/s (kHz) carrier signal and demodulating the incoming signal from the distant end back to baseband speech. Various telephone instruments were connected to these mainframes to be able to initiate and receive calls and to switch between clear and scrambled speech. An auxiliary unit was also available that enabled up to three telephone instruments to share one Frequency Changer mainframe and allow any of the users to 'hold' the mainframe unit for a forthcoming secure call and prevent the other users from using it at that time. This system started to be deployed through the war department network both at home and in the field from early 1940 and modified (four wire operation) Frequency Changers were built for use with radio communication. Tropicalized versions of the equipment were also manufactured for use in areas of high moisture or humidity.

During the war this equipment was known as a 'frequency changer' and then a 'scrambler' and most of the equipment was manufactured at the GPO factory in Holloway (code FH), North London, when TMC (Telephone Manufacturing Company) made the system available to commercial customers from the late 1950's, they branded the system 'Secraphone.'

The telephone instruments were based on a standard British design current at the time known as the '300' series. These instruments had a black bakelite body and were fitted with a green handset to identify them as a scrambler. The green handsets were either made of molded Urea Formaldehyde or Diakon (Lucite) but due to wartime shortages many of the handsets were black and painted green to identify them quickly. Bizarrely, the receiver (earpiece) cap was Black in the majority of cases due to the fact that the high efficiency receiver used was only available with a black cap during the wartime period.

The telephone instrument was not fitted with a dial, as the call was normally initiated by a switchboard operator elsewhere. Just below the handset, are two buttons that are used to switch between SECURE and CLEAR modes. They are commonly labeled SECRET and ENGAGE FOR SECRET or words to that effect."[98]

[Note: Since General Patton's vans were delivered to him in June of 1944, it is probable it would have been equipted with the SA5063/1 or a variant.]

### Technical Notes on the Scrambler Phone

"SA5063/1 was introduced in February 1944 for use on LB (C.B.S. 2&3) and Magneto systems (plus long lines on CB/Auto systems), this instrument consisted of a modified Tele.No.394 fitted with a Key No.303B switch assembly, 12 way line cord with a BT No.6 (20 way with metal lid) and a Green 164 handset. Due to wartime shortages Tele No.396 chassis's were sometimes used in these instruments also. The SA5063/1 was used either on a direct exchange/PBX line or with a SA5050 Auxiliary Unit to allow up to three sets of multiple.

The SA5063/1 instruments wired in parallel could access a single Frequency Changer unit. The primary difference between the SA5063/0 and the SA5063/1 is that the latter had additional security switch contacts so that other instruments wired in parallel could not eavesdrop on a scrambled conversation.

The SA5063/1 were all factory made as the 394 chassis was modified and partially hard wired to the Key No.303B. The SA5063/1 was fitted with two push buttons and a label marked SECRET and ENGAGE FOR SECRET (later SCRAMBLE and HOLD SCRAMBLER) but the

ENGAGE FOR SECRET had no function if the instrument was connected to a direct exchange line. No third button could be fitted on these instruments as there were no spare switch contacts in the central position on the Key No.303B although there is record of later labels marked PRIVATE, NORMAL, ENGAGE FOR PRIVACY suggesting that a button was fitted in this position to release the other functions without having to replace the receiver.

The phones were not a stand alone scrambler unit. They had to have a frequency changer mainframe consisting of a wooden or metal chest containing the tube based circuitry to modulate the signal and scramble or descrambled the signal into normal speech patterns. By 1944 they had introduced a unit what would run on 110 volts, which would work with most Army generators. The Patton Van and work trailer had such generators.

### Frequency Changer No 6AC

Introduced in January 1944, this CV1052 tube based unit had a power supply designed to run on either 100-110v/200-250v AC or 12v DC (via a vibrator circuit) for use in instances of main power unavailability or failure.[99]

When completed General Patton received three of the converted shop vans, he received one and the other two went to Chief of Staff Hugh Gaffey and Assistant Chief of Staff Hobart Gay. Patton envisioned a highly mobile army that would not stay in place for very long and at a moment's notice headquarters could become a highly mobile caravan. The name "Caravan" stuck and was used to mean the "Patton HQ van" specifically and his entire Third Army headquarters, when they were on the move.

[Note: The "caravan" term was used by the British before U.S. use. Patton's vehicle list from Africa included 2 "caravans."]

Patton was wearing a shoulder holster and had done so since the invasion. He wrote home to Beatrice that it would get him in the mood for battle. Owing as he was wearing a shoulder holster, he had to be carrying his M1911 .45 cal. ACP pistol. It had ivory grips with three stars embedded in the grips on both sides.

[Patton]
**June 11, 1944 Sunday**

At 1030 Gay, Codman and I went to Peover Chapel and presented Vicar Green and the two Wardens with an American flag and a bronze plate inscribed: "This flag is placed here to commemorate the fact that the Commanding General and his Staff and Members of the American Third Army worshipped here during the Second World War, 1944."

To avoid any chance of publicity, only the Vicar and the two Wardens were present. The flag and plate will not be put in place until the existence of the Third Army is published.[100]

General Gay, Col Codman and General Patton presented the rector of the Episcopal Chapel, which is situated just in rear of Peover Hall an American Flag and a plaque that Third Army Headquarters enjoyed the privilege of worshiping God in this historical chapel. Patton had done this at Casablanca and Palermo as well. The plaque and flag were accepted in the name of the Church by Vicar Green. General Patton asked that the matter be kept secret until after the departure of headquarters of Third Army. General Gay so noted in the Third Army log that General Patton had done the same thing in similar ceremonies, in the English Episcopal church, Casablanca, Morocco, and in the English Episcopal Chapel, Palermo, Sicily.

There was still a great deal of shuffling around for available space to allow for sufficient hospital to be established to administer to the wounded. Many of Patton's Third Army units were moved to facilitate this.[101]

[Smith]

Map distribution on the Continent was covered by an Operations Memorandum published 11 June. This memorandum outlined the procedure for distribution of maps in the United Kingdom to troops leaving for the Continent, both build-up or in assault, as well as for distribution on the Continent. This depot closed operations at ALTRINCHAM on 3 July and opened on the Continent in France after the arrival of Headquarters Third U.S. Army.

Several relief models were constructed to study Western France and certain fortified islands. Third U.S. Army having no model making detachment, the models were constructed by three enlisted men of the Army Topographic Battalion. Photographs were made of the models and halftone reproductions made at a final scale of approximately 1/500,000. These models were used extensively by staff sections for planning and later in operations. They were forwarded to the War Department after operations extended beyond their area of coverage. The halftone "model mosaics" made from the originals were distributed down to and including regiments. They were also later used to supplement and illustrate G-2 Order of Battle reports and the "OVERLORD" War Report.

At about the same time the terrain models were being constructed, considerable interest was demonstrated in third dimensional Vectography and, at the request of the A.C. of S. G-2, an officer from the Topographical Subsection was assigned the task of investigating facilities for their production in large quantities. Visits to LONDON and HIGH WYCOMBE, England, revealed a plant in the process of completion capable of producing 75,000 vectographs per month. These facilities were utilized by the G-2 Section for several orders of considerable size and the results were received with enthusiasm. However, the eventual fast pace of the campaign, coupled with the fact that vectographs could only be supplied from the United Kingdom, made their use impractical.

Prior to leaving the United Kingdom it was realized that there should be a reproduction unit with Army Headquarters to take care of the many small rush jobs required. It was believed that there would be many situations when the Engineer Topographic Battalion, because of its space requirements and relative immobility, would be located at a considerable distance from Army Headquarters. In forming this reproduction detachment, it was decided to take a press trailer with a Harris 20" x 22" 112" lithographic press, a camera van and a 2 1/2-ton truck, together with the necessary personnel consisting of one officer and nine enlisted men, all from the Army Topographic Battalion. This detachment proved to be of immense value in turning out rush jobs for Army Headquarters and in relieving the Army Topographic Battalion of many small jobs which might have interfered with the larger reproduction work of the battalion.

During this entire planning phase the training of all Third U.S. Army engineer units in the United Kingdom was continuously checked and coordinated. Periodic inspections were made and deficiencies in training corrected as rapidly as possible. Training activities were largely concentrated on Bailey bridging, construction and maintenance of roads, mines and booby traps, including the use of the non-metallic mine detector, and waterproofing of vehicles. The Engineer Battalion of the 2nd French Armored Division was trained in the use of Bailey and U.S. Floating Bridging.

Procurement directives covering the acquisition of real estate, billeting, and hiring of civilian labor were drawn.[102]

[Gay]
**June 12, 1944 Monday**

Generals Patton, General Gaffey, Ordnance Officer, Artillery Officer, representatives from the G-3 and Lt. Col Codman departed by air to the Western Range at 0900. Upon arrival they were given a demonstration of the 76 mm gun in the medium tank that was put on by the 6th Armored Division. (Major General Grow) It was decided that Third Army would accept 76 mm guns in sufficient quantity to equip three (3) battalions only. General Patton and company return by air to Peover at 1430.[103]

[Patton]
**June 12, 1944 Monday**

I went to Salisbury Plain by air to test the 76mm tank gun. This is an extremely accurate weapon, very easy to control, but kicks up such a blast and quantity of smoke that you cannot see the tracer on the AP shell until you have reached a range of 1500 yards. Since you get no burst from an AP, it is vital to see the tracer, and in the fighting in the hedgerows of France that tracer must be seen under 200 yards.

This gun was developed when we were fighting in the desert. Like many of

our developments, it has come into existence too late. However, since we
must utilize the weapon, we have decided to put it in the separate tank
battalions. We have also asked for 500 replacement tanks, M-4s with .75s.

There is a great deal of talk from France that the 75 mm. will not
penetrate the Panther tank nor the Tiger tank. I have personal knowledge
that they will penetrate the Tiger and, I think, the Panther.[104]

Patton still retained his sense of humor when writing home to Beatrice. He wrote that he had
read in the paper that the Germans had stated that General Patton was commanding 59 divisions
in France. Ever mindful that he should stay away from any publicity of any kind, Patton, wrote.
"It was a distinct shock to me. I will probably have to explain it in the morning."[105] This was a
confirmation that operation Fortitude was working and the Germans truly believed that General
Patton would still be leading the main invasion effort at the port of Calais. This was incredible
considering that the Normandy invasion had been underway for 6 days and pouring men and
materials on to the continent of France constantly.

[Gay]
**June 13, 1944 Tuesday**

Staff meeting was held at 1100 and G-2 gave a long discussion in reference
to the enemy possibilities as it refers to Operation Overlord.

General Patton attended the Exhibition of American Arms and Equipment at Manchester. He
then spoke to assembled Provost Marshal, Division and Corps, of Third Army.[106]

[Patton]

I went to see an exhibition of British weapons at Manchester. All the
officers and soldiers connected with the exhibition are wounded and not
useful for further front line service.[107]

[Gay]
**June 14, 1944 Wednesday**

A Staff meeting was held at 1100 and the tactical situation of Operation
Overlord was discussed. Colonel Miller of the 9th Air Force gave an
assessment of air operations to date. The staff including General Patton.
Met again at 2000 to go over a planned presentation of Operation Overlord
pending a visit of high ranking personnel visiting in the next few days.
Mistakes in the operation were so noted so as not to be repeated. One

mistake that stood out was the overloading of enlisted men with too much equipment.[108]

Told the Chief of Staff to have the staff ready to give a briefing on the present state of battle, the general plans for use of the Third Army and special plans on "Swordhilt" and "Chastity".

General Patton ordered a general assembly of the 3rd Army Headquarters and assembled was an honor guard manned by the 503rd MP battalion and participating to their left was the now official 61st Army Ground Forces Band. The Honor Guard marched forward and dipped the Third Army Colors. At that moment the Army chaplain came forward and officially blessed the flag of the Third United States Army, read some scriptures and prayed.[109]

[Gay]<br>

**June 15, 1944 Thursday**

The regular staff meeting was held at 1330 and the presentation was rehearsed. Colonel Bratton and an advanced detachment moved to Braemore to make preparations for the movement of HQ, TUSA, Group "X" to that place.[110]

[Patton]

The second dry run on the briefing was better. Lady Leese asked Mrs. Beck, Colonel Codman and me to see a play in Manchester called "Africa Star". It was very funny and excessively vulgar. At the end of the play the leading man, Leslie Henson, made a curtain speech and said the wife of the Commander of the British Eighth Army and the Commander of the American Seventh Army in Sicily were in the audience clapped for a long time. We then went backstage to meet the cast, and when we came out to get in the car there was quite a crowd, everybody all clapping and cheering. Such is fame. We took the ladies to a very nice dinner, arranged by Codman, at the Midlands Hotel and stopped at Tabley House and saw the Leicester-Warrens, who are charming and completely dried up. Lady Leese is their daughter. I told them about Mrs. Constantine-Smith and they were much amused. She is a strong Peace Party person, and is a card.[111]

[Allen]

G-2 Intelligence reported that there was a buildup in lodgment area of 11 US divisions, and 18 British divisions. There were now 171,738 US troops in France and 234,060 British troops which totaled 395,798 which had landed. The Germans were reported to have 14 ½ divisions in contact.

183

Third Army was now almost ready for operation.

Third U.S. Army Divisions lined up in the United Kingdom as follows:

DATE ASSIGNED
DIVISION THIRD U.S. ARMY FURTHER ASSIGNED TO DATE
5th Infantry* XV Corps 2 Jan
8th Infantry* XV Corps 2 Jan
4th Armored 1 Feb XV Corps 20 April
5th Armored 3 March XX Corps 9 March
6th Armored 3 March XX Corps 9 March
90th Infantry 5 March (Attached to First US Army, 27 March - 30 July)
79th Infantry 4 April VIII Corps 8 April
83d Infantry 4 April VIII Corps 8 April
28th Infantry 14 April XX Corps 14 April
2d French Armored 21 April (Attached) XII Corps (Attached) 20 May
35th Infantry 26 April XV Corps 5 May
7th Armored 26 April XX Corps 5 May
80th Infantry 11 June XII Corps 15 June

* Units assigned directly to Corps by European Theater of Operations, U.S. Army as Headquarters Third U.S. Army was in the United States on this date.[113]

[Gay]
**June 16, 1944 Friday**

Staff meeting was held at 1100. Again the tactical situation was discussed regarding Operation Overlord. Squadron commanders O'Farrell and Lambert, R.A.F. from Cranage Field, were dinner guests of General Patton.[114]

[Gay]
**June 17, 1944 Saturday**

A staff meeting was held at 1100. The daily situation of Operation Overlord was presented. Maj. Gen Silvester, commanding General of the 7th Armored Division paid an official visit to General Patton. General Gay had quite a few administrational duties to handle, which included being a go between Generals while the chief of staff was away. Arrangements were made for General Patton to speak to the assembled officers and non-commissioned officers of the 7th Armored Division on Wednesday at 1400, June 21, 1944. Colonel Bratton made arrangements with General Gay by phone to move the advanced elements of Third Army called Group "X" Hq., TUSA, to move to Braemore area Sunday, 18th of June.[115]

[Patton]

D plus 11
General Silvester, Commanding the 7th Armored Division called to report in. General Gaffey and Colonel Codman flew to Hull to inspect the 2nd French Armored Division. They think it will do well. Just heard that Major General Barton, 4th Division, and Major General McKelvie, 90th Division, had been relieved by Collins for failure to go fast enough.

    (1) Also that all spare colonels in First Army had been expended and we had to send four of ours.[116]

I doubt either the expediency or justice of such wholesale beheadings. It creates fear and lack or self-confidence. I once read a book called, "Lincoln or Lee," by an English officer, General Maurice, in which he showed that while Lee practically never relieved a general, but finished the war with those whom he started, Lincoln changed every time he had a failure, hoping for a miracle. Lee, on the other hand, was content to know the capacities, or lack of capacity, of his generals and used them accordingly.

    1 Gen. Barton was still in command of his division on July 6. B.A.P. He was sent home on December 27th after the Bulge for rest and recuperation.[117]

Colonel Tattersall, who runs the exhibition of weapons, called. Gaffey and I called on the Prime Minister of New Zealand, who spent the night with friends at Knutsford. I will send him some cars and an escort to take him to Burtonwood Airport in the morning. He seems unnecessarily unassuming.[118]

June 18, 1944 Sunday: General Patton and Gay attended church services at the chapel. General Gay was running the administration of details leading up to the activation of the move out of Third Army. He spoke with XV Corps and dealt with a French Ambulance of the 2nd French Armored Division slated to be assigned to Third Army. First Army called and requested four colonels to be taken from Third Army and assigned to 1st Army to replace losses of colonels on the battlefield. Colonels Carter, Reed, Brinson and Cornog names were given. At 1630 General Patton left for London on Official business according to General Gay's daily log.[119]

[Gay]<br>

**June 19, 1944 Monday**

The Chief of Staff called Third Army Headquarters and made arrangements for General Patton to speak to the 35th Division on Wednesday at 1030 and gave the coordinates of the airfield where the Army Commander should land.

News of one of the first casualties of Third Army was received on this date. Colonel Guenther, Chief of the P and PW Section was killed by a pilotless plane (German V1 Rocket) He was killed in a church in London.

Arrangements were made by XX Corps to test flame throwers on medium tanks of the 6th Armored Division. General Patton returned from his official visit to London. Major General Cook paid an official visit and remained as the dinner guest of General Patton. The scheduled speech to the 35th Division by General Patton was cancelled due to the impending move out of the division.[120]

[Patton]
**June 19, 1944 Monday**

Just heard on the radio at 0800 that the 9th Division has reached the west coast of Cherbourg Peninsula near Lessay. Hope so. I dreamed of Paddy Flint last night about 0300. Very vivid --- we were sitting on a roof mending a flagpole with concrete, and had some cooked ducks in a basket, which apparently we intended to eat while sitting on the roof. What this has to do with crossing the peninsula, I don't know.

Yesterday I asked for Col's. T. Q. Donaldson, Bob Sears, and again for Gordon Rogers as extra colonels.

The following data on the current operations in Normandy is of interest. The period covered is from the 6th to the 12th of June for the American Forces and from the 6th to the 10th for the British Forces.

| CASUALTIES | U.S. | BRITISH |
|---|---|---|
| Killed | 1,503 | 776 |
| Wounded | 8,163 | 3,239 |
| Missing | 4,225 | 2,854 |
| Total | 13,891 | 6,869 |

It must be remembered that during this period the size of the two armies was identical. Prisoners of war captured as of June 15, 1944: U. S., 8,513; British, 7,052.

Further data in the Italian Operations from September to June in losses are as follows:

| CASUALTIES | U. S. | BRITISH | FRENCH |
|---|---|---|---|
| Killed | 11,368 | 5,017 | 3,943 |
| Wounded | 43,487 | 23,068 | 16,000 |
| Missing | 8,723 | 9,740 | 1,268 |
| Total | 63,578 | 37,825 | 21,219 |

|                  |          |         |         |
|------------------|----------|---------|---------|
| Prisoners of War | 20,978   | 5,942   | 5,942   |

In this operation the British and American forces were about equal. The French were about one-half of either of the others. It is interesting to note that the proportion of killed to wounded is as 1 to 4 in Italy; in Normandy it is nearer 1 to 5.

Left for London by plane at 1630 and arrived at 1800 and saw Hughes. Inspected a place where one of the pilotless planes hit. It took all the leaves and many or the small branches off the trees for at least an acre, broke windows for some two blocks each way, and destroyed a large house.

The destruction varies from the center outwards. A large monastery, or nunnery, near where the bomb hit was obliterated, and the houses for about a block away had the windows broken. We heard quite a few during the night. The plane in flight sounds like a normal plane with a bad cold. When the noise stops there is a pause or about 10 seconds, and the explosion. The detonation is not very loud, but this may be due to the fact that they were not very close.

Saw a buzz bomb pass over the end of Mount Street just after breakfast. It looked very much like a small Spitfire and was going extremely fast. They are said to do 400 m.p.h. This bomb hit some distance away. Shortly afterwards, one hit very close in Oxford Street.

I went to Headquarters FUSAG, where they know nothing. I ordered a pair of trousers at Weatherills. Later I helped decorate W. H. Simpson with the Legion of Merit. Lee Scowden, Hulen[121], Hughes[122], Stearhs[123] and myself, all members or the Class of 1909, were there. Air Marshal Lee-Mallory is very anxious to see me, so I called on Smith to see if I should go. He said to do so unless I felt Mallory should call on me, as I am the senior. Such a thought had never entered my head. He said that if I did go I should listen carefully to what Mallory said and then tell him. The visit did not come off, as Mallory could not be there at the time I could. I think he is trying to get me interested in some airborne operations, and as I care very little for General Browning, the British Airborne man, I was glad not to see him. I think these planes will get peoples nerves in time.[124]

[Gay]<br>**June 20, 1944 Tuesday**

There was a staff meeting held at 1100 and the tactical situation was discussed regarding Operation Overlord. General Gaffey left the HQ and made an official visit to the headquarters of the XV Corps.[125]

[Patton]

Still we are not in it. Codman got back from London where Harkins says that they propose to put 4 corps or 4 divisions each in the First Army. That leaves little for me but I still hope for the best. "Hope Springs Eternal".[126]

[Gay]
**June 21, 1944 Wednesday**

General Summers, assistant division commander of the 80th Division paid an official visit to General Patton. He was accompanied by the Chief of Staff and A.C. of S., G-4, 80th Division. A staff meeting was held at 1100. Colonel Miller, Ninth Air Force, described in considerable detail the pilotless planes (German), a few specimens of which had been taken practically intact by the ground units of the British Air Force.

General Patton spoke to the assembled officers and selected non-commissioned officers of the 7th Armored Division. The copy of which is the same as all of the other speeches and is kept in the possession of Lt. Col. Codman.[127]

[Patton]

Flew to Tidwith and spoke to the entire 7th Armored Division. Later, talked intimately to all field officers. The Division gives a very favorable impression. I talked to all enlisted men who had served under me previously. There were about 250 of them from the old Second Armored Division, so I had them to one side and had a little talk with them. They were mostly senior non-commissioned officers and glad to see me.[128]

[Gay]
**June 22, 1944 Thursday**

The first indication that the advanced group "X" of Third Army should begin to prepare to move out. It was their job to establish the advanced Hq. to help direct the army onto the continent and move to the areas assigned. This was a huge undertaking as it had to land, move past a battle in progress and stage in an area that could be under fire at any moment.  General Gay and his aide-de-camp moved out to meet the advanced group as it prepared to cross the channel.[129]

[Patton]

Colonel Nixon, of the Ordnance Department, gave me some very interesting data today. It is a comparison between our estimates for the operation in France, which were made without knowledge of what actually happened in Italy, as compared with what actually did happen in Italy from the 23d of April to the 9th of June.

Rounds per Gun per Day

| TYPE | ROUNDS | NO. OF GUNS | OUR ESTIMATE |
| --- | --- | --- | --- |
| 3-inch | 7.7 | 360 | 42 |
| 105 | 87.4 | 530 | 59 |
| 155-how. | 41.9 | 160 | 33.3 |
| 155 gun | 33.4 | 96 | 33.3 |
| 8-inch how. | 27.7 | 48 | 33.3 |
| 8-inch gun | 27.8 | 4 | 25.0 |
| 240-how. | 23.3 | 12 | 25.0 |
| 81-mm.mortar | 21.3 | 696 | 25.0 |

With the exception of the 3-inch gun, which is an anti-tank weapon, our estimates were very close to actual and were very much above what ETOUSA is making for the operation in Normandy. I am sure that their estimates for ammunition are too low, especially in the case of 81-mm mortar shells. This may have very serious results. Called Hughes on the Scrambler and gave him data.

Made out efficiency reports for Corps Commanders, and Gaffey, Gay, Codman and Stiller.[130]

June 23, 1944 Friday: Preparation were made to proceed to the marshaling area and General Gay gave orders that the entire caravan and kitchen equipment should be kept together. Since the area was crowded, it was agreed to meet at the last available time prior to departure.

Major Sutton was the liaison to General Bradley's command, called FUSAG, which stood for First United States Army Group. He was assigned to TUSA, which was Third United States Army. He reported back to General Patton and presumably briefed Patton on operations and what the advanced part could expect.[131]

[Patton]

Nothing new. General Gullion  spent the night. He had a British female, Major McDonald, with him and I sent her to the hotel. She had the largest legs I ever saw that were not fat. He has not aged a bit since he was a cadet, although he is 64, nor, in my opinion has he gained any intelligence. When he graduated he stood at the bottom of his class.

General Gay and Captain Murnane left for France this morning.[133]

June 24, 1944 Saturday: Headquarters at Peover was beginning to attend to last minute details. Inventory of supplies to be left and taken were made. All of the supplies to be left were directed to the proper authority as the next group would occupy the Peover facilities. Guards would need to be left in place until the facilities could be turned over to the proper authorities.

The Provost Marshal announced that he would be in-convoy commander of advanced Group "X" move and that appropriate assignments be made for the forthcoming moves.[134]

In the last week of June, a G-2 Section memorandum outlining the function and policies of the Army Photo Center was concurred in by the commanding officer, 10th Reconnaissance Group. The A.C. of S. G-2 (Air) and the 10th Group commanding officer agreed to a daily photographic cover of the Army front to a depth of ten miles at 1/15,000. Pinpoints of artillery locations, bridges, and known or suspected enemy locations were to be taken on a larger scale. In slow-moving or static situations, photographic reconnaissance would be employed to the utmost, while in fluid or mobile situations tactical reconnaissance would be employed. In this period, the Engineer Technical Intelligence team reported for duty, its mission being to search for and examine captured enemy material and to send to higher echelons any new-type equipment for evaluation.[135]

[Patton]

Took occasion to compliment the staff on their work at the staff conferences this morning. I do this from time to time. As a matter of fact, I consider the staff of the Third Army better than that of the Seventh Army. The top men in each section are practically the same, and the number twos are better than we had in the Seventh.[136]

[Patton]
**June 25, 1944 Sunday**

Third Army is about to enter the War. At the 1100 staff meeting, the Chief of Staff that sections should be prepared to move in convoy to a new location on Thursday June 29th.

General Patton attended Church Service accompanied by Lt. Col. Codman. He then departed at 1500 by car to visit the 35th Infantry Division and attend the artillery fire demonstrations by the Corps artillery, XX Corps.[137]

Hear that Cherbourg has been entered, but that fighting still goes on in the streets. Had intended to fly to Tavistock in Cornwall, Headquarters 35th Division, but the weather was too bad so we drove, leaving at 1545 and arriving at 2400. It is about 350 miles by road. In the morning we will meet Ike at Exeter. Codman and I had dinner at Bristol. It is pretty badly destroyed.[138]

June 26, 1944 Monday: There was a staff conference held at 1100. Arrangements contingent as to time and route authority received from WBS for movement of the "X" Echelon, HQ, TUSA, discussed. At 1400 there was a conference of march group commanders and final arrangements of Group "X" echelon was completed.

The PRO (public relation office) prepared biographies of the three General Officers, HQ TUSA.[139]

[Patton]

Drove to Exeter and met Ike, his boy John, Kay and Lt. Colonel Gault, his British aide. We drove all over Cornwall, stopping to inspect units in the 35th (Kansas) Division. Ike made an inspection by walking through the ranks and talking briefly to numerous men. He tries to find points of common interest with them and is clever at it. Then he gets the loud speaker and tells the soldiers to fall out and gather around. He talks very familiarly to them but uses I, mine and me too much, usually exhorting them to fight well, "So that we can end this war and I can go home and go fishing."

"Fabius back to his plow." The men seem to like it and usually clap and cheer a little.

It is the style of an office seeker rather than that of a soldier. Two movie and two still photographers accompany him and take shots of his conversations and get the names of the men he is talking to. I presume these are later sent to the home town of that person, which I think has a very good effect. His theory is that by this method one gets on a level with the men. A Commander cannot command and be on the same level. At least that is my opinion. I try to arouse fighting emotion --- he tries votes --- for what?

However he was very pleasant. I had dinner with him on his special train and slept on it, getting off tomorrow at Salisbury at 0550.[140]

June 27, 1944 Tuesday: The daily briefing was held at 1100. The move was to be done with three separate convoys. There was a 'Y" echelon and a "Z" echelon and commanders were designated to command the convoys to the embarkation areas.[141]

The 2890th Engineer Technical Intelligence Team, consisting of three officers and six enlisted men, joined the Engineer Section, being attached to the Intelligence Subsection. The mission of this team was to search for and examine captured enemy materiel and to send to higher echelons for further examination and evaluation samples of any new type equipment located. The team was also immediately to disseminate to troops any information of value pertaining to new types of enemy technical engineer material.[142]

[Patton]

General Walker, Commanding General XX Corps, met me at Salisbury and we drove to see a firing problem by the Corps and Division Artillery of the XX Corps. I saw a 240mm Howitzer for the first time. It throws a 360 pound shell 25,000 yards but weighs 50 tons and is not very accurate.

There are only 2 guns to a battery and each battery has to have a scoop shovel to make the emplacements. It also has to be moved on two vehicles. The gun positions were well selected, dug in and camouflaged, but, the guns were too close together and generally in line. The local defense weapons were not out far enough in spite of all my directions on the subject. There was only one dummy battery, very badly done. There was no way to quickly remove the camouflage nets in case they catch fire.

Colonel Condor's group was an exception. He was with me in the desert and in every fight to Messina. I was disgusted with the rest and told them so.

Flew back to Peover.[143]

Lt. Col. Robert Allen placed in his journal an assessment of non-support of British General Montgomery. He stated, "Interesting Fact, I've met no English Officer who (is) very enthusiastic about Monty, and none of ours who served in North Africa or Italy very keen about him either. British seem to consider him a publicity hound. USA'ers a credit grabber."[144]

June 28, 1944 Wednesday: General Patton and the Chief of Staff departed at approximately 0900 to inspect the French 2nd Armored Division. Colonel Matthews, G-1, was acting as Chief of Staff in their absence.

The daily staff conference was held at 1100. The Provost Marshal informed the staff that final arrangements were made for the moving of "X" echelon. All questions were answered about the movement. There was a situation briefing by G-3 and G-2, the ordnance officer presented a twenty minute motion picture of the new type of mine destroyers operating attached to an M4 tank. At the conclusion the ordnance officer announced that a number of them had been assigned to Third Army.[145]

Patton loved good music and knew the importance of a good Army band. He arranged for the 6th Cavalry Regimental Band to be transferred intact on this date. They were redesignated the 61st Army Ground Forces Band.[146]

[Patton]

Inspected the French 2d Armored Division near Hull. We had hoped to fly but it was too thick, so we drove. It took nearly 4 hours.

Wherever we went there were guards of honor. The equipment was in good shape, the men clean and well turned out. The Mess is filthy and there

were six men to a small pyramidal tent with no beds nor mattresses. All
the men were well and anxious to fight. I wore my two French pins and they
gave me another. Gaffey and Codman were along. Called on the Leicester-
Warren's to say goodbye. General Cook spent the night. All the trucks
leave in the morning at 0600.[147]

June 29, 1944 Thursday: Army Headquarters* The movement of Echelon "X" commenced at
0400. Group "X" of Headquarters was directed to move by motor transport to Breamore.

Army Headquarters moved by motor from Peover and Toft Camps to the area around
BREAMORE, nineteen miles west of Southampton.[148]

[Patton]

Took my extra clothes to the Stockdales at Fern Hill, Alderley Edge,
Cheshire. We gave them a barrel of Marsala Wine which Colonel Sears had
captured in Sicily and sent to us. We also gave some to the Leicester-
Warrens.
      We hear from Harkins that FUSAG wants to run a show scheduled for
Third Army, as a task force run by them. Gaffey went to London to try and
stop it.[149]

June 30, 1944 Friday: Operation at Peover was closed at 0800. General Patton departed for
Breamore CP by plane at 1000.[150]

[Patton]

Took off in a B-26 for Breamore House (Hampshire), arriving at 1330 at
an operational airfield with a group of P-47s on it. They have been up
daily and have had only one casualty, and that from Anti-air. Breamore
is said to be the finest example of Elizabethan architecture in England.
It is huge. About 100 years ago it was gutted by fire and all the paneling
burned. Some of it has since been replaced. There is an old Saxon Church
near here; that is, there are fragments of a Saxon Altar. The present
church is built out of bits of flint and is at least a thousand years
old. It is the same construction as the Chateau Gaillard in Normandy. I
was very pleased when I spotted the original Saxon window and afterwards
confirmed this by reading a book on the church. Owner, Sir E. Hulse, is
a brigadier in the RAF in the Far East. Family is broke.[151]

G-1 Section reported Third Army strength at 264,843.[152]

July 1, 1944 Saturday: The Third Army Headquarters had now moved to Breamore and the war
room was set up and at 1100 hours, the staff meeting started. General Patton attended the meeting
as it was a planning meeting and all preparations had to be exactly right as there was little time to

correct problems. General Gaffey arrived from London at 1830.[153]


[Patton]

Dropped a blackout cover on my toe and will probably lose the nail. Fortunately, Sgt. Meeks' feet are bigger than mine by several sizes, so I am wearing one of his boots, which keeps the pressure off my toe.  Harkins states that we will not go to France until the end of July. This is a very bad disappointment.

The Montague girl, the daughter-in-law of the man who rents Breamor House, has just been killed in an automobile accident. We sent some flowers and a car to take her father and mother-in-law to the scene of the accident. She ran into one of our SOS trucks. Her husband, who is Montague's son, is fighting in Italy, and the parents have futile hopes that he can get back to the funeral. They asked me my opinion, and I could not be very encouraging.[154]


Willie, who was unaware of the war and where he would be following his master, found a lady friend at Breamore. Willie decided to have a love affair with his lady friend in a most public moment. Willie later was seen roaming the grounds with his new found love and many talked of his quite public display of affections as they would have had they had same encounter themselves with a lady friend of their own.[155]

## Order of Battle

Few people understand what the continent of Europe was about to become given the number of American troops that were about to pour into France. General Dwight David Eisenhower was soon to become the commander in chief of the largest army ever assembled on the continent of Europe. His Command was called Supreme Headquarters Allied Expeditionary Forces simply called SHAEF for short. In fact, it was not just a single army but a mass of many armies.  There were actually three complete armies assembled in a group command. General Bradley was the 12th Army Group commander. His Army Group was comprised of the First, Third and Ninth Armies and the two air forces; the US Strategic Air Forces and the Allied Expeditionary Air Forces.  General Bradley's opposite was British General Montgomery who commanded the 21st Army Group. He was also the ground commander for the invasion. These commands were just that: Headquarters commands with large staffs. They had to be since they had huge numbers of men and materials under them they had to move and engage in combat. The largest fighting forces under an Army command were Corps. Each Army would have from two to four corps established under it. Three corps was the TOE best suggestion but necessity and the fog of war was always to trump the paper organization. The Table of Organization of July 1st was to have seven corps in the ground forces and three corps in the air forces. Third Army was to have the Fifteenth, Twelfth and Twentieth Corps assigned to it. A corps had several divisions assigned to it. They could be Armored, Infantry or Airborne. These divisions and even the corps were considered to be fluid and could be moved and reassigned to other corps or armies depending on the battlefield situation. As of July 1st Third Army was to have the 5th, 8th and 35th Infantry divisions and 4th Armored Division which were to be assigned to 15th Corps. The 80th Infantry Division and the 5th Armored Division were slated to be assigned to the 12th Corps. The 28th Infantry Division and the 6th and 7th Armored Divisions were to be slated to the 20th corps. Assigned directly to 3rd Army Headquarters was first I Tank destroyer brigade, the 33rd Field Artillery Brigade and the 38th Anti-Aircraft Brigade. All of this was on paper and put out on a chart issued by the War Department's statistical branch on July 1st 1944. Needless to say, this organizational chart was soon obsolete and changed probably before the ink was dry. It does, however, give a sense of the proposed organization of forces that were to come ashore or were coming ashore at that date. All of this was carefully planned out, and the units were stationed in England ready to depart and land in France. The actual number of men and materiel in all of SHAEF was only known in generalities and paper authorized strengths never equaled real strengths in the field. Either real or paper strengths still presented a formidable task of moving all of it into Europe. General Patton was aware of all of the logistical issues and commanded his Third Army from the top down and the ground up. No detail was too small to be ignored.[156]


July 2, 1944 Sunday: The daily staff meeting was held at 1000 and the G-3 presented the outline of the First Army Attack Plan. Staff sections were alerted for a move on approximately the 5th of July.

 At 1600 orders were received directing the move to begin on or about the 4th of July. General Hobart Gay, Assistant Chief of Staff, in a hurry to get back to England from France and apparently unable to catch a flight arriving close enough to the staging area at Breamore, returned from visiting the front in France by way of a British PT Boat. General Gay brought news that some of the artillery assigned to Third Army's VIII Corps was torpedoed while heading toward France and received heavy losses. He arrived at Third Army Headquarters at Breamore 1630.


There was a special staff meeting called which all Echelon chiefs were called to attend at 1830 hours. The final instructions for the move were issued with regards to water proofing, spotting for loading, and general arrangements for convoy movement to the loading zone.

 General Patton addressed the conference briefly.[157]


[Patton]

We were called up over the telephone this morning from the BUCO (Build Up Command Office) Headquarters stating that we leave for France on the 5th. I do not understand the significance of this, but it is apparently correct. Hughes came down to lunch and was as pleased as we were. Wrote a paper, which he will get to Ike, showing the striking similarity between the Schlieffen Plan and the situation we now occupy in Normandy. All we have to do is to change the pivot from Alsace to Caen, and you have it.

By landing at Morlaix with two infantry and one armored division, we can
make a rear attack on the Germans confronting the First U. S. Army, and
then driving on to the line Alencon-Argentan, and thereafter on Evreux
or Chartres, depending on circumstances, we will really pull a coup. On
the other hand, if we play safe and keep on attacking with articulated
lines driving to the south, we will die of old age before we finish. I
dressed my paper up with the names of Scharnhorst, Clausewitz and Moltke
so as to catch Ike's eye. I hope he reads it. I have no ambition to be
credited with the idea so long as I get the pleasure of executing it.
It is a good paper. However, the same thing could be affected by placing
one or two armored divisions abreast and going straight down the road,
covering the leading elements with air bursts. I am sure that such a
method, while probably expensive in tanks, due primarily to mines, would
insure our breaking through to Avranches from our present position in not
more than two days. This plan would have the advantage of not requiring
setting up an amphibious operation. On the other hand, it is so bold that
it would never be approved.[158]

Verbal orders were received from higher headquarters to prepare for immediate movement to
the Continent.[159]

July 3, 1944 Monday: The 1100 staff meeting was held. General Gay explained the tactical
situation as it existed and as it pertained in particular to the VIII Corps. General Gay explained
that the drive south was to start at 0600 with the four corps abreast, the VIII was on the right.
Patton's Corps commanders, Maj. Gen. Walker, Maj. Gen. Haislip and Maj. Gen. Cook, came to
Headquarters. In addition, British Major General Miller came to headquarters.

Note, the interest in the Corp's attack commencing in France was part of the planned
maneuvers to create a tactical situation to allow a breakout of Third Army, which would be
Operation Cobra. The 1970 movie suggested it was not known to General Patton until he arrived
at General Bradley's CP in France. This was not true and it was the reason Third Army was not
landed immediately along with all of the other troops under Bradley's command. It was not yet
known how long it would take to achieve a space large enough to assemble the 3rd Army for a
breakout but it was part of the plan now in progress.

News arrived that Col. Neil Fickett, Commanding Officer of the 6th Cavalry Group, had
been injured in an accident and hospitalized. Colonel Cornog was given the temporary assignment
to command the Group, which Patton considered essential to his communication network.

[Patton]

Hughes left and I had Walker, Cook and Haislip for lunch and final
movement instructions. General Miller, British, who used to be Alex's
"HQ" in Sicily also came. Called General Lee at 1430 on phone to ask for
an increase of 6 officers and 63 enlisted men for Corps Headquarters. The
number of officers has been doubled and the number of men increased by

60% with no added housekeeping help. When I phoned I heard Lee tell his
secretary that he did not wish to be disturbed at a conference. She then
said he had stepped out. I said, "I just heard his voice and will either
speak to him now or call General Eisenhower and report the affair." Lee
came on the telephone, very suave as usual. His rank has gone to his
head. The soldiers say SOS means "shit on a shingle." They may be right.
I called on Captain Montague, the lessor of Breamore House whose daughter
had been killed in a motor accident.[160]

Late in the afternoon, the staff of Third Army was given word that there would be a late staff meeting at 1730 hours. Col Wallace wrote in his book that this "was highly unusual and so close to the anticipation of becoming operational, there was great excitement in the air. The staff section chiefs were assembled and at exactly 1730 hours, General Patton strode quickly but quietly in and took his place before us. He looked over for a brief moment at his staff and said, "Gentlemen, the moment for which we have all been working and training so long has at last arrived. Tomorrow we go to war! I congratulate you. And I prophesy that your names and the name of Third Army will go down in history – or they will go down in the records of the Grave Registration Bureau. Thank you and Good Night!"[161]

### Jean Gordon

July 4, 1944 Tuesday: Everett Hughes met Patton as he arrived to meet Jean Gordon, Bee's niece. She was in the ARC, which stood for American Red Cross, and was in the Doughnut Girl Clubmobile program. They were to have dinner at the Dorchester Hotel with the American Society in Eylon, which was run by a Mr. Harvey D. Gibson, Red Cross Commissioner in Great Britain, and there was also in attendance the head of the British YWCA.(Young Women's Christian Association). There was talk about the Allied Clubs (set up to assist the soldiers away from home) and Mrs. Gibson commented that General Hughes was "a breath of fresh air," and he, J.P., his female aide, Miss Gordon and Patton went out for drinks. Hughes remarked in his diary that she was "quite a gal" and George "did not want her presence known."[162]

[Author's note. There were at least two good reasons for Patton not wanting his niece's presence known. The first of which were the ever-present accusations that she and her uncle had more than a casual relationship and were intimate, which was vehemently denied by the men around Patton both during and after the war. The second reason was that she could be used by the enemy if captured and it was not a good idea to let anyone know who was related to whom in time of war, as there were spies everywhere. Operation Fortitude depended on the spies watching Patton's every move.

There was, of course, much more to this. In 1936, when Patton was assigned as G-2 in Hawaii, he has been infatuated with Jean. There was widely believed to be a love affair going on between her and "Georgie" and Beatrice was sure of it. There is no evidence that the affair continued after that, no real evidence that it occurred and no evidence it did not; it remains one of pure speculation, but it seemed to be real at the time and would fuel much speculation each time they were seen together. Patton himself tended to suggest he was intimate with her to his friend Everett Hughes. Jean was the daughter of Beatrice's half-sister Louise and was the same age as Bea's daughter Ruth Ellen. Both of Patton's daughters had grown up with their cousin Jean and she had been a bridesmaid at both of the daughters' weddings. Whether she was having an affair with her uncle or not, Ruth Ellen, Beatrice and Everett Hughes believed it to be.][163]

### The Doughnut Girls

The Red Cross Doughnut Girls were not an unorganized group of unsupervised young ladies who just showed up to serve doughnuts. Quite the contrary. This program was approved and endorsed by General Eisenhower. It was uniformed, had specific training and there was a rigid requirement to be accepted. "In planning for the European offensive, General Dwight D. Eisenhower asked the ARC and Gibson to make Clubmobile services available to his forces as soon after the invasion as possible. Eisenhower expressed the belief that Clubmobile services were well suited to provide morale support to the highly mobile invasion force. Early in 1944, ARC leaders began implementing plans for this new mission that would require an innovative design for the trucks and the logistics of transporting and disbursing thousands of pounds of supplies. In the end, ten Clubmobile groups were planned for deployment to the continent."

Qualifications:

1. At least twenty-five years of age, and 29 preferably not more than thirty
2. Well educated, including at least two years of college education, and to have had some work experience.
3. Had to be in good physical health, display an acceptably upbeat and positive attitude and social skills.
4. Only attractive women were selected for service with the ARC.

It was highly recommended the women be single as they were in or near a combat zone. The American Red Cross ARC Doughnut "Girls" carried the informal rank of captain, which was granted to ensure that in case of capture they would be treated as officers. The work was difficult and daily work required women to load flour bags, carrying coffee urns, stocking the vehicles with supplies, preparing donuts and coffee in massive amounts for hours at a time, and driving large trucks through unfamiliar and ill-suited territory. These tasks were complicated by weather, often cold and wet. They had to prepare service for 500 men at a time and cook 1000 doughnuts to accommodate them. This required 70 pounds of flour, 12 pounds of coffee and the other ingredients to prepare to serve and service the troops.

The training was also difficult. They had to learn to drive the converted GMC 6x6 truck, do maintenance, and maneuver it in field conditions.

The women were expected to maintain their uniforms, hygiene and camp equipment in the field under the same adverse conditions as the soldiers the field. They would have to bath in the field, learn to shampoo their hair in a helmet and still be "glamorous to the GI" to remind him at home, when he did get a chance to stop and get a doughnut.

They also had to be aware of their surroundings. In the ETO, they often could find themselves in areas they could have to defend themselves. Though not spoken off, many would have access to firearms. (Ramsey, Julia A. "'Girls' in Name Only: A Study of American Red Cross Volunteers on the Frontlines of World War II," Master's Thesis, Auburn University, 2011.)[164]

[Patton]

Went to London at 1430 and arrived at 1700 to see Hughes. He was very dubious about my going to France, as he feared I would not be wanted when I got there. He had a similar experience the first time he went. I found that the order to go to France is simply in consonance with the program of shipment, and the advance in time is due to the fact that more shipping is available than had been contemplated.

Had a very pleasant night in spite of the "Flying Dutchmen" who came in quite regularly. We will leave for France by air on the morning of the 6th. Sent Gay on ahead to pick a place for our headquarters.[165]

Echelon "X" moved from Breamore Hall into the embarkation area and started boarding LST's and MT's destined for the Continent.

Well into the night, the Third Army Headquarters moved in hundreds of vehicles toward the shore of England at Southhampton to be loaded into LST ships.

[Note: There is complete list of exactly what was transported by ships on this date in the index section in the back of the book. This list was taken from the After Action Reports dated on the 5th of July. It is a great interest to historians as it outlines exactly what the headquarters of Third Army was composed of, how many men were assigned and their duties. It also gives the official designation of the vehicles assigned to Third Army. The Third Army headquarters was to be completely mobile, camped under canvas and camouflage netting and capable of rapid mobility at a moment's notice—and it was. No other Army in history was so designed up to this point in modern warfare. It became a model to follow in years to come.]

July 5, 1944 Wednesday: NEHOU, FRANCE. General Gay departed by air at 1040 for the Continent and arrived at the landing strip, Omaha beach, at 1130. He immediately went to FUSA (First United States Army; General Bradley's command) for the purpose for receiving directions as to where to select bivouac areas. He was told that it should be placed in the triangle Ste. Sauveur-Bricquebec-Barnesville, but if it extended out of this triangle to some extent, it would make no difference. From Hq. FUSA, General Gay went to HQ, Special Engineer Brigade and contacted General Gaffey and VIII Corps Hq. From 1900 until dark they walked the selected bivouac areas for Hq. Third Army.

General Patton returned to Breamore Hall.

[Patton]

Went to see Ike at 1500. He was just back from France and seemed cheerful, but a little fed up with Monty's lack of drive. He is swinging over to take personal command of the fighting, but is still temporizing. He cannot bring himself to take the plunge. His current plan is for four American armies, with one small American army for Montgomery, as the British have reached their limit of 14 divisions; Bradley to have three large American armies with me on the southern flank. Why an American army has to go with Montgomery, I do not see, except to save the face of the little monkey. Six "Flying Dutchmen" hit near 22 Mount Street between 5:45 PM and 8:00 PM, all near enough to shake the place. Left for Breamore at 8:45. I was glad to leave London.

General Patton wrote in his diary his soldier's prayer on this date.

A SOLDIER'S PRAYER

By

Lt. General G. S. Patton, Jr.

God of our Fathers, who by land and sea has ever led us on to victory, please continue your inspiring guidance in this the greatest of our conflicts.

Strengthen my soul so that the weakening instinct of self-preservation, which besets all of us in battle, shall not blind me to my duty, to my own manhood, to the glory of my calling, and to my responsibility to my fellow soldiers.

Grant to our armed forces that disciplined valor and mutual confidence which insures success in war

Let me not mourn for the men who have died fighting, but rather let me be glad that such heroes have lived.

If it be my lot to die, let me do so with courage and honor in a manner which will bring the greatest harm to the enemy, and please, oh Lord, protect and guide those I shall leave behind.

Give us the victory, Lord.[166]


Echelon "X", HQ. TUSA completed its embarkation and Echelon "Y" HQ. TUSA in part moved to Breamore Hall.

On July 5th, the headquarters staff of Third Army loaded onto LSTs for France. They disembarked at Utah Beach, traveled over the beaches and were directed by 3rd Army MPs toward the Apple Orchards at Nehou, approximately 15 miles south of Cherbourg.

Concurrently, in England, the next elements of Patton's Third Army Headquarters began to move.[167]


**Swashbuckling, Sulfur-breathing, Pearl-handled "Superman"?**

March 25th, 1945

Thoughts jotted down during the flight back: It is strange how imperfectly and incompletely the hard, bright light of modern publicity reveals the character of those on whom it is directed. Take General Patton. What impression of him as a man has the public received from the press? Primarily, I should think, a kind of two-dimensional colored cartoon of a swashbuckling, sulfur-breathing, pearl-handled "superman" packaged in tinsel and labeled Old Blood-and-Guts. It is fair to say the General has done little to discourage this type of portraiture, and on occasion has even played up to it. Skill in public relations as such has never been his forte. His whole being is concentrated on the job in hand; his standards, values, and preoccupations antedate the technique of present-day publicity. For what seems to have escaped most contemporary journalists is the fact that General Patton is not a contemporary figure.

To be sure, he has contributed to the science of warfare professional proficiency of the highest modern order. More significantly, however, and it is this that sets him apart, he brings to the art of command in this day and age the norms and antique virtues of the classic warrior. To him the concepts of duty, patriotism, fame, honor, glory are not mere abstractions, nor the shopworn ingredients of Memorial Day speeches. They are basic realities - self-evident, controlling. Bravery is the highest virtue, cowardice the deadliest sin.  For him, seeking the bubble reputation even in the cannon's mouth holds no hint of irony, and death upon the battlefield is a consummation devoutly to be wished. In the time of Roger the Norman or in ancient Rome, General Patton would have felt completely at home - with one important qualification having to do with an overriding characteristic of the General himself.

I am sure you are aware of the quality I have in mind.  To those close to him it is obvious.  To his commands in the field it is a quality sensed rather than perceived. To the public at large it has been overshadowed by the publicized version. And yet the voltage of that quality was potent enough to galvanize hundreds of mothers, fathers, grandparents, wives, sisters into pouring their hearts out on paper.  I refer, of course, to the voluminous mail which flooded our headquarters at Palermo after the two soldier-slapping incidents, and which it fell to me to classify.  It was not a difficult job.  There was no middle ground.  Every letter was either for the General or against him.  The letters of protest, in many cases both obscene and anonymous, channel themselves to ringing the changes on "You are a cowardly so-and-so for striking a defenseless enlisted man." The pro-General letters, mostly from relatives of servicemen, also bore a close resemblance one to all other. "I want you to know we are proud our son is serving in your Army," a typical letter ran. "From the newspaper accounts we are not clear as to exactly what you did and why, but we want you to know we are for you.  Keep going and God bless you."

In the first tabulation, all communications from personal friends of the General were eliminated. The results: letters of protest, 11%, letters in support, 89%.

It seemed to me at the time - and still does - that even more striking than the decisive percentages was the fact that not one of those who expressed their good will had the opportunity or the possibility of knowing at firsthand that side of the General's nature which remain thoroughly unpublicized: the side of his nature which on countless occasions in Africa, Sicily, France, Luxembourg, and now Germany impelled him to visit, unheralded and unsung, the wounded of our field and base hospitals.  Not one of his correspondents had seen him standing, or sitting, or kneeling by a bedside or cot, the hand of a desperately wounded soldier in his - the murmured words of encouragement and the pain in his own eyes, the measure of this man's innate humanity and kindliness. Yet, surely, if mysteriously, these correspondents must have sensed the quality which seemingly eluded the commentators and the politicians - the quality of compassion. The simple truth of the matter is that all his life General Patton has been obsessed with an almost neurotic aversion to suffering and cruelty in any and every form. It is this quality - so difficult, nay, impossible to square with the business of war making - which sheds light upon some of the contradictions and anomalies of the General's character.

The tough vocabulary, the emphasis on frightfulness, the simulated rages, so many symptoms of the conflict between his inner nature and the demands of his chosen medium. The disparity sometimes, though not often, leads him astray. After bawling out a delinquent in his own inimitable manner it is not unusual for the General to remark, "A good cussing-out is the only way. I've got to make them more scared of me than they are of the Germans."

Well, on such matters one doesn't argue with the General, but when you come right down to it who, other than the enemy, is scared of him? Not his staff, nor his household, nor his drivers and orderlies. Not his dog, at whom in public he thunders and in private croons a kind of baby talk. Not the exhausted division commander whom the General has brought back to his own quarters, patted on the back, put to bed, and, a day or two later, sent off refreshed, rejuvenated, recharged - confident in the knowledge that whatever is in store, he will be backed to the hilt. Certainly not the tanker or the rifleman up front to whom the name of Patton means the captain of the winning team, a captain who demands much, but nothing that he himself has not done or is not prepared to do. No, other than the congenital shirker, the phony, and the misfit, I can think of no one under his command who has reason to be unduly scared of the General. His gift for leadership is based not on fear but rather upon a dynamism of total dedication and communicable humanity.

There are signs that already the old gory legend of the profane, hard drinking, hard-living primitive is beginning to wear thin, and since, upon inspection, even its superficial aspects fail to pass muster, future biographers and historians should have little difficulty in piercing its speciousness. The General's language - picturesque; when addressing troops, freely sprinkled - mostly for laughs - with god-dams, S.O.B.'s, a few four-letter words, and those scatological rather than pornographic, as our old friend, le professeur Louis Allard, used to say of Rabelais. In more than two years under the same roof, tent, or sky, I have never heard the General tell a really sacrilegious or dirty story or encourage the telling of one. Alcoholic intake? Except on very rare occasions, an average of one whiskey-and-water before the evening meal, and possibly (when and if available) a glass of wine with it. The fair sex? Any serious interest on the General's part in any women other than the members of his own family would be news to me.  Tobacco? Here we are on thin ice, for, to the General, cigars could indeed be a dissipation.  His nicotine tolerance is low and tobacco irritates his throat. However, a household conspiracy organized by Charley Odom in which humidors and cigar boxes are mysteriously emptied or just disappear has proved reasonably successful in holding him down to three or less stogies a day.

What does that leave? Gluttony perhaps? Well, the General's breakfast consists of cereal, two eggs, tea, and toast.  Lunch, one course usually, cold meat or hash, and a dessert.  Dinner, soup, an entree or roast, vegetables when available, dessert, coffee.  Since the beginning of the French campaign, he has on trips to the front eliminated lunch entirely, as a waste of time. This means that Al and I are reduced to concealing dry rations in our pockets with the hope of nibbling them unnoticed. To this end a division latrine often serves a useful and double purpose.

Only once since North Africa do I remember the General taking any particular interest in food, other than that it be simple, wholesome, and not too hot.  It was upon our return to the royal palace at Palermo after that rugged alfresco session up in the mountains and olive groves of Sicily.  It was our first sit-down dinner with knives and forks and a tablecloth in weeks.  The meat was overcooked and one of the vegetables burned.

"What we need is a good caterer," the General said. "I wish I could remember the name of the man who used to produce those chicken croquette lunches around Myopia before the war."

"Creed?" I hazarded.

"That's the man," the General said. "Find out where he is and get him over here by air right away."

It took thirteen months and as many top-priority cables for the General's requisition to catch up with Captain Edward Creed on duty at the Quartermaster School, Fort Lee.  Since joining us at Etain, he has reorganized not only the General's mess but the entire system of food supply and service to all Third Army hospitals.  In terms of morale dividends, the Captain has already proved a blue-chip investment.

And now I see the airstrip ahead so will close this rather rambling letter with an incident having perhaps a certain bearing on the foregoing. It was early morning in our first Normandy apple orchard and I had knocked on the door of the General's trailer.  He had finished shaving and was standing before the glass pensively stroking his jaw.

"Codman," he said without turning round, "I wish to hell I had a real fighting face."

 "I should have thought it was a reasonable facsimile," I began.

"No, no, no," he said impatiently. "You are either born with a fighting face or you are not. There are a lot of them in Third Army, Paddy Flynn, Stiller, and many others. Having practiced for hours in front of the mirror, I can work up a fairly ferocious expression, but I have not got, and never will have, a natural-born fighting face."

And there for the moment let us leave the General's unresolved problem - the reconciliation of the fighting soldier and the gentle man.

Codman, *Drive* 270 -275

[1] Blumenson, *The Patton Papers* Vol.2 450-451; D'Este, Eisenhower, *A Soldier's Life* 591-594.

[2] Blumenson, *The Patton Papers* Vol.2 450-451.

[3] Patton, Diary entry May 4, 1944.

[4] Patton, Diary entry May 5, 1944.

[5] Allen, Journal entry May 5, 1944.

[6] Third Army. After Action Reports, Vol.2 Staff Reports, Section Reports, G-3 Part 4.

[7] Diaz family collection.

[8] Patton, Diary entry May 6, 1944.

[9] Sweetman, Bill, *The Great Great Book of WWII Airplanes*, pages 317-367

[10] Patton, Diary entry May 7, 1944.

[11] Allen, Journal entry May 7 1944.

[12] Rohmer 42-43.

[13] Patton, Diary entry May 8, 1944.

[14] Third Army. After Action Reports, Vol.2 Annex Section.

[15] Allen, Journal entry May 8, 1944.

[16] Patton, Diary entry May 9, 1944.

[17] Patton, Diary entry May 10, 1944.

[18] Allen, Journal entry May 10 1944.

[19] Patton, Diary entry May 11, 1944.

[20] Rankin.

[21] Patton, Diary entry May 13, 1944.

[22] Hughes, entry May 14-16,17, 1944.

[23] Patton, Diary entry May 13, 1944.

[24] Patton, Diary entry May 14, 1944.

[25] 301st Signal Corp Battalion 30.

[26] Diaz family collection.

[27] Blumenson, *The Patton Papers* Vol.2 456; D'Este, *Patton: A Genius for War* 595-596; Hirshson 568.

[28] Patton, Diary entry May 14, 1944.

[29] Blumenson, *The Patton Papers* Vol.2 456; D'Este, *Patton: A Genius for War* 595-596; Hirshson 568.

[30] Patton, Diary entry May 16, 1944.

[31] Patton, Diary entry May 17, 1944.

[32] Patton, Diary entry May 18, 1944.

[33] Third Army, After Action Reports Vol.1 Planning in the United Kingdom 13.

[34] Polk, James H.World War Letters and notes of Colonel Polk 40-41; 63.

[35] Patton, Diary entry May 19, 1944.

[36] Third Army, After Action Reports, Vol. 2

[37] Patton, Diary entry May 20, 1944.

[38] C. C. Smith, *My War Years, 1940-46: Service on Gen. Patton's Third Army Staff* 45.

[39] Allen, Journal entry, May 21, 1944 entry.

[40] Patton, Diary entry May 22, 1944.

[41] Third Army, After Action Reports, Vol.1 Planning in the United Kingdom 13.

[42] Allen, Journal entry May 22, 1944.

[43] Allen, Journal entry May 23, 1944.

[44] Patton, Diary entry May 24, 1944.

[45] Third Army After Action Reports, Vol.1 Planning in the United Kingdom 13.

[46] Allen, Journal entry, May 24, 1944.

[47] Patton, Diary entry May 25, 1944.

[48] Patton, Diary entry May 26, 1944.

[49] Third Army, After Action Reports, Vol.1 Planning in the United Kingdom 13.

[50] Patton, Diary entry May 27, 1944.

[51] Allen, Journal entry, May 27, 1944.

[52] Spires 36-40.

[53] Matricardi, Paolo, Angelucci, Enzo, *Complete Book of World War II Combat Aircraft* 1933-1945, Military Press, New York page 273.

[54] Patton, Diary entry May 28, 1944.

[55] Third Army, After Action Reports, Vol.1 Planning in the United Kingdom 13.

[56] This is a verbatim copy of an original speech given by General Patton on May 29, 1944 that is a part of the author's personal collection. It was written originally hand-written then transcribed via manual typewriter. There is little evidence that the original speech started out as the movie speech does by starting out "No Bastard ever won a war by dying for his country, He won it by making the other poor dumb bastard die for his". General Patton may very well have used those words but not in his speech. In fact, out of three original speeches taken down on three different days, he starts the speech as it begins on this day. Colonel Codman was instructed to keep a copy of the speech in his briefcase at all times. Patton does differ in a few words in each speech, but very little in format.

[57] Patton, Diary entry May 29, 1944.

[58] Patton, Diary entry May 30, 1944.

[59] Gay, Log Diary 389.

[60] Patton, Diary entry May 31, 1944.

[61] Third Army, After Action Reports, Vol.1 Planning in the United Kingdom 13.

[62] Gay, Log Diary 389.

[63] Gay, Log Diary 393.

[64] O. N. Bradley and Blair., Clay 243

[65] Hirshson 477; Blumenson,*The Patton Papers* Vol.2 461-462.

[66] Third Army, After Action Reports, Vol.2 Planning in the United Kingdom 14.

[67] Patton, Diary entry June 1, 1944.

[68] Patton, Diary entry June 2, 1944.

[69] Third Army, After Action Reports Vol.2  Planning in the United Kingdom 14.

[70] Allen, Journal entry, June 2, 1944.

[71] Blumenson, *The Patton Papers* Vol.2 463.

[72] Patton, Diary entry June 3, 1944.

[73] Gay, Log Diary 393.

[74] Gay, Log Diary 393.

[75] Patton, Diary entry June 4, 1944.

[76] Patton, Diary entry June 5, 1944.

[77] Gay, Log Diary 393.

[78] *Politics Magazine* 226-227; Province, *The Unknown Patton* 26-37; Hair collection, Patton's Speech at Camp Bewdley, near Stourport, England. Original Patton Speech.

[79] Third Army, After Action Reports, Vol.2 Planning in the United Kingdom 14.

[80] Third Army, After Action Reports, Vol.2 Staff Reports, Section Reports, G-2, Overview of Section Organization, Part 2, 1-55.

[81] Patton, Diary entry June 6, 1944.

[82] Allen, *Lucky Forward: The History of Patton's Third U.S. Army* 73.

[83] Gay, Log Diary 394.

[84] Gay, Log Diary  395.

[85] The St. Laurent beach.

[86] The Varreville beach.

[87] Patton, Diary entry June 7, 1944.

[88] Patton, Diary entry June 8, 1944.

[89] Gay, Log Diary 396.

[90] Gay, Log Diary 397-398.

[91] Patton, Diary entry June 9, 1944.

[92] Gay, Log Diary 398

[93] Patton, Diary entry June 10, 1944.

[94] Patton would use this mobile headquarters throughout the war; it survived and is now displayed at the Patton Museum in Fort Knox, Kentucky. On the side of the door to the Patton Van at Fort Knox used to read an except from *War As I knew it*, Patton's autobiography. It was from a footnote in the book. The whole of the footnote read, "One of the very few written accounts was a footnote in *War As I Knew It*, attributed to Col. Paul Harkins, He wrote in part, "His parlor, bedroom and bath were a converted Ordinance trailer [Van], entered from the rear after climbing a steep set of steps. The steps were corrugated iron and were a great hazard to Willie, the General 's dog. After Willie had lost several of his toenails in the corrugations, it became necessary to cover the steps with boards. Inside, there was a desk with side drawers, electric light, two telephones, and other necessary office fixtures. The general has a small map board, which he referred to seldom, if ever. He did not keep the situation posted in his living trailer; it was posted in his office trailer. There was a small closet for clothes, a small washstand and cabinet for toilet articles, and a built-in bed at the far end of the van. A radio was installed in an upper panel inside the truck, which the general used frequently to listen to broadcasts. He never used radio in talking to his commanders. Even during the most rapid advances, the Signal Corps usually kept up with wire communication.  Once in a while it was necessary to use radio telephone, which was handled over a regular telephone system installed in the truck. One of the two telephones, - incidentally, it had a green receiver-was a direct line to General Bradley and General Eisenhower. This particular telephone had a device supposed to scramble the words as they passed over the wire and come out spoken at the other end.  Most of the General's oaths [profanity] were used at this device. It seemed he could never get it in phase and complained that it scrambled his words before he uttered them. All electrical devices were run by a mobile generator than furnished electricity for the headquarters group. The office trailer was a long, moving van type of truck, fitted inside with a desk, map boards and telephones. It was located in camp close to the general's living trailer. The General preferred to use the two trailers for living and work, and it was not until the winter set in that he moved inside. When spring came in 1945, while moving through Germany, he favored his truck house for sleeping and used it even though his office was in a building and his meals served indoors."; *also see* Patton's diary entry of July 12, 1944.

[95] G. S. Patton, George S. *Patton Papers*, BOX ? Patton Correspondence File; Blumenson. *The Patton Papers*. Vol.2, 466.

[96] Inside the Turret Newspaper, Fort Knox, Kentucky. Friday, May 7, 1965

97 Patton, George S. Jr., *War As I Knew It.* Paperback Bantam Books New York 1947 page 291

98 Grant, Andy, *Scrambled, Everything that you need to know about scramblers but were afraid to ask,* Telecommunications Heritage Journal, Issue Number 99, Summer 2017, ISSN 1353-0097. Pages 11-15 with additional information added by Andy Grant.

99 *Ibid.*

100 Patton, Diary entry June 11, 1944.

101 Blumenson, *The Patton Papers*, Vol.2 466; Gay, Log Diary 399.

102 C. C. Smith, *My War Years, 1940-46: Service on Gen. Patton's Third Army Staff* 37.

103 Gay, Log Diary 399-400.

104 Patton, Diary entry June 12, 1944.

105 Blumenson, *The Patton Papers.* Vol.2 467.

106 Gay, Log Diary 400.

107 Patton, Diary entry June 13, 1944.

108 Gay, Log Diary 402.

109 G. S. Patton, George S. *Pattton Papers* Collection, Oversize Albums (Container 62), Box OV 19 1944-1946; Diaz family collection.

110 Gay, Log Diary 403.

111 Patton, Diary entry June 15, 1944.

112 Allen, Journal entry June 15, 1944.

113 Third Army, After Action Reports, Vol.1 Planning in the United Kingdom 10.

114 Gay, Log Diary 403.

115 Gay, Log Diary 405.

116 Handwritten notation added by B.A.P.

117 Handwritten notation added by B.A.P

118 Patton, Diary entry June 17, 1944.

119 Gay, Log Diary 406.

120 Gay, Log Diary 407.

121 Col. Frank Hulen.

122 Col. Thruston Hughes.

123 Col. C. P. Stearns.

124 Patton, Diary entry June 19, 1944.

125 Gay, Log Diary 407.

126 Patton, Diary entry June 20, 1944.

127 Gay, Log Diary 408.

128 Patton, Diary entry June 21, 1944.

129 Gay, Log Diary 409.

130 Patton, Diary entry June 22, 1944.

131 Gay, Log Diary 409.

132 Brig. Gen. A.W. Gullion.

133 Patton, Diary entry June 23, 1944.

134 Gay, Log Diary 411.

135 Third Army, After Action Reports, Vol.1 Planning in the United Kingdom 18.

136 Patton, Diary entry June 24, 1944.

137 Gay, Log Diary 411.

138 Patton, Diary entry June 25, 1944.

139 Gay, Log Diary 412.

140 Patton, June 26, 1944.

141 Gay, Log Diary 413.

142 C. C. Smith, *My War Years, 1940-46: Service on Gen. Patton's Third Army Staff* 39.

143 Patton, Diary entry June 27, 1944.

144 Allen, Journal entry June 27, 1944.

145 Gay, Log Diary 414.

[146] Third Army, After Action Reports, Vol.1 Planning in the United Kingdom 16.

[147] Patton, Diary entry June 28, 1944.

[148] Third Army, After Action Reports, Vol.1 Planning in the United Kingdom 16.

[149] Patton, Diary entry June 29, 1944.

[150] Gay, Log Diary 414.

[151] Patton, Diary entry June 30, 1944.

[152] Third Army, After Action Reports, Vol.1 Planning in the United Kingdom 16.

[153] Gay, Log Diary 415.

[154] Patton, Diary entry July 1, 1944.

[155] R. J. Stillman 39.

[156] Allen, *Lucky Forward: The History of Patton's Third U.S. Army*, Index, Back of illustrations, front

[157] Gay, Log Diary 415-416.

[158] Patton, Diary entry July 2, 1944.

[159] Third Army, After Action Reports, Vol.1 Planning in the United Kingdom 16.

[160] Patton, Diary entry July 3, 1944.

[161] Wallace 4; Gay, Log Diary 416.

[162] Hughes, Diary entry July 4, 1944.

[163] R. H. Patton 233-236.

[164] Ramsey, Julia A. "'Girls' in Name Only: A Study of American Red Cross Volunteers on the Frontlines of World War II," Master's Thesis Auburn University, 2011.

[165] Patton, Diary entry July 4, 1944.

[166] Patton, Diary entry July 5, 1944.

[167] Gay, Log Diary 416-417.

# BIBLIOGRAPHY


11th Armored Division History. "Thunderbolt Commanding Generals, Brigadier General Charles Solomon Kilburn." n.d. 11th Armored Division History, Legacy Group. http://www.11tharmoreddivision.com/history/Generals_History.html#kilburn.

301st Signal Corp Battalion. *History of Company A, January 20, 1943 to September 15, 1945*. Munich: US Army Signal Corps, 1945.

514 Quartermaster Group. *Patton's Wheels, Story of the Quarter Master Trucks in Third Army*. Original document - Author's personal collection. St. Paul Imprimerie, Luxemburg: Third Army, 1945.

667th Engineer Topographical Company Detachment. "Third Army, Officer Mess Menu, Hotel Kaiserhof." 1944: Third Army Headquarters, n.d.

*A Day with General Patton*. Dir. 166th Signal Photo Company; NR#2 TSgt A. Statt, Ca. 26/8/44.

Allen, Robert S. "Memorandum to Commanding General, Third United States Army." The Robert Sharon Allen Papers, Box 27, Folder 13. Madison, WI: Wisconsin Historical Society Archives, 29 April 1945.

Allen, Robert S. *Lucky Forward: The History of Patton's Third U.S. Army.* 1st printing. New York: The Vanguard Press, 1947.

Allen, Robert S. "Robert S. Allen Collection; RSA Journal 1,2,3,4, 1944-1945; National Infantry Museum & Soldier Center, 1775 Legacy Way; Columbus, GA 31903 Unpublished typed (transcript transferred from Patton Museum, Fort Knox Kentucky)." n.d.

Allphin, Dempsey. *Two of Us Ain't Goin'*. CITY: Writers Club Press, 2001.

Alvarez, David. *Allied and Axis Signal Intelligence in World War II*. Portland : Frank Cass Publisher, 1999.

Andrews, Curt. "The Story of General George S. Patton, Jr." Warrior D M Circa 1965-66: Pgs.

"The Anchora Delta Gamma." Menasha, WI: George Banta Publishing, March 1945. 75.

Axelrod, Frederick. *Patton: A Biography*. Palgrave Macmillion, 2006.

Ayer, Frederick, Jr. *Before the Colors Fade, Portrait of a Soldier, George S. Patton Jr*. Second Printing. 1964.

Baron, Richard, Baum, Abe (Maj.), and Goldhurst, Richard. *Raid, The Untold Story of Patton's Secret Mission*. G.P. Putnam and Sons, 1981.

Blumenson, Martin. *Patton: The Man Behind the Legend*, 1885-1945 . New York: Morrow, 1985.

Blumenson, Martin. *The Patton Papers*. Vol. 2. Boston: Houghton Mifflin Company, 1987.

Blumenson, Martin. *The Patton Papers*. Vol. 1. Boston: Houghton Mifflin Company, 1987.

Bradley, Omar N. *A Soldiers Story*. Henry Holt and Company, 1951.

Bradley, Omar N., and Blair, Clay. *A General's Life Story, An Autobiography by General of the Army Omar N. Bradley*. New York: Simon and Schuster, 1983.

Brown, Walter L. *Up Front with U.S.; Day by Day in the Life of Combat Infantryman in General Patton's Third Army*.1979.

Bryant, Arthur. *The Years of Endurance, 1793-1802*. 1st . London: Collins, 1942.

Buechner, Howard A., Colonel, Medical Corps A. U.S. Dachau Retired. *The Hour of the Avenger*.

Limited Edition. Metaire: Thunderbird Press, Inc., 1986.

Butcher, Harry C., Captain USNR Aide-de-Camp. *General Dwight David Eisenhower, My Three Years With Eisenhower 1942-1945*. 1st Printing. Kingsport Press, 1946.

Codman, Charles R. *Contact*. 1st edition. Boston: Little Brown and Company, 1937.

Codman, Charles R. *Drive*. Boston: Little Brown and Company, 1957.

Crismon, Fred W. *US Military Wheeled Vehicles*. Crestline Publishing Company, 1983.

Dailymail, Online. "The Genocide Generals: secret recordings explode the myth they knew nothing about the Holocaust." n.d. Dailymail Company UK. Published by Associated Newspapers Ltd. http://www.dailymail.co.uk/femail/article-469883/The-Genocide-Generals-secret-recordings-explode-myth-knew-Holocaust.html.

Davis, Benjamin O., Jr. *American*. Washington, D.C.: The Smithsonian Institution Press, 1991.

D'Este, Carlo. *Eisenhower, A Soldier's Life*. New York: Henry Holt and Co., 2002.

D'Este, Carlo. *Patton: A Genius for War*. New York: Harper Collins, 1995.

Diaz family collection. "Diaz, Gregorio A. CWO; Bandleader, 61st Army Ground Forces Band, Third U.S. Army." n.d.

Diaz, Gregorio A. CWO, Bandleader. "Remarks to the 6th Cavalry Regiment by Colonel Edward M. Fickett. 6th Cavalry Regiment, 61st Amy Ground Forces Band, Third U.S. Army." December 31, 1943.

Dietrich, Marlene. *Marlene*. Ed. translated from the German by Salvator Attanasio. 1st Edition. New York: Grove Press, 1989.

Eisenhower, David. *Eisenhower: At War 1943-1945*. New York : Random House, 1986.

Eisenhower, Dwight D. *At Ease, Stories I Tell My Friends*. 1st printing. Doubleday, 1967.

Eisenhower, Dwight D., General. Wyden, Barbara. Papers: Gen. Dwight D. Eisenhower Headquarters Diary, Supreme Headquarters, Allied Expeditionary Forces. European Theater. Ed. Personal Secretary to the General written for General by Kay Summersby. Unpublished; Library Abilene Kansas Accession 01-19 Processed by JWL (Date Completed: November 20, 2001) , 1944-1945.

Eklund, Coy. Lt. Col. "World War II Journal, G-1 Headquarters, Personal Diary." Cav. Assistant, Army G-1 Headquarters Third, n.d.

Essame, H. *Patton: A Study in Command*. New York: Scribner's, 1974.

Ethell, Jeffery L., Grinsell, Robert, Freeman, Roger, Anderton, David A., Johnson, Fredrick A., Sweetman, Bill, Vanags-Baginskis, Alex, Milkesh, Robert C., and Wantanable, Rikyu. *The Great Book of World War II Airplanes*. New York: Bonanza Books, Wing and Anchor Press, 1984.

Farago, Ladislas. *Patton: Ordeal and Triumph*. New York: Obolensky, 1963.

Farago, Ladislas. *The Last Days of Patton*. New York: McGraw-Hill, 1981.

Fitzharris, Joseph G. *Patton's Fighting Bridge Builders: Company B, 1303 Engineer General Service Regiment*. Texas A&M University, 2007.

Fletcher, Marvin E. *America's First Black General: Benjamin O. Davis Jr., 1880-1970*. University Press of Kansas, 1989.

Flourie, Harland. *Battle Cry Magazine*. August 1957, 1 ed.

Forty, George. *The Armies of George S. Patton*. London: Arms and Armor, 1996.

Fox, Don M. *Patton's Vanguard: The United States Army Fourth Armored Division*. McFarland and Company, 2003 .

Frankel, Nat and Larry Smith. *Patton's Best: An Informal History of the 4th Armored Division*. New York: Hawthorn Books Inc., 1978.

Gawne, Jonathan. *American Tactical Deception Units in the European Theater 1944-1945*. Havertown: Casemate, 2002.

Gay, Hobart, General Chief of Staff. Log Diary. U.S. Army Military History Institute Army Heritage and Education Center; photocopy of diary covering the period from July 1943 through Oct 1945. . Carlisle, PA: Army Heritage Center Foundation, n.d.

"General George Patton Interrogates a SS General, 1944." 2008. Eyewitness to History. www.eyewitnesstohistory.com.

"General Patton's War Letters to Frederick Ayer." The Atlantic Monthly. January 1948.

GlobalSecurity.org. "White Phosphorus (WP)." n.d. GlobalSecurity.org. 2013. http://www.globalsecurity.org/military/systems/munitions/wp.htm.

Grant, Andy. "Scrambled: Everything that you need to know about scramblers but were afraid to ask." Telecommunications Heritage Journal, Issue Number 99, Summer 2017, ISSN 1353-0097. Pages 11-15

Green, Michael and Gladys Green. *Weapons of Patton's Armies.* MBI Publishing Company, 2000.

Hair, Denny. "The 64th Anniversary of General Patton's Death." Heidelberg Germany, U.S. Army Medical Department (MSAMH). 2009.

Hair, Denny. "Patton's Speech at Camp Bewdley, near Stourport, England. Original Patton Speech (Original)." Author's personal collection, 31 May 1944.

Hair, Denny. Press release, 13 April 1944, Number 1912 Headquarters, European Theater of Operations, United States Army. Author's personal collection, 31 May 1944. http://www.pattonthirdarmy.com/HeidelbergTrip.html.

Hair, Denny. "The Rescue of the Lipizzaner Horses: A Personal Account." HAUTE ÉCOLE The Official Magazine of the Lipizzan Association of North America 20.4 (Spring/Summer 2012): 9-10.

Hancock Reed, Charles, Colonel. "The Rescue of the Lapizzaner Horses: A Personal Account (November 4, 1970)." 05 01 2008. 2d Dragoons. http://history.dragoons.org/2008/01/05/the-rescue-of-the-lipizzans-a-personal-account/.

Harkins, Paul D. *When the Third Cracked Europe: The Story of Patton's Army Times.* Harrisburg, PA: Stackpole Books, 1969.

Harratt, Tony Staffordshire. *14 Liaison Squadron.* England: unpublished manuscript, August 2001.

Hatch, Alden. *George Patton: General in Spurs.* New York: Julian Messner, Inc., 1950.

Hays, Robert. *Patton's Oracle Gen. Oscar Koch, as I Knew Him: A Biographical Memoir.* Lucidus Books, a division of Herndon-Sugarman Press, 2013.

Heefer, Wilson A. *Patton's Bulldog: The Life and Service of General Walton H. Walker.* White Mane Books, 2001.

"Hicks Body Company Maintenance and Parts Book: Body Mobile Shop Truck Built for the Ordnance Department," Hicks Body Company, Inc. Lebanon, Indiana, 1941.

Hirshson, Stanley P. *General Patton: A Soldier's Life.* New York: Harper Perennial, 2003.

Historical Section G-3 Third Army Headquarters. "Brief Summaries of Operation, August 1 1944 through 8th May 1945." 1945.

History of the Sixth Cavalry Regiment, Sixth Cavalry Group at Home and Abroad. Germany: Frankische Presse Plant, January 1947.

Horan, James, Frank, G., Morison, Samuel Eliot, and Forester, C.S. *Battle: True Stories in Combat in WWII.* Saturday Evening Post. Doubleday Inc., 1965 .

Hughes, Everett Strait. Everett Strait Hughes Papers, BOX I:2 Diary notes, 1942-1956.

Washington, D.C.: Manuscript Division, Library of Congress, n.d.

Hymel, Kevin. *Patton's Photographs*. Dulles: Potomac Books, 2006.

Irzyk, Albin F. Brigadier General (Ret). *Gasoline to Patton: A Different War*. Oakland: Elderberry Press, Inc , 2005.

Irzyk, Albin F. Brigadier General (Ret). *He Rode Up Front for Patton*. Pentland Press, Inc, 1996.

Jeffers, H. Paul. *Command of Honor: General Lucian Truscott's Path to Victory in World War II*. New York: Nal Caliber, 2008.

Jocquot, Ruth. "Former Secretary to Patton says Toughness Mostly Legend." Journal Every Evening Newspaper, Wilmington Delaware, Thursday August 23, 1945 page 2

Karlsch, Rainer. *Hitler's Bombe*. Munchen: Deutshe Verlags-Ansalt, 2005.

Kipling, Rudyard. *Rudyard Kipling's Verse: Inclusive Edition, 1885-1918*. Ed. John Henry Nash. Garden City: Doubleday, Page & Company, 1922.

Klien, Jerry. "Patton Ghost, Tough Breed, 2nd Cavalry Colonel Recalls." Peoria Star Journal 1963.

Kneece, Jack. *Ghost Army of WWII*. Gretna: Pelican Publishing Company, 2001.

Koch, Oscar W, and Hays, Robert G., Brigadier General. *G2: Intelligence for Patton*. Atglen: Schiffer publishing Ltd., 1999.

Korson, George. *At His Side: The American Red Cross Overseas in WWII*. New York: Coward-McCann, Inc., 1945.

Lande, D.A. *I Was With Patton*. St. Paul, Minnesota: MBI Publishing, 2002.

Lewin, Ronald. *Ultra Goes to War*. McGraw-Hill Book Company, 1978.

Mauldin, Bill. "My Confrontation with General Patton." Life Magazine 6 August 1971.

Mauldin, Bill. *The Brass Ring: A Sort of Memoir*. W W Norton & Co Inc., January 1971.

McDermott, William V. *A Surgeon in Combat European Theatre-World War II, Omaha Beach to Ebensee 1943-1945*. New Hampshire: William L. Bauhan, 1997.

McHugh, Vernon D. *From Hell to Heaven: Memoirs from Patton's Third Army*. Pennsylvania : Dorrance & Company Ardmore, 1980.

McLaughlin, J. Kemp. *The Mighty Eighth in WWII: A Memoir*. Lexington: University Press of Kentucky, 2000).

McLean, Cynthia K. *A Life on Horse Back, Stories of Spencer Kimball McLean as told to Cynthia K. McLean*. Unpublished. Cynthia K. McLean, 2006.

Mellor, William C. *General Patton, The Last Cavalier*. Logmans Canada Limited, 1971.

Mellor, William. *Patton, Fighting Man*. New York: Putnam, 1946.

Meredith, James Howard. "Hemingway's U.S. 3rd Army Inspector General Interview during World War II." 22 March 1999. The Free Library. 10 January 2014 http://www.thefreelibrary.com/Hemingway's U.S. 3rd Army Inspector General Interview during World...-a05486.

Miller, Merle. *Plan Speaking: An Oral Biography of Harry S. Truman*. Berkley Publishing Corporation, 1974.

Mitgang, Herbert. "At War With The Stars And Stripes, Army Newspapers in World War were Unofficial, Informal, and More than the Top Brass Could Handle." American Heritage Magazine, Online Collections, Travel, and Great Writing on History April 1971.

Morgan, Marjorie Lee, ed. *The Clubmobile: The ARC in the Storm*. St. Petersburg: Hazlett Printing and Publishing, Inc., 1982.

Newman, Larry G. "General Patton's Premonition, An account of a press conference at which the General sounded a grim warning." The American Legion Magazine July 1962.

Nye, Roger H. *The Patton Mind: The Professional Development of an Extraordinary Leader.* Garden City: Avery Publishing Group, Inc., 1993.

Odom, Charles B. *General George S. Patton and Eisenhower.* Tallahassee: Rose, 1985.

Odom, Charles B., Col. Consultant in Surgery to the Surgeon Third U.S. Army. *WWII Medical History: 3rd United States Army, WWII.* http://history.amedd.army.mil.

Olewiler, B.J. *A Woman in a Man's War.* Xlibris Corporation, 2003.

O'Neill, James H., Brigadier General, retired. "The True Story of the Patton Prayer." The Review of the News. Third Army, 6 October 1971.

O'Neill, James H., Brigadier General, retired."The True Story of the Patton Prayer." Review of the News, 6 October 1971: 29-40.

Pageant Magazine Staff. "Patton's Souvenirs." Pageant Magazine 5 November 1945: 78-81.

Parson, Lain. *The Encyclopedia of Air Warfare.* New York: Thomas Y. Cromwell Company, 1975.

Patterson, Michael Robert, Webmaster. "Benjamin O. Davis, Brigadier General, United States Army." n.d. Arlington National Cemetery Website. http://www.arlingtoncemetery.net/bodavis.htm.

*Patton.* Francis Ford Coppola and Edmund H. North. Dir. Franklin J. Schaffner. Perf. George C. Scott. Prod. Frank McCarthy. Twentieth Century Fox Film Corporation, 1970.

Patton, George S. George S. Patton Papers Collection, Patton Diary 1943-1945 BOX 3 Annotated transcripts. Washington, D.C.: Manuscript Division, Library of Congress, n.d.

Patton, George S. George S. Patton Papers, Patton Letters Home, Beatrice. Washington, D.C.: Manuscript Division, Library of Congress.

Patton, George S. George S. Patton Papers, Patton Correspondence File, Letter to Fredrick Ayer. Washington, D.C.: Manuscript Division, Library of Congress, Jan. 14th 1944.

Patton, George S. George S. Patton Papers. Patton Diary 1943-1945 Box 62, Folder 2, Photograpgh of Patton's C-47 tail section. Washington, D.C.: Manuscript Division, Library of Congress, n.d.

Patton, George S. George S. Patton Papers Collection. Oversize Albums (Container 62), Box OV 19 1944-1946. Washington, D.C.: Manuscript Divison, Library of Congress, n.d.

Patton, George S. Patton Papers; Finances, Letter to Frederick Ayer, May 1945. Vols. Box 14, Folder 19. Washington, D.C.: Manuscript Division, Library of Congress, n.d.

Patton, George S., Jr. *War As I Knew It.* Boston: Houghton, Mifflin, 1947.

Patton, Robert H. *The Pattons: A Personal History of an American Family.* New York: Crown Publishers, 1994.

Pearl, Jack. *Blood-and-Guts Patton: The Swashbuckling Life Story of America's Most Daring and Controversial General.* Derby: Monarch, 1961.

Peck, Ira. *Patton.* New York: Scholastic, 1970.

Perry, Milton F. and Parke, Barbara W. *Patton and His Pistols: The Favorite Side Arms of General George S. Patton, Jr.* Harrisburg: Stackpole, 1957.

Persico, Joseph E. *Piercing the Reich: The Penetration of Nazi Germany by American Secret Agents During World War II.* New York: The Viking Press, 1979.

Petesch, Angela. *War Through the Hole of a Donut.* Madison: Hunter Halverson P, 2006.

Politics Magazine. August 1945: Volume 2, No.8 226-227.

Polk III, James H. *World War II Letters of Colonel James H. Polk 1944-1945.* Oakland: Red Anvil Press, 2005.

Polk, James H. General. "You Might As Well Die a Hero." ARMY. December 1975 : 41-42.

Price, James Frank. *Troy H. Middleton: A Biography*. Louisiana State University Press, 1974.

Pogue, F.C., Interview with Lt. General Walter B. Smith, Ambassador to Russia, at the Old State Department Building, 9 May 1947. George C Marshal Foundation, 1600 VMI Parade, Lexington, Virginia

Province, Charles M. *Patton's One Minute Messages: Tactical Leadership Skills for Business Managers*. Novato: Presidio Press, 1995.

Province, Charles M. *Patton's Third Army*. New York: Hippocrene, 1992.

Province, Charles M. *The Patton Principles*. San Diego: CMP Productions, 1978.

Province, Charles M. *The Unknown Patton*. New York: Hippocrene, 1983.

Puryear, Edgar F., Jr. *Nineteen Stars*. Washington: Coiner Publications, 1971.

Ramsey, Ann. "Abbeville Man Drove for Patton." Wiregrass Today Sunday 26 December 1986.

Ramsey, Julia A. "'Girls' in Name Only: A Study of American Red Cross Volunteers on the Frontlines of World War II"; A thesis submitted to the Graduate Faculty of Auburn University in partial fulfillment of the requirements for the Degree of Masters of Arts in History. Auburn, Alabama, August 6, 2011.

Rankin, Fred Wharton, Brigadier General. Medical Department United States Army in World War II, Activities of Surgical Consultants, Part II Surgical Consultants to Field Armies in Theaters of Operations, Chapter XV, Third U.S. Army, Charles B. Odom, M.D. U.S. Army Medical Department, Office of Medical History. Book and Documents retrieved January 03, 2014 at http://history.amedd.army.mil/booksdocs/wwii/actvsurgconvoli/CH15.htm, n.d.

Rexford, Oscar Whitelaw. *Battlestars and Doughnuts: World War II Clubmobile Experiences of Mary Metcalf Rexford*. The Patrice Press, 1989.

Ripley, Tim. *Patton Unleashed*. MBI Publishing , 2003.

Rogers, Russ. *Historic Photographs of General George S. Patton*. Turner Publishing, 2007.

Rohmer, Richard. *Patton's Gap*. New York: Beaufort Books, 1981.

Rommel, General Field Marshal Erwin. *Infantry Attacks*. Trans. U.S. Army Translated from German by Lieutenant Colonel G.E. Kidde. Original English translation 1944, Washington, The Infantry Journal 1944. Potsdam: original publisher, Ludwig Voggenreiter Verlag; published and distributed in the public interest by authority of the Alien Property Custodian Under License No. A-196, 1937.

Rosevich, Joseph D. "The Patton Nobody Knew." *Saga True Adventures for Men Magazine*. April 1953: 24-27, 94-96.

Royle, Trevor. *Patton: Old Blood and Guts*. London: Weidenfeld & Nicolson, 2005.

Ruane, Michael E. "Toe-tapping Patton march is finally recorded, to the joy of composer's." 29 November 2013. The Washington Post. http://www.washingtonpost.com/local/to-the-joy-of-composers-son-a-toe-tapping-march-for-patton-is-finally-recorded/2013/11/29/267d6da6-51ec-11e3-a7f0-b790929232e1_story.html.

Sasser, Charles W. *The African American 761st Tank Battalion in World War II: Patton's Panthers*. New York, London, Toronto, Sidney: Pocket books Printing, 2005.

Semmes, Harry H. *Portrait of Patton*. New York: Appleton, 1955.

Sixth Cavalry Group. *History of The Sixth Cavalry Regiment: Sixth Cavalry Group at Home and Abroad*. Germany: Frankische Presse Plant, January 1947.

Smith, C. Cabanne. *My War Years, 1940-46: Service on Gen. Patton's Third Army Staff*. Houston, 1989.

Smith, Walter Bedell. *Eisenhower's Six Great Decisions: Europe 1944-1945*. Longman's Green and Co.

1956.

Sobel, Brian. *The Fighting Pattons.* Westport: Praeger Publishers.

South, Betty. "We Called Him 'Uncle Georgie.'" The Quartermaster Review January/February 1954.

Spires, David N. *Patton's Air Force: Forging a Legendary Air-Ground Team.* Washington, D.C.: Smithsonian Institution Press, 2002.

Stansell, Partick and David Doyle. "Allied - Axis, The Photo Journal of the Second World War." No.6. 2-17.

Stanton, Shelby L. *Order of Battle, U.S. Army World War II.* Presidio Press, 1984.

Stillier, Alexander Chapman, Service number 01010000, United States Army Service Record, DOD, Freedom of Information Act.

Stillman, Richard J. and Riggs, Mary F. *General Patton's Best Friend: The Story of General George Smith Patton, Jr. and His Beloved Dog, Willie.* New Orleans : R.J Stillman Company, 2001.

Stillman, Richard J. *General Patton's Secret Missions: Little Known Facts About Intriguing Experiences of Old Blood and Guts.* New Orleans: R.J Stillman Company, 2005.

Stillman, Richard J. *General Patton's Timeless Leadership Principles.* New Orleans: Stillman Co., 1997.

St. John, Jeffery, Editor The New American, American Opinion Magazine, Reflections on a Fighting Father, A son and Daughter Remember General George S. Patton Jr., The New American, December 16, 1985. Pages 27-34.

Stowe, Leland. "Old Blood and Guts off the Record." Esquire Magazine October 1949.

Summersby, Kay Morgan. *Eisenhower Was My Boss.* Werner Laurie Books, 1949.

Summersby, Kay Morgan. *Past Forgetting: My Love Affair with Dwight D. Eisenhower.* New York: Simon and Schuster, 1976.

Swanson, Brandon. "They Saved Horses: The Casualties of Operation Cowboy Finally Get Their Due." The Prague Post,10 May 2006.

The Fourth Armored Division. *From the Beach to Bavaria.* Munich, Germany: US Army G-3 Historical Section, 1946.

*The Holy Bible: King James Version.* Dallas, TX: Brown Books Publishing, 2004.

The Royal Household. *Order of the Bath.* 2008/2009. 16 June 2013 http://www.royal.gov.uk/MonarchUK/Honours/OrderoftheBath.aspx.

Third Army. "After Action Reports Vol.1 ."

Third Army. "After Action Reports, Vol. 2." May 1945.

Third Army Headquarters, Historical Section G-3. "Third US Army G3, The Campaign of France, Avalanches, Brest, to the Moselle 1 August-24 September 1944 ." Brief Summaries of Operation. July 9th, 1945.

Third Army Printing. *In Action With the 277nd Signal Pigeon Company.* Munich, Germany: F Bruckmann KG, printer, 1945.

Third U.S. Army and Third U.S. Army Headquarters. "Third United States Army, Crossing the Rhine, Office of the Engineer, 652nd Engineers." Confidential Report. 1945.

Third US Army G3, Historical Section G-3 Third Army Headquarters. "Brief Summary of Operation, August 1, 1944 through 8th May 1945." 22 of March through April 21, 1945. 1945.

Toland, John. *The Last 100 Days.* New York: Random House, 1965.

Totten, Ruth Ellen Patton. *The Button Box: A Daughter's Loving Memoir of Mrs. George S. Patton.* University of Missouri Press, 2005.

US Army Military History Institute, Senior Officers Oral History Program, Project 81-G. Hobart Raymond Gay, Lieutenant General, USA Retired, Interview by Willard Wallace, Colonel, USAR 1981 Pages 27-30

U.S. Army. "American Red Cross Activities in the European Theater." The General Board Report, Study No. 5. November 1945.

U.S. Third Army., Headquarters. *In Memoriam. George S. Patton, Jr. General, U.S. Army.* Bad Tolz, Germany, 1946.

Ulrich, Andreas. "Hitler's Drugged Soldiers." May 2005. Spiegel Online. http://www.amphetamines.com/nazi.html.

Van Creveld, Martin. *Supplying War: Logistics From Wallenstein to Patton.* 2nd Edition. Cambridge University Press, 2004.

Valley Morning Star Newspaper. Harlingen, Texas "Valley Man describes Patton, Christian Soldier." Eberhardt, Glenn, Reporter, Sunday November 1, 1970 , page A10

Venditta, David. "I've Got This Top-secret Message: An Interview with Andrew V. Cisar." 05 June 2004. The Morning Call. http://articles.mcall.com/2004-06-05/news/all-andrewcisar_1_tommy-guns-trailer-front-door pgs 1-3.

Wallace, Brenton G. *Patton and His Third Army.* Harrisburg: Military Services Publishers, 1946.

War Department. "TM 11-281 War Department Technical Manual, Radio Sets SCR-399-A and SCR 499-A." War Department, March 1945.

Wedemeyer, Albert C., General. *Wedemeyer Reports.* Third Printing. New York: Henry Holt and Company, 1958.

Weigley, Russell F. *Eisenhower's Lieutenants: The Campaigns of France and Germany, 1944-1945.* Bloomington: Indiana University Press, 1981.

Wellard, James Howard. *General George S. Patton, Jr., Man Under Mars.* New York: Dodd, Mead, 1946.

Wellard, James Howard. *The Man in a Helmet: General George S. Patton.* London: Eyre & Spottiswoode, 1946.

White, Margaret Brourke. *Dear Fatherland, Rest Quietly: A Report on the Collapse of Hitler's Thousand Years.* New York: Simon and Schuster, 1946.

Widmer, Jack Lt.Col. "Damn It Don't Quote Me." *True, The Man's Magazine* 20.16 (1947): 25-27, 112 -115.

Williams, Mary C. *United States Army in World War II, Special Studies Chronology 1941-1945.* Washington D. C.: US Government Printing Office , Reprinted 1960.

Williams, Vernon L. *Lieutenant Patton and the American Army in the Mexican Punitive Expedition 1915-1916.* Austin: Presidial, 1983.

Williamson, Porter B. *I Remember Patton's Principles.* Tucson: Arizona Lithographers, 1979.

Williamson, Porter B. *Patton's Principles: A Handbook for Managers Who Mean It!* New York: Simon & Schuster, 1979.

Wilson, Dale E. *Treat 'Em Rough: The Birth of American Armor, 1917- 1920.* Novato, CA: Presidio Press, 1989.

Winterbotham, F. W. *The Ultra Secret.* Harbor and Roe Publishers, 1974.

XX Corps personnel. "XX Corps: Its History and Service in World War II." 1946.

Yeide, Harry. *Fighting Patton: George S. Patton Jr. Through the Eyes of His Enemies.* Zenith Press, MBI Publishing Company, 2011.

Zalga, Steven J. *Leadership Strategy: Conflict George S. Patton.* Oxford, UK: 2010.

Zorn, Chaplain George L. "Third Army, Church Bulletin, Garrison Theater Chapel."
Telephone Lucky 19. Third Army printing, 22 November 1944.

Made in the USA
Monee, IL
26 December 2024

75447170R00139